Praise for
Isabelle Huppert, Modernist Performance

"Florence Jacobowitz effectively brings together insights gleaned from a wide range of scholarly, journalistic, and filmic sources. Her writing style is exquisite, making the book accessible to a wide audience and a pleasure to read for academics. The descriptions of ideas, films, performance details, and more are clear and engaging; the observations about the films also reveal a significant depth of insight and compassion."

—Cynthia Baron, author of *Modern Acting: The Lost Chapter of American Film and Theatre*

"Florence Jacobowitz provides us with a compelling, innovative, in-depth study of this wonderfully intelligent and versatile actor. Isabelle Huppert is often perceived as cold and detached as a performer, but she is so much more than that, and Jacobowitz's meticulous investigation into what she terms Huppert's modernist performance style deeply enriches our understanding and appreciation of this complex artist."

—Susan Hayward, professor emerita, University of Exeter

"Close analyses of an impressive range of the star's challenging films underpin the argument for the distinctiveness of Isabelle Huppert's performance style here. These accessible, informative accounts locate Huppert in the context of her contemporary collaborators and explore how we can read her work against earlier modes of star performance."

—Edward Gallafent, professor emeritus of film studies, University of Warwick

"In a deft examination of Isabelle Huppert's modernist performances, Jacobowitz reveals how Huppert's enigmatic, yet creative acting styles elicit viewers' critical engagements with cinema and the feminine."

—Homer B. Pettey, professor emeritus, University of Arizona, and coeditor of *French Literature on Screen*

Isabelle Huppert,
Modernist Performance

Isabelle Huppert,
Modernist Performance

Florence Jacobowitz

Foreword by Serge Toubiana

Wayne State University Press
Detroit

© 2024 by Wayne State University Press, Detroit, Michigan 48201. All rights reserved.
No part of this book may be reproduced without formal permission.

ISBN 9780814348932 (paperback)
ISBN 9780814348949 (hardcover)
ISBN 9780814348956 (e-book)

Library of Congress Control Number: 2023949849

On cover: *Une affaire de femmes* (*Story of Women*) by Claude Chabrol © 1988 mk2
Productions / Films A2 / Films du Camelia / Sept. Used by permission.
Cover design by Tracy Cox.

Published with the assistance of a fund established by Thelma Gray James of Wayne
State University for the publication of folklore and English studies.

Wayne State University Press rests on Waawiyaataanong, also referred to as Detroit, the
ancestral and contemporary homeland of the Three Fires Confederacy. These sovereign
lands were granted by the Ojibwe, Odawa, Potawatomi, and Wyandot Nations, in
1807, through the Treaty of Detroit. Wayne State University Press affirms Indigenous
sovereignty and honors all tribes with a connection to Detroit. With our Native
neighbors, the press works to advance educational equity and promote a better future
for the earth and all people.

Wayne State University Press
Leonard N. Simons Building
4809 Woodward Avenue
Detroit, Michigan 48201-1309

Visit us online at wsupress.wayne.edu.

*For my family, Shimon, Yonah, Nina, Yishai, Ella, Frieda,
and Jim, with love*

Contents

Foreword		ix
Acknowledgments		xiii
	Introduction	1
1	Modernist Performance: Une modernité de jeu	33
2	Huppert and Godard: Acting Degree Zero	59
3	A Woman's Film: *Une affaire de femmes*	81
4	Huppert and Bovarysme: "Archetypes of Dissatisfaction"	99
5	*La Pianiste* and the Modernist Melodrama	115
6	Reading *Elle*	139
7	Celebrating the Outlier: *Villa Amalia, L'avenir, In Another Country*	153
	Notes	179
	Bibliography	195
	Index	201

Isabelle Huppert, the Art of Secrecy

Foreword by Serge Toubiana

Recently, I was invited by the Premiers Plans Festival in Angers to host a masterclass with Isabelle Huppert. Knowing her for a long time and having a friendly relationship with her, I gladly accepted the invitation. Before our conversation on January 27th, the festival had screened *La dentellière* (*The Lacemaker*), directed in 1977 by Swiss filmmaker Claude Goretta—a film that had introduced Isabelle Huppert to a wide audience in France and around the world. Up until then, Huppert had played various supporting roles in different films, but in *La dentellière*, she took on the lead role of Béatrice, a shy and introverted young woman. Isabelle and I entered the darkened room a few minutes before the end of the screening. Suddenly, I was transported back many years when Isabelle Huppert had that round, pale, and timid face with freckles. An innocent face where emotions passed through in a kind of emotional neutrality. Goretta's film undeniably marked a pivotal moment in her artistic journey, as if it had identified her, in her paleness, her silence, and in her most secretive self. Goretta had captured Isabelle Huppert in her intimate truth—a young woman focused inward, silent and melancholic.

The final shot of the film carried me away with its strength and impact: silent, enclosed within herself, Béatrice slowly turns her head until her look meets that of the viewer, in what is known as a *camera look* (*regard-caméra*). I immediately thought of another film that also ends with a camera look, *Les 400 coups* (*The 400 Blows*), François Truffaut's debut film. Young Antoine Doinel (played by Jean-Pierre Léaud) runs to the beach after escaping from the juvenile delinquency centre. He runs for a long

x   Foreword

time, finally reaching the seashore (we can guess that he is discovering it for the first time), and wades into the water before turning around to meet the viewer's look. The word "FIN" appears on this freeze-frame.

What is the significance of such a look? Fixing the camera's eye is like making the viewer a witness. By looking at the viewer, Antoine Doinel (Jean-Pierre Léaud) and Béatrice (Isabelle Huppert) share with them the enigma of their existence. Their camera looks challenge us, soliciting us to enter the intimacy of their characters and discover their secret or mystery. Béatrice's look—that of a young hairdresser who failed in her love story with François (Yves Beneyton), the young man she met during the film, and who finds herself locked alone in a psychiatric hospital—seems to say to us: my discomfort is *also* yours. My intimate unhappiness is *also* yours, and you are responsible for it. My madness or melancholy, my solitude—*you are responsible*.

Beyond engaging the viewer, the camera look also involves the intimate relationship between the actor/character and cinema. Looking at the camera, a gesture usually considered forbidden in film grammar, is more or less akin to establishing complicity with the act of recording. Isabelle Huppert can say to herself: I am in front of the camera, playing my role, embodying Béatrice, this young woman lonely and struggling with her inner turmoil, but I am not fooled by the cinematic apparatus, or at least I am *aware* of it. I also know what is behind the décor or the *dispositif* (apparatus), and I am its accomplice. This intimate knowledge has to do with the work of the *cinematic unconscious* (*l'inconscient cinématographique*), which Isabelle Huppert has, in my opinion, consistently embodied in most of the films she has been in since *La dentellière*. She knows almost as much as the one filming her (the director) about this fascinating and complex relationship that binds the actress (or actor) to the mechanical eye that observes her. With this camera look, Isabelle Huppert not only challenges the viewer by inviting them to share her most secret intimacy but also identifies with cinema itself as a neutral recording machine of the visible or the real. It is as if the actress, looking directly into the camera's eye and beyond that into the spectator's eye, signifies that she intimately understands the very mechanism of cinema, sharing with it what constitutes the art of moving images. By freezing the image with this camera look, Isabelle Huppert inscribes her intimate complicity with the director who watches her. Since this 1977 film, it seems to me that there is a kind of *secret pact* between Isabelle Huppert and the directors she works with (and she has appeared in about 120 films): You film me, of course, but on my side, I know or recognize you, and we play the same game on equal terms. Cinema, the art of revelation, operates on both sides of the camera, on an equal footing between the actress and the one directing. Isabelle Huppert is an actress who has decidedly positioned herself on the side of the auteur, hence the mise-en-scène. She obviously performs with her co-stars in films directed by Goretta, Chabrol, Benoît Jacquot, Godard, Pialat, Cimino, Haneke, Ozon, or Hong Sang-soo, not to mention Werner Schroeter, Patricia Mazuy, and many others, but *above all*, she performs with her directors: those *who watch her*. Behind each character she embodies, whether an abortionist, criminal, prostitute, judge, Madame Bovary, or the average woman-on-the-street, in drama or comedy, Huppert is *also* an actress who intimately knows the cinema's secret and facilitates the viewer's access to it. The mystery of cinema, the secret of that big eye that looks and inspects the characters' souls deeply, Isabelle Huppert has lived and embodied it passionately for so many years. In one of her latest films, *Sidonie au Japon* (*Sidonie in Japan*), directed by Élise Girard, Isabelle Huppert's title character arrives in Osaka, invited by her Japanese publisher to promote a novel she wrote a few years earlier, dealing with the death of her husband. Sidonie discovers Japan, conforms to the local life codes or customs, often silent, as if this journey were the best way for her to mourn her late husband. The film holds surprises poetically, even comically. The actress is excellent in the role of a silent and secretive woman who lets herself be invaded by the Japanese tranquility. With Isabelle Huppert, the mystery in cinema does not exhaust itself; it constantly regenerates. And this is likely to last for a long time.

February 7, 2024, written for Florence Jacobowitz

Translation by Justin Baillargeon, PhD

Acknowledgments

I dedicate this book to the memory of Robin Wood and Andrew Britton, critics, teachers, colleagues, and friends to whom I am profoundly indebted. Their criticism was informed by the assumption that great art speaks to lived social experience and can change the way one perceives the world, opening up an awareness about life that doesn't readily find expression otherwise. Their valuation of the radical collaborations of Dietrich and Sternberg, Rossellini and Bergman, the cinema of Max Ophüls, stars like Garbo, as forerunners of a modernist cinema within the framework of narrative films, changed the way I envisioned the cinema, as did their welcoming attitude toward popular culture and the recognition of its potential to be as creative and significant as great art and literature. The commitment to women-centered directors, genres and stars, considering the interdependence of all these factors in a reading of a film, the importance of close readings as a central means of critical evaluation, are evidenced in this project.

I am grateful to Richard Lippe and have enjoyed a long, creative, collaborative partnership and friendship that has been invaluable. His willingness to discuss and read my work and provide honest and intelligent comments is much appreciated.

Thanks to the team at Wayne State University Press, and specifically Marie Sweetman, for supporting and publishing this atypical approach to Huppert's work. The fact that the Press has reprinted a number of Robin Wood's books as well as publishing the indispensable *Britton on Film* makes me feel that it is an appropriate choice for me.

Thanks to Serge Toubiana for his foreword; I am honored to have it. Thanks to Isabelle Huppert for agreeing to use her likeness on the cover, and to mk2 films and Anne-Laure Barbarit for permission to use the image xiv Acknowledgments

from Claude Chabrol's *Une affaire de femmes*. I am grateful to David Klein for helping me with the cover design. Professor Paul Socken's assistance with the French translations is appreciated. I also thank Anders Gatten for helping me with the images in the book.

INTRODUCTION

This book is an attempt to place my response to an actor, Isabelle Huppert, who has been important to me since I first saw a number of the early films in which she featured as a central protagonist. Claude Goretta's *La dentellière* (*The Lacemaker*, 1977), Claude Chabrol's *Violette Nozière* (1978), Michael Cimino's *Heaven's Gate* (1980), and Jean-Luc Godard's *Sauve qui peut (la vie)* (*Every Man for Himself*, 1980) were the beginnings of this journey. I cannot say that I ever separated the actor from these films. They spoke to me because they articulated the contradictions and realities of my experience, raising questions about a woman's place in a culture still heavily patriarchal despite the radical changes engendered by the social justice movements of the 1960s and, particularly, feminist politics. If the personal is political, the cinema and its dramatization of the personal was where struggles of lived experience were imagined and envisioned. I identified with Huppert's tendency to appear guarded, a suggestion of melancholy, a more minimalist approach to expression and acting. Huppert always retains a mystery, not in an essentialist sense of unknowability, but an insistence on privacy, a refusal to offer a full explanation, as if there may not always be a clear reason or motivation to account for what a person wants and what is risked in attaining it. There is a reluctance to reveal herself fully, as if by doing so there is a danger of losing control. Huppert was sought out for projects from early on in her career because of her presence and style of performance, which perfectly suited the tensions these films explored, regarding the woman's insistence on self-expression in a culture reluctant to cede her the freedom she seeks. The emphasis on autonomy that comes to define Huppert's image is complemented and supported by a style of performance that upends the mainstays of women and fictional representation and their implications of power and control. Huppert's disruption of the expectations of

2 Introduction

identification, her refusal to surrender herself fully to the viewer, frees her from a tradition of objectification and invites a distinctive approach to her characters. Understanding this strategy is essential to this project.

Over the years the paradoxes attributed to Huppert's persona have been noted and acknowledged—her ability to be present yet absent, inviting intimacy without encouraging familiarity, strong and vulnerable, estranging and humanizing—without attributing these to a methodology of performance. Huppert has discussed her ideas about acting and performance consistently and intelligently, and what emerges is a distinctive, coherent style that leans toward modernism, "une modernité de jeu," challenging traditional ideas about characterization, acting, viewer identification and the pleasures of spectatorship in fictional narrative cinema.[1] Huppert's distinctive approach to characterization, for example, using aspects of her self in the construction of a character instead of offering the illusion of a fictional being existing apart, complicates a discussion of performance, as it implies a level of agency and participation on the part of the actor that exceeds an interpretation of the script. In an interview for *Elle* (2016), Paul Verhoeven commented, "I think there is always a mystery to her acting. I have never seen an actor or actress add so much to the movie that was not in the script."[2] Directors have often given her this leeway in her conception and presentation of the character and the role, and one can argue, as Verhoeven does, that it is a contribution that she brings to the film. The directors who understand and incorporate what she offers—a presence defined by intelligence, resistance, and autonomy supported by a style of performance that demands an active, analytic viewer—collaborate with her to create films that use the persona and the person to shape the role and the character and the viewer's relationship to the narrative. This book presents a thesis about a style of performance, fine-tuned and layered over the course of a long career and collaborations with numerous artists/auteurs, some of them more key to her development, who have contributed to this modernist style of performance across a broad spectrum of films, most of which (excluding some by, for example, Jean-Luc Godard, Werner Schroeter, Hong Sang-soo) more or less adhere to the basic protocols of narrative realist cinema, even when they are on its radical edge. Huppert's tendency to make space for the character alongside her self, to resist effacing who she is in the creation of the character, anchors one's reading of her characters in the present, an extrapolation that politicizes her work and supports the films' intention that the viewer refer the ideas raised to one's own life. Huppert's intelligence, confidence with her sexuality, and commitment to her desires infuses these characters, producing a subtle self-reflexivity that becomes increasingly pronounced as her career develops. She comes to signify resistance, the freedom to pursue what you want, however catastrophic the results, the anti-victim. The idea of the woman insisting on deciding her destiny is not new to women's fiction but takes on new relevance in the wake of the ruptures opened up by the women's movement and the reality of the backlash against freedom, equality, choice—issues still resonant. All of Huppert's great films can be read as a repudiation of a lingering, anachronistic, classist patriarchal society.

Modernist Performance

Huppert's development of a modernist style of performance must be contextualized within a consideration of the European art film and its emphasis on directorial authorship, a zeitgeist drawing from postwar existentialist thought and the political movements of social change that influenced postwar European cinema. The insistence on individual agency as a means toward self-determination and the advocacy for freedom from the oppressive ideologies of various social institutions that conspire to eliminate freedom and choice form a political basis for Huppert's women-centered films. If the modernist agenda is to "authentically express the experience of the contemporary world," as Clement Greenberg has suggested, Huppert's oeuvre explores women's experience in the present—with its tensions, contradictions, and ambiguities left intact.[3] Although there is a range of what constitutes modernist art and modernist performance, one can identify key tenets that identify modernism in postwar theater, literature, visual arts, music, and cinema, including a tendency toward minimalism and abstraction, a reconception of characterization and acting, an attention to the construction of style and representation, and an invitation to a more critically aware viewer. Modernist drama, literature, and cinema move away from immersing the audience in the illusion of a coherent, predictable world through identification with characters one "knows" who are defined for the reader/spectator.[4] Psychology is abandoned, and

4   Introduction

motivations are opaque, muted, and replaced by ambiguity, mystery and complexity.[5] An emphasis on interiority—unconscious motivations, mental states, an idea of time that is disjunctive—disrupt the semblance of verisimilitude. A sense of disconnection, alienation, and ennui are recurring thematic tropes. Often landscapes or milieux can be as formative to the meaning of the film as dialogue and plot, contextualizing the character's individual experience in relation to the outer world.[6] Characters are placed within the totality of the film, and meaning is dependent on a consideration of the whole.

Huppert's distinctive style of performance can be located within this tradition. Instead of creating a fully defined character, psychologically explained through the exteriorization of emotions and motivations, Huppert creates something very different. Her reluctance to transform herself into a character, to disappear into an imitation of a person one can access for the duration of the narrative, challenges expectations of identification, resisting the attendant implications of appropriation and the fantasy of availability and ownership typically offered in the illusion of inhabiting another person.[7] Instead, Huppert's characters often leave gaps that defy a full explanation of motivation, exposing a substratum of contradictory impulses, where defiance or protest emerges. Huppert has mentioned her affinity with Nathalie Sarraute's conception of characterization and the invitation to the reader to experience the characters' interiority, revealing states with their impulses and contradictions instead of explaining motivation and psychology.[8] Like Sarraute's or Duras's protagonists of *le nouveau roman*, the characters' actions can be motivated by abstract, subconscious states that are not always contained by consciousness or controlled by morality. This invites a different mode of viewer engagement—one that is active and participatory, as meaning is elusive, ambiguous, and less pronounced. Huppert's remarkable ability to exteriorize what is ineffable and to reveal interiority has been fundamental to her collaborations with Claude Chabrol and Michael Haneke, among others. One can trace a direct relationship between le nouveau roman and Chabrol's conception of *Violette Nozière* or Claire Denis's *White Material* (2009) in the films' privileging of states of mind not governed by the logic of consciousness or linear time.

The modernist performance style associated with Bresson's actors as "models" evidence elements shared with Huppert's, however more austere.

Communicating a state of mind in Claire Denis's *White Material*.

The movement away from exteriorized expressivity,[9] the emphasis on interiority without psychological explanation, the resulting opacity, the ideal of neutrality, the overlay of actor and character, informed the conception of acting and characterization of directors like Godard, elements that Huppert claims were discussed in preparation for her role as Isabelle in *Sauve qui peut (la vie)*.[10] James Quandt points out Godard acknowledged his "*Histoire(s)* proceed from a Bresson axiom in the Notes: 'Don't show all aspects of things. Leave a margin of the undefined,'" an idea that Michael Haneke shares.[11] Haneke claims that Bresson's Balthazar, "the screen 'hero'[,] is not a character who invites us to identify with him, who experiences emotions for us that we are allowed to feel vicariously. Instead, he is a projection screen, a blank sheet of paper, whose sole task is to be filled with the viewer's thoughts and feelings."[12] Balthazar is clearly the extreme example, but the unwillingness to explain or exteriorize emotions, to leave gaps, allows the "actor" to subvert the pleasure of emotional identification with a character that can be appropriated by the viewer and fully understood, avoiding an uncritical involvement in the narrative. The perception of "blankness," "opacity," and "absence" often associated with Huppert is an intentional modernist strategy of creating a space for the spectator to assess one's "thoughts and feelings" in dialogue with the work. It also points to what is not easily visible. Huppert suggests that "an actor is aware that what is hidden is as important as what is shown," and, in her work with Benoît Jacquot, for example, she relies on the director to delicately reveal what is hidden, the "veiled" unconscious.[13] Antonioni's modernist characters have been described as "abstractions" and "embodied themes rather

6   Introduction

than flesh-and-blood people."[14] Instead of knowable characters whose actions are "explained" by psychological motives, they are "indeterminate, less unified ciphers whose emotional lives and thought processes were ambiguous, if not polysemic."[15] Patrice Chéreau's idea of Huppert as "the abyss as blank page" suggests a similar idea.[16] One must creatively fill in spaces and ellipses through critical reading.

The nouveau roman, Bresson's oeuvre, Antonioni's modernist cinema, Brechtian theater: all insist on an active, engaged critical spectator willing to explore the narrative intellectually as well as emotively. Huppert's films elicit a different kind of identification but are not without pathos and emotion. Her ability to humanize complex characters while, at times, estranging the spectator suggests that identification is solicited and used to invite an engagement with a character's position, the alienation or sense of entrapment placed within the overall social context of the film. Andrew Higson makes the same point with regard to Brecht's strategy of distanciation: "It is a means of foregrounding the ideas or the ideological processes at stake in the action, rather than encouraging the audience to become inextricably bound up in the psychological predicament or emotional state of the character performing the action. It is a means of linking the individual to the social as well as, or rather than, to the 'inner self,' and the discrete action to its historical context."[17] The pleasure offered is in identifying with the woman's agency—the demand for personal fulfillment and the refusal of the standard consolations of victimhood, acceptance, and renunciation. The pathos of Madame Bovary's decision to commit suicide is dependent on one's identification with her *prise de conscience* and her understanding, finally, of how a masculine hierarchy thwarts women's self-realization. The spectator must actively read and participate in the creation of meaning, as the film places her trajectory within a social world that impinges on her life and, by extension, women's lives. Brecht's idea that the actor "demonstrates" as opposed to "becomes" a character applies to Huppert's insistence against creating the semblance of being a "person" separate from her self.[18] Her characters, therefore, always imply her presence.[19] Since her earliest projects, Huppert seemed to intuitively understand this, developing a style both instinctive and controlled, straining the illusion of creating a character who is someone distinct and clearly defined.[20] This is central to her modernist style; by using aspects of herself she disrupts the illusion that underlies identification and not only references herself but also the relationship between actor and spectator. By not disappearing into a fictional other whom one can inhabit throughout the narrative, the fantasy of appropriation imbricated in the pleasures of identification through the gaze is obstructed, implying an awareness that the character is a construction. Huppert's characters don't cancel out identification so much as redefine the terms. One identifies with a position without the illusion of "becoming" the character. As Huppert explains, "Even though I don't believe I'm like Emma Bovary, a lot of her feelings are close to me. And that's why it's a masterpiece, a monument. Flaubert created the archetypal woman. Since I too am a woman and not a monkey, I feel close to her turmoil, her emotions, hesitations, her idealism, selfishness, and her dissatisfaction. But she's not me. I'm not a provincial woman married to a doctor trying desperately to be another person."[21] Similarly, the spectator doesn't "become" Emma, but can still identify with her sense of ennui and the conflicted feelings it engenders.

The melodrama and the woman's film open a space for the utilization of modernist strategies, and Huppert's women-centered films are related to these genres. Andrew Britton argues that the "anti-naturalism of the melodramatic tradition and its tendency to conceive of characters as exemplary embodiments of objective social forces and contradictions in an implicitly didactic and polemical mode, were very readily available for Brechtian inflection."[22] In *Screening Modernism*, András Bálint Kovács points out the modernist characteristics of the melodrama, citing Antonioni's *Eclipse* (1962), among others, as modern melodramas about the condition of alienation and existential "nothingness."[23] Characters are often more abstracted, less psychologically realized, and understood in their placement within their surroundings, communicating a sense of their alienation from prescribed social roles. Films as diverse as Michael Haneke's *La Pianiste* (*The Piano Teacher*, 2001), *White Material*, and *Elle* (2016), for example, draw from the traditions of the Gothic melodrama. The generic tropes of madness, illness, or hysteria as expressions or manifestations of powerlessness, familial dysfunction, alienation from oppressive social dictates, an identification with the outlier are vivified by Huppert in the films' distinctly feminist iterations of classic generic concerns.[24] The New Wave directors'/critics' recognition of the work of filmmakers like Hitchcock and Rossellini as precursors of modern cinema and forerunners of the idea of a cinema that would render contemporary reality in a way that

8   Introduction

expresses the experience of modern life is illustrative of the acknowledgment of a continuity between the New Wave and cinematic practices that draw from a history of genres like the melodrama.[25] The woman's dream of changing the reality of her existence, her sense of entitlement to do so—the backbone of Bovarysme—is fundamental to the woman's novel and film and is particularly pronounced in the Chabrol collaborations as well as Rithy Panh's underrated *Un barrage contre le Pacifique* (*The Sea Wall*, 2014) or Denis's *White Material*, which set these thematic concerns within colonialist settings. These films must be placed within a context that considers the relationship between performance and genre, and how a modernist reconception of identification and performance can utilize the conventions of the woman's film to investigate the woman's position in contemporary social life.

The European art film develops in conjunction with the idea of authorship, the privileging of the director as the creative artist responsible for the film. Astruc's idea of the *caméra-stylo* suggests a conception of a personal cinema of ideas, abstract thought and intellectual expression, the "essay" film.[26] *La politique des auteurs* expanded this idea of the essay to include fiction, and the director, as metteur en scène, "writes" through the cinematic visualization of the film.[27] Huppert's most significant work has been with directors whose personal vision fully informs the film. She acknowledges the creation of characterization exists in tandem with mise-en-scène, as part of the totality of the work of art. Understanding camera placement, mise-en-scène, as a "partner" to her conception of character extends the idea of authorship to something more collaborative,[28] evident in her comment "I furrow my film inside those I pass through."[29] This suggests the latitude she sees herself being given to participate in the creative process. Many of the directors she works with seek her out with the understanding of what she offers, utilizing her contribution and conception of characterization within the entirety of the film. She increasingly performs in films written explicitly for her, creating a character informed by who she is, in conjunction with the director's vision of the film. Huppert's tendency to create characters who leave blanks to be filled in, whose motivations can be unconscious and unacknowledged by the character, are felicitous in the art film and its unique conception of the cinema, where the point may be to explore ideas and raise questions or present existential arguments with an engaged, active viewer. Huppert's seven films with Claude Chabrol, seven with Benoît Jacquot, four with Michael Haneke, three with

Hong Sang-soo, and two each with Bertrand Tavernier, Jean-Luc Godard, and Werner Schroeter evidence the partnerships between a director and an actor whose presence and style of performance is central to each project.

A book about an actor and performance is also one about the spectator who is "reading" the work. Understanding performance through close textual readings demonstrates the interdependence of authorship, star persona, genre, politics, crucial to a discussion of Huppert and acting. In *Elle*, Michèle is inscrutable if one isn't placing her within the broader social context the film painstakingly sets up, particularly as it is a film that doesn't adhere to the expectations of a traditional realist narrative. She is, however, intelligible and generates pathos if one is willing to read the character within the terms of the film, mise-en-scène, the arc of its narrative, the conventions from which it draws. This study presents a thesis about a style of performance supported by the presence of an actor who has come to signify a feminist approach to acting and characterization. Select films explore this thesis, the idea being to elucidate a methodology that can be applied to the many films in which Huppert has appeared. As ideas and theories should be tested against critical practice, I have chosen close readings as a means of illustrating the significance of Huppert's performance to the meaning of the film. To extract performance from a context that recognizes the confluence of authorship, genre, and, crucially, critical reading is to reduce the discussion of an actor's performance style and presence to a list of facial and hand gestures, the occasional outburst or generalizations related to recurring character traits such as cold, perverse, inexpressive, mad, or monstrous, that risks solidifying clichés into ends in themselves.[30] Performance must be placed within the entirety of the work of art and the meaning it invites. *Violette Nozière*, *La Pianiste*, and *Elle* risk being drained of their enormous complexity and pathos if one is unwilling to actively read them, considering mise-en-scène and a language of conventions to which they creatively refer. Readings are, of course, not limited to mine; a great work of art allows for multiple readings as diverse as its audience.

The following short readings of *La dentellière* and *Violette Nozière* evidence the beginnings of Huppert's modernist style of performance. *Heaven's Gate* is included as a Hollywood auteurist film that, performance-wise, adheres to the conventions of American cinema and the western/ melodrama. Although atypical in terms of Huppert's style, it illustrates characteristics that became essential to Huppert's persona, particularly her characters' insistence on self-definition: Ella Watson is both central to the community and characterized by her outsider status. The film celebrates Ella's challenge to traditional conceptions of a woman's place by presenting her as a woman who is independent, resilient, outspoken, at ease with her sexuality, and unconventional, regarding her love relationships as friendships. Cimino utilizes Ella as an emblem of possibility, which accounts for the gravitas accorded her assassination at the end of the film, summarizing the sense of loss that permeates the film's vision of America. Cimino's insistence on casting Huppert as Ella was prescient to what she comes to signify.

La dentellière

Huppert's early films often address a young woman's desire for sexual freedom and self-determination, struggles within the family and the repression of female sexuality. Bertrand Bier's *Les Valseuses* (*Going Places*, 1974), *La dentellière*, *Violette Nozière*, Benoît Jacquot's *Les ailes de la colombe* (*The Wings of the Dove*, 1981), and Joseph Losey's *La Truite* (*The Trout*, 1982) are transitional coming-of-age narratives, where the protagonist struggles

Acting as being: Pomme in *La dentellière*.

Introduction 11

to move from the presexual virgin/child to a sexually independent person. Huppert describes *La dentellière*—which brought her international attention and recognition—as the film that changed how she was perceived as an actress.[31] Huppert's character, Béatrice, known as "Pomme," is a young working-class woman who meets and falls in love with François (Yves Beneyton), a *haut bourgeois* university student. Although the narrative trajectory is somewhat anomalous to what Huppert's persona comes to signify as an anti-victim, or at least one who expresses herself, as Pomme is destroyed by her lover's rejection, her naturalistic performance, remarkable for a kind of unaffected minimalism, already demonstrates a form of acting degree zero that Godard sought. Pomme is a character who communicates who she is through gestures over thoughts or words, revealing herself by the way she eats an apple, how she enjoys her ice cream on the terrace of a café while on vacation, or her manner of walking or being. It is riveting to watch her because hers is a performance so self-effacing and subtle that it appears almost effortless. Though this restraint suits the conception of Pomme, a person rarely treated as a subject of interest, as the epilogue notes, whom one passes by without really noticing, Huppert's performance never seems acted or overtly demonstrative. François, the student of Marxism and semiotics, is offered as a more familiar figure of identification to the viewer, until he loses interest in Pomme and discards her. His attraction to her virginal, unspoiled innocence is also a self-affirmation of his genuine radicality and soon becomes his fear of her difference, and François abandons Pomme as a failed experiment after gaining her trust and deep affection. The scene where he leads her blindfolded to the edge of a precipice, a game based on complete trust, dramatizes the relationship, which he later betrays. Pomme becomes a victim of François, who uses and then tires of her; lacking the means to articulate her feelings of betrayal and loss, she sinks into a depression, a victim of his pursuit and precipitous rejection. "I thought you wanted to change," he argues, tiring of the fantasy and her failure to conform to the project, misreading her silences in his criticism of her inability to express herself. François only sees the image he wishes to construct to suit his needs and therefore cannot read the subtlety of her gestures, her means of expression—putting a stone on a grave, preparing food, ironing and folding, the everyday signs of caring for someone. Pomme's fragility and victim status are somewhat undermined by her gaze toward the camera at the end

12 Introduction

An ending that demands to be read: *La dentellière*.

of the film; in a long take, the camera slowly approaches her from behind as she is seated at a table mechanically knitting, then turns and rests alongside her, at which point she stops and turns to look directly at the camera. It is a moment that is disjunctive and almost accusatory, implicating the viewer in François's treatment of her, reminiscent of Antoine Doinel's confrontational gaze at the end of François Truffaut's *Les 400 coups* (*The 400 Blows*, 1959). It is a moment that solicits an interpretation and a reassessment of how one stereotypes women like Pomme and why she is at the center of the narrative.

Pomme's minimalist naturalism, melancholy, the references to an image in a genre painting, is further developed by Godard in his *Scénario de Sauve qui peut (la vie)* (1979), where he compares framing and body movements in the film "comme chez Bonnard," and particularly in the idealization of the working-class virgin in *Passion*. The grace of everyday gestures, the deglamorization of the character, the emphasis on honesty and transparency, and, most importantly, the aim for neutrality over expressivity and acting as subtraction is already present in *La dentellière*, as is the story of a male who projects his desires onto the woman and his inability to see her outside of his needs. The inscrutability of the woman as a reflection of the male ego is a theme Godard foregrounds and elaborates, though the central female characters in *Sauve qui peut (la vie)* and *Passion* (1982) express a resistance to their obfuscation and subordination.

Violette Nozière

Huppert's first collaboration with Chabrol, *Violette Nozière*, introduces themes that came to define their body of work and significant aspects of Huppert's persona and approach to characterization. *Violette Nozière*, like *Une affaire de femmes*'s Marie Latour (*Story of Women*, 1988), achieved notoriety for a criminal act, but Chabrol inverts their singularity, suggesting they are an extreme of the norm, typical women whose actions are a response to their oppression, heightened at a time when fascism with its masculinist ethos is dominant or on the rise. Chabrol, like Haneke, was influenced by Hitchcock, who also locates criminal deviance within a social framework and often, particularly, the family. Alice White of *Blackmail* (1929), the two Charlies of *Shadow of a Doubt* (1943), *Marnie* (1964), and Norman Bates of *Psycho* (1960) are variants of the type, divided psyches trying to negotiate the sexually repressive contradictions of the family and the culture. Like Alice White of *Blackmail*, Violette's dividedness, the state of contradiction she cannot reconcile, is visualized in her costume—the clean-scrubbed appearance of the schoolgirl who lives at home (her innocence emphasized in the photograph of her confirmation) and the sexual vamp who emerges at night. When Violette is diagnosed with syphilis, she worries that her parents will find out that she is sexually active and enlists her doctor to avoid implicating herself; instead, she convinces her parents that it is a hereditary illness they all share. *Violette Nozière* might be considered an iteration of the American 1970s horror movie—rite-of-passage films where protagonists like Regan of William Friedkin's *The Exorcist* (1973) or Carrie of Brian De Palma's *Carrie* (1976) threaten to acquire a sexual identity in a patriarchal world fearful of the girl-child becoming an empowered sexual being. The characters' duality, both angelic and demonic, fuels the horror of the narrative. The emergent night side—sexual, violent, independent—expresses the cultural fear of change and the loss of patriarchal control in both the family and the culture at large. Violette Nozière's trial was considered a trial of the family; the fantasy of parricide or killing the father, or usurping his place or what he represents, and the complementary unconscious unwillingness to relinquish the mother and female empowerment are themes that persist throughout Huppert's films. Violette's mask-like inscrutability suggests that she acts without full awareness of what drives her or the implications of her actions. Although

The divided self: Violette in *Violette Nozière*.

her motivations are not psychologically explained, the film invites a psychoanalytic reading of the themes of the child's/adolescent's inability to achieve a sexual identity as demanded by the culture.

Violette takes on a visually feminized lover, Jean Dabin, and usurps the dominant role in the relationship, taking pleasure in providing him with money and stealing petty cash and jewels from home to supplement his increasing demand.[32] The escalating stakes for bigger sums and Jean's query of an inheritance, along with the complications of her illness, the pressure to marry, and the context of a culture that promotes the myths of love, romance, and the conspicuous consumption of fashion, travel and leisure all contribute to Violette's solution to murder her parents. She protests what she sees as the pettiness of familial life by creating a fantasy of grandeur to realize her vision with a plan to travel to Les Sables-d'Olonne in a Bugatti, while releasing herself from familial obstructions. In many ways, Violette is an adolescent prototype of Madame Bovary, a character whose aspirations are fed through popular culture and its myths of romance, along with a sense of entitlement and ambitions of upward mobility as an escape from the boredom and entrapment in which she

Introduction   15

finds herself. Moments where Violette stages her desires in front of the mirror in the hotel room she rents are like Madame Bovary's enactments of her romances in the garden, both of them locked in their own subjectivity, escaping the mediocrity they reject. Their transgressions are provoked by an ever-increasing accumulation of discontent that they cannot fully understand. Although Violette never achieves the clarity and prise de conscience that Emma Bovary and Marie Latour reach, her final denunciation of the jury of patriarchal men who judge and condemn her, cursing them as pitiful bastards who disgust her, suggests an awareness of her experience of oppression.

Violette Nozière is structured as a flashback following Violette's murder attempt. The narrative is presented in fragments where dreams, memory, and fantasy freely intermingle, illustrative of Violette's states of mind as opposed to explaining her motivations in a narrative that follows causal logic, placing great emphasis on the unconscious. Violette is never presented as a psychologically plausible character with whom one can identify. Was she raped by her father as she claimed, or simply responding to the investigator's insinuation?[33] Jean Carmet's characterization and presentation of M. Nozière as a benign presence whose intentions are, at best, ambiguous in this regard don't directly support the accusation. Instead, the confined, claustrophobic space of the working-class home, where privacy is nonexistent, and the father steals glances at his daughter's naked body as she washes herself, or the parents' attempts to muffle their lovemaking— "You'll wake *la petite*"—within earshot of Violette, suggests the way sexuality permeates the small apartment despite the efforts to deny, contain, and control it, and the emphasis on hygiene and cleanliness fail to compensate for the dirtiness of sexual needs. Casting the adult Huppert in some scenes as a child bouncing on her father's lap or as a nine-year-old left to her grandmother's care, feeling abandoned and shut out of her parents' secrets, underlines the choice of presenting states of mind over reality and Violette's perception of herself as both an adult and a child. The train whistles that mark the narrative evoke Violette's father and an association with his railway work as an engine driver, just as the recurring references to the sea (*la mer*) and its similarity to the word for mother (*la mère*) suggest that Violette's desire to go to the sea or her dream of her lover emerging from the sea, hint at unconscious coded expressions of maternal yearning, dream associations that ask to be deciphered. Violette's robberies, like

16   Introduction

those of Hitchcock's Marnie, are acts rooted in a subconscious place that are meaningful beyond the need for money. Violette's misreading of the responses to her actions—surprised when a man mistakes her for a prostitute when she rifles through his wallet after sex, offended by a man's sexual advances after entering his car late at night asking to be taken to the sea, or her surprise at her guilty verdict—suggests her disengagement from the world around her as well as from herself. Huppert's flat, opaque, matter-of-fact presentation of Violette suppresses the expressive flourishes one might expect of a character who decries mediocrity, visualizing instead her subconscious reality. Huppert's remarkable ability to dramatize contradiction and a layered interiority that Violette herself cannot access or explain is key to her portrayal of the child/woman struggling to become an adult, in a performance that was acknowledged at Cannes with her award as Best Actress. A critic from the *Washington Post* at the time of the film's release complained about Huppert's inexpressiveness and opacity, and the failure to clarify Violette's motives, as if the unwillingness to explain or facilitate identification is a fault of the performance or director instead of an intentional strategy of the filmmaker and his film.[34] Huppert later claimed that Chabrol "liberated me from any idea of character," encouraging a complex portrayal that involved "showing" versus "explaining," acknowledging ambiguity and revealing states of mind that defy coherent motivation.[35] She remains enigmatic and eludes direct identification; she is only comprehensible within the social context the narrative creates.

Violette's ultimate recuperation into society and success at regaining her mother's devotion underlines the point that, despite the surrealists' celebration of her crime as a liberating enactment of instinct and the subconscious, she was never overtly a political rebel, but a person responding to her familial and inequitable social conditions. (In fact, Violette's appreciation of her newfound celebrity is obliquely suggested in the scene in prison near the end of the film, where she hums the tune of the popular song written about her.) Nevertheless, Huppert's performance, within the context of the film, reveals the crime to be a subconscious act of self-liberation. As Andrew Britton argues, the fantasy of phallic erasure, or the reconstituting of the family without the father, as an expression of power and independence, is a central preoccupation of the woman's film and a recurrent one in many of Huppert's subsequent films—*La Pianiste* (2001); *Elle* (2016); Diane Kurys's *Coup de foudre / Entre Nous* (1983); Chabrol's *L'ivresse de*

Violette's subconscious memory/dream of sexual contradictions in the family. Violette and Baptiste Nozière (Jean Carmet) in *Violette Nozière*.

pouvoir (*Comedy of Power*, 2006), with the pointedly named protagonist Jeanne-Charmant Killman; Jacquot's *Villa Amalia* (2009); *White Material* (2009); and *Un barrage contre le Pacifique* (2008), to name a few—as is its corollary, the woman's unwillingness to relinquish close female friendships and love relationships, as seen in *Une affaire de femmes* (1988), Chabrol's *La Cérémonie* (1995), and *Coup de foudre*.[36] In addition, the blurring of boundaries and power dynamics between Huppert's characters and a son or younger male as an alternate or a substitution for the husband/father/lover in films such as Jacquot's *L'école de la chair* (*The School of Flesh*, 1998), Christoph Honoré's *Ma mère* (*My Mother*, 2004), Joachim Lafosse's *Nue Propriété* (*Private Property*, 2006), Luc Bondy's *Les fausses confidences* (*False Confessions*, 2017), or Bavo Defurne's *Souvenir* (2016) with its subversive theme song "Joli garçon, je dis oui!," or as dependents who cannot navigate the world without the mother, as in *White Material* and Haneke's *Happy End* (2017), are further examples of films that explore the fantasy of a rejection of the father. Many of Huppert's films use her persona's emblematic autonomy to challenge the oppressive regulations of a patriarchal, classist culture

18 Introduction

and its implications for the woman who resists, even when the release results in violence and monstrous acts. At times Huppert is conflated with perverseness or amorality and the taboo, which, in her greatest films, are placed as responses to the culture in the way madness is understood in the woman's novel as a reaction to the woman's nullification and entrapment.

Heaven's Gate

The critical dismissal of *Heaven's Gate* in North America in 1980 is by now well documented. Excepting lone voices like Robin Wood, who discussed it with the seriousness it deserved, claiming its original version to be "among the supreme achievements of the Hollywood cinema," and an appreciative reception in England and France, the film is only belatedly receiving its due, particularly following its restored and remastered release by Criterion in 2013.[37] Isabelle Huppert was cast in a major role as Ella Watson, after Hollywood stars including Jane Fonda and Diane Keaton turned it down. Cimino fought to have his heroine played by Isabelle Huppert after seeing *Violette Nozière* at the Paris Cinema in New York, despite the studio's vigorous objections to her being unknown in America, her accented English, and the perception of her as "too young," "too French," and "too contemporary."[38] Huppert was a felicitous choice for Cimino's depiction of Ella, who is conceived as a modern woman, both within and outside of history. Considering Huppert's career, it is a performance and characterization that is anomalous in the way it conforms to the conventions of Hollywood practice. When Marlene Dietrich agreed to appear in the comeback role of Frenchy, a saloon entertainer in the western *Destry Rides Again* (1939), there were doubts whether the role suited the performance style with which she became associated in her collaborations with Josef von Sternberg, where her characters were not psychologically driven, didn't explain motivations, or satisfy traditional expectations of identification and were aligned with artifice and stylization more so than realism. Dietrich's performance style was defined by an ironic detachment and her presence, which always reminded the viewer that the character was also Dietrich. Dietrich's Frenchy, like Ella, is also an immigrant and a life force in the community—expressive, energetic, as capable and demanding as the "the boys in the back room." The viewer's identification with the character is intensely felt with her death, like Ella's, at the end of the film. Her absence is a loss that haunts the resolution of the narrative, marking the emptiness of the ideologically sanctioned couple of Destry and Miss Tyndall. Unlike the recognition of Dietrich's success in adopting an entirely different conception of performance in *Destry Rides Again*, Huppert's significant performance as Ella was sadly lost in the fallout of the film's controversial identity as a disaster.

Heaven's Gate utilizes the conventions of the western to present a commentary on the founding of America and the precariousness of the democratic principles that define it, but it is also a meditation on the impending changes that were to characterize the conservatism of Reaganite America and the consequences of privileging economics over liberal ideals. The film is based on the shocking historical events of the Johnson County War, when cattle baron financial interests protected by the governor and the president resulted in the sanctioned murder of American homesteaders by an American mercenary militia, setting the tone of irretrievable loss that permeates the film. As Billy Irvine (John Hurt) sums up, "I guess in principle everything can be done." The film begins with the ritualized Harvard graduation of James Averill (Chris Kristofferson) and Billy Irvine, and their graduating class's idealistic enthusiasm for social betterment. The spirit of reconstruction is celebrated while also subtly undermined in Billy's humorous valedictory summation: "We disclaim all intention of making a change in what we esteem, on the whole, well arranged"—a declaration of the ruling class's reluctance to make any concessions that would endanger their privilege and dominance. *Heaven's Gate* is less James's story of an individual's lost opportunities to enact social change and a complacency that neither he nor Billy can ultimately overcome as it is a statement about democracies that are, in fact, divided by the disparity between the rich who enjoy money and power and the poor who are at their mercy. The film is both an elegy and a wistful imagining of the utopian potential of what might have been: a frontier community of diverse European immigrants united by a promise of freedom and equality, unbound by the traditions of privilege and class.

Ella is central to that envisioning of a young country open to new, fresh possibilities. Ella's energy, vivacity, and originality are exactly what makes her so appealing and ultimately untenable to the status quo. Her

20   Introduction

distinctive identity defies the categorizations of the western and its masculine, puritan ethos, where the woman is an adjunct to the male and his needs, either sexual, related to male pleasure, as the saloon entertainer or whore, or necessary for domesticity and settlement, as the wife or schoolmarm. Ella straddles both distinctions, as she is a madam/prostitute who runs a brothel in the town of Sweetwater but who is also committed to settlement and marriage. Her establishment is a no-nonsense profit-making business, open to accepting cash or cattle for payment in advance. Nate Champion (Christopher Walken) also prostitutes himself to the Stockgrowers Association for money and the potential of the upward mobility he seeks, and Ella justifies taking payment from him despite her affection for him because, she explains simply, she likes money. The scene where Ella is maintaining her books and Nate tells her he enjoys watching her write figures emphasizes her identity first and foremost as an ambitious, practical, self-sufficient member of the Sweetwater community, a character who diverges from social expectations or stereotypes. Steven Bach reported that the *Los Angeles Times* arts editor Charles Champlin reconsidered his original condemnation of the short version of the film at the time of the release of the longer one and recognized Ella's autonomy, noting how she was "not so much ... the stereotyped whore with a heart of gold but ... an independent woman with her own code."[39] Perhaps as a French immigrant Ella can more easily challenge American puritanism and is unencumbered by guilt or propriety; she is at ease with her sexuality and the unconventional situation of loving two men at once, explaining simply, "I can manage it." *Heaven's Gate* unusually supports this possibility and even suggests a kind of friendship between the men, as when James is out cold in Ella's bed and Nate, almost tenderly, carries him back to his room; their relationship is further solidified in Nate's farewell note addressed to both Ella and James when he realizes he is dying. Ella is also building a future in a new country she wants to be a part of and is direct about her practical choice to accept Nate's proposal, explaining to James, "You buy me things, he asked me to marry him," understanding that James hesitates to make a personal commitment that would demand stepping beyond the strict parameters of his class. James acknowledges his apartness from the community that, as its marshal, it is his job to protect, telling Ella, "It's more your country than mine anyway." The film foregrounds Ella's devotion to her community by her refusal to leave Sweetwater despite the danger to her, and her participation in all major communal events, culminating in her frontline riding and shooting in the circle of the final battle. Ella's fearless crossing of gender lines is symbolically punished by her inclusion on the death list, justified as her complicity for accepting stolen cattle. The scene of the rape and murder of the prostitutes culminating in Ella's brutal rape begins with her warning the man who uses his gun to lift up her skirt, "If you don't stop, I'll bend that iron around your head," and then, smoking a cigarette, proceeds with business, calmly declaring the rules of payment, well aware of her danger and their identity as paid assassins. The rape is a declaration and an enactment of power, as is Canton's (Sam Waterston) stalking and murdering of Ella following the final battle, which has no narrative logic following the cavalry's rescue of Canton and his mercenaries, except as a statement of power, which her independence threatens.

Cimino's *Heaven's Gate* is a western but is also akin to the European art film in its complete investment in the director/auteur's aesthetic vision, which never subordinates form and style to plot and characters. Cimino references John Ford as a director of westerns aware of the significance of location to meaning, and, one might add, the importance of set pieces like weddings, dances, or funerals.[40] The profound physical beauty of the landscape, magnificently visualized in the remastered version of the film, is necessary to understanding the citizens/immigrants, their fierce desire to work the land and develop the country despite the terrible consequences of their persecution, and the hate and callousness that greets them. Ella's

Ella shooting back at the empowered all-male militia, challenging social hierarchies as both a new immigrant and a woman in *Heaven's Gate*.

22   Introduction

and Nate's homes, though vulnerable, signify their joy as new Americans, where Ella pours coffee and bakes pies in her attempts to embrace her Americanness, and Nate papers his home as an expression of planning a future. Ella's subtle response to Nate's pride in his home—she tells him it is beautiful and softly wipes a tear from her eye—is touching in the way she perfectly understands and empathizes with Nate's commitment and his attempts, as he explains, "to civilize the wilderness." *Heaven's Gate* is architecturally built to privilege significant communal events—the opening graduation ceremony and dance, the entire community gathered for their portrait followed by the Sunday dance at Heaven's Gate, the final battle for Sweetwater's self-preservation. Excepting the Harvard sequence, which is referenced in James and Ella's waltz at Heaven's Gate, Ella's prominence in these scenes reflects her centrality to the film. Her act of showing off her newly acquired birthday gift in a rambunctious ride, emphasized by several shots taken from a mobile camera mounted on the buggy, on the day of the public gathering for a photo that documents and celebrates the homesteaders (like the dance at Heaven's Gate that later follows), doesn't particularly advance the narrative so much as communicate the utopian promise of Sweetwater through energy, vitality of movement, and an irrepressible sense of fun and pleasure. The Sunday dance at Heaven's Gate (the hall referencing a utopia where the rich cannot enter) and the visual presence of David Mansfield as the fiddle player John DeCory and his band, is a statement of Americana that stands at the heart of the film; it foregrounds the film's score, which blends indigenous American music with strains of the waltz, communicating a distinctively American democratic music and dance, and a tradition it leaves behind. The dance declares a celebration of a nonhierarchical diversity and inclusiveness. Ella joins in, arm in arm, in a kind of free-form roller-skating dance that makes a statement of equality, freedom, and community.

The scene following the carnage of the final battle, where Ella and James prepare to leave, wordlessly dressed in travel clothes that suggest wedding attire, is presented as almost dreamlike, cryptic and more symbolic than real. Canton's ambush and killing of Ella sums up the resistance to social change underlying the narrative, punishing James for his betrayal of his class and eradicating the promise Ella represents of a different America. James's cri de coeur, "Oh, Ella, don't die," weeping as he lifts her up, is the film's final emotional statement of a catastrophic loss. The last scene on the yacht in Newport, where James is adrift with the unnamed beautiful Harvard woman (Rosie Vela), is a dramatization of his life following the defeat of the Johnson County War—stasis and containment, a mortuary of stillness and lifelessness summarizing the sense of mourning, personal loss, and lost ideals.

Cimino utilizes Huppert's presence to embody Ella's independence and courage to articulate her needs and act on them, crossing gender lines in her affinity with traditional masculine activity and agency, elements that became key to her persona. Although one can argue that Cimino's use of characters is atypical in the way their development does not dominate or take precedence over the "story" of the betrayal of democratic principles and ideals, they do conform to American expectations of performance and characterization. Unlike the minimalist naturalism of *La dentellière*, where the character is presented through her physical presence, the pared-down neutrality and quasi-documentary self-referencing aspects of the Godard films, or *Violette Nozière*'s abstracted unconscious states and opacity, Ella is a character whose motivations are clear to the viewer and forthcoming; she is direct and expressive, and there is no ambiguity about her. Although Huppert brings a contemporary aspect to Ella, she creates a psychologically realized character who is offered as one of the key figures of identification, who exists fully apart from the actor. There are no gaps in explaining who Ella is and what she wants. At times this availability to the viewer accompanies a kind of fantasy of appropriation, most notable in the scene where Ella bathes in the river following her heated carriage ride that seems to be included to offer an opportunity for a kind of traditional form of visual pleasure while evoking Huppert's association with nature and naturalness. Other scenes are more ambiguous, such as when Ella first sees Jim and tears off her clothes as a response to his query of how she manages to conduct her business and bake pies at once, illustrating Ella's sense of humor, self-possession, and comfort with her sexuality rather than her objectification for the viewer, naturalizing her sexuality and nakedness. Huppert's offhand, blasé delivery of the comment about the photographer—"It's always the skinny guys that surprise you"—is another example of her dry wit and ease with sexuality. One of Ella's most charming moments is when she runs out, covered only in a blanket, to see her new carriage, and, touched by the gesture, comments on its beauty and says, "I can't stop crying. I feel I finally got somewhere. I'm so happy I could bust,"

Ella's unrestrained whoop of joy: *Heaven's Gate*.

and then lets out a loud, spontaneous whoop of joy. Overall Huppert's Ella is a vital American heroine who challenges the western's conventional typologies to perfectly realize the film's yearning for reinvention. Huppert's youth and contemporariness, and her accent which marks her as a French immigrant—the characteristics that concerned the studio—are precisely those Cimino needed to extend his critique beyond history, to an America still divided by the same disparities.

The chapters that follow were chosen to be illustrative of salient aspects of Huppert's style and the development of her career. Chapter 1 expands on what constitutes Huppert's modernist style, setting a basis for the readings of Huppert's oeuvre as explored through specific films. Huppert's articulate, intellectually rigorous elucidation of her modernist approach over the course of her career is invaluable to this book, as it outlines a singular methodology that defines her distinctive style. The chapter offers examples of precedents of modernist performance styles, suggesting a tradition that evidences shared aspects of Huppert's style. Chapter 2 examines Godard's modernist ideas about acting and characterization, which become evident in elements of Huppert's performance style as it developed. Godard's promotion of a pared-down acting style emphasizing interiority over outward expressivity, along with his use of the actors' personas and histories to inform and enrich their identities as fictional characters, contribute to a textured work that complicates the exploration of gender relations and the male consciousness at its center.

Chapters 3 and 4 discuss Chabrol's collaborations with Huppert, arguably the most significant of her career—hence the inclusion of a discussion of two of their films. Chabrol's films, less overtly experimental than those by other New Wave directors, follow the semblance of a more traditional narrative but are modernist in significant ways, particularly in the influence on Huppert's ideas of characterization. His notion that the actor reveals an interiority, exposing layers that complicate the reading of motivation, eschews psychological explanations outwardly expressed and creates an elusiveness that demands a reading of the character within the social context of the film. A central theme of both *Une affaire de femmes* and *Madame Bovary*—the self-indulgent, ambitious woman who prioritizes her desires, wanting the freedom men enjoy, incognizant of the repercussions it will unleash—presents an archetype that underlies many of their collaborations. *Une affaire de femmes* is a sublime work of art and perhaps Huppert's greatest film in its perfect integration of its feminist politics and its star's presentation of a role. Marie is an ordinary homemaker in line with the ideology of her times, until she decides to offer women illegal services and enjoy the benefits and freedom it offers her. The film relies on Huppert's ability to create a character who is complexly human: impulsive, greedy, contemptuous, biased, selfish, both a caring mother and a disdainful wife. She is unreflective and misjudges the exigencies of the Vichy regime. Marie becomes a clear-sighted heroine by the end of the film, when she condemns the patriarchal system that oppresses women like herself, a progression dependent upon Huppert's ability to acknowledge her presence in the role, creating a heroine of great pathos. Madame Bovary's unhappiness, ennui, and restlessness, engendered by the emptiness she cannot satiate, recasts Flaubert's heroine in a modern interpretation that takes on new relevance in the wake of the women's movement. Huppert's intelligence and intuitive perceptiveness emphasizes the awareness that characters like Marie or Madame Bovary gain by the end, which imbues these films with force and resonance.

Chapter 5 places Haneke's *La Pianiste* within the traditions of the melodrama and a hierarchical repressive social framework. Haneke claims to have written the part of Erika for Huppert, and it is a symbiotic collaboration. Haneke's tendency to reject psychological explanation, retaining a mystery that asks the spectator to fill in the spaces and remain critically active, perfectly suits Huppert's performance style. *La Pianiste* draws from the genre of the melodrama, deconstructing the myths of romantic love and examining the tropes of suffering, self-immolation and madness, without

26   Introduction

allowing the spectator's indulgence of the pleasures of a shared victimhood. Huppert expresses Erika's estrangement and struggles to navigate the culture through a remarkable precision and economy of expression and body language, revealing a complex interiority without "explaining" her; her performance is a tour de force, at once elusive and touching, as it humanizes Erika without inviting direct identification, demanding a reading of a woman entrapped within a social structure that almost destroys her.

Paul Verhoeven's controversial *Elle* presents an analysis of the politics of male dominance and the misogyny it produces. Chapter 6 investigates an approach to understanding the film that demands an active spectator. While concerned with objective reality, more importantly it explores symbolic territory, a reality that is both conscious and unconscious. Despite the emotional terrain, *Elle* invites a distanced perspective from the heroine, contributing to a tone that at times borders on absurdity and a sly humor reminiscent of Buñuel. Acknowledging the horror that underlies bourgeois normality connects Michèle, like Haneke's Erika or Chabrol's Violette, to Hitchcock's traumatized, detached child-adults (Marnie, Uncle Charlie, or Norman Bates), alienated from the social world and frozen in time, unable to achieve an identity that allows for caring and intimacy. *Elle*'s trajectory consists of a woman freeing herself from predation and oppression, reversing herself from victim to agent, in control of her life. Huppert's ability to expose layers of consciousness, to elicit empathy while estranging Michèle from the spectator through a conciseness of expression and an unwillingness to fill in the gaps, is essential to understanding *Elle*.

The final chapter presents three films that utilize the metaphor of an existential journey to explore a woman's place, featuring women reexamining their lives and forging new directions in the quest of self-definition and fulfillment within cultures still dominated by patriarchal values. These films are structured around the female protagonist and are specifically dependent on Huppert's iconic presence and style of performance to explore questions pertaining to the woman's position as an outsider, either figuratively or literally. Films that are centered on a woman choosing to abruptly leave a relationship or a professional identity that is no longer fulfilling, negotiating the uncertainties of losing aspects of her identity as a mother or wife or daughter, expressing her autonomy in a culture defined by male privilege all use Huppert's iconic identity as a woman who resists prioritizing social expectations over her own needs, without

Introduction   27

compromising herself in the process. These films depend on Huppert's ability to create characters using aspects of her persona and her person, in a way that references a woman's understanding of performance and role-playing, and how art speaks to life. The image of forging an independent path becomes a central metaphor for women's autonomy, one emblematic to what Huppert has come to represent.

Huppert's long and varied career associated internationally with the postwar art film, an art form highly dependent on a director's vision, also includes significant work in theatrical performance and important collaborations with theater directors like Robert Wilson and Ivo van Hove, as well as a career in art and commercial-fashion photography, demonstrated in the impressive array of celebrity photographers assembled in the collection edited by Ronald Chammah and Jean Fouchet, *Isabelle Huppert: La femme aux portraits* (*Woman of Many Faces*), or individual photographers such as Carole Bellaïche and Nan Goldin, among many others. Over the years, Huppert's presence on social media such as Instagram attests to her present-day identity as an international icon. This book focuses on her work with select film directors with whom she has collaborated. It is beyond the scope of this project to include her theatrical career, in part because of the importance of attending these productions live. I have had the privilege of seeing Robert Wilson's *Quartett* (2009), Benedict Andrews's *The Maids* (2014), and Trip Cullman's *The Mother* (2019) in New York, and these performances complement essential elements of Huppert's modernist style and her persona in films yet are also more highly stylized. *The Mother*, for example, emphasizes abstracted states over a mimetic representation of a psychologically defined character with whom one is invited to identify without qualification. Robert Wilson and Darryl Pinckney's modernist *Orlando* (1993) further explores the parameters of gender constructs, utilizing Huppert's image as someone who challenges these definitions and can conceive of characters abstractly. Jacques Lassalle's *Medea* (2000), uses Huppert's ability to expose extreme behavior as part of the human condition, to present a feminist exploration of a mother's decision to kill her children. It is difficult to discuss performance style and iconic meaning without the idea of a star's presence and persona, which permeates all facets of Huppert's career. She is increasingly sought out for projects that depend on her iconic presence and its feminist implications of self-determination, resistance to appropriation, and anti-victimhood;

28   Introduction

many of her cinematic collaborations, Werner Schroeter's *Deux* (*Two*, 2002), *Une affaire de femmes*, *La Pianiste*, *Villa Amalia*, *L'avenir* (*Things to Come*, 2016), *White Material*, and Ira Sachs's *Frankie* (2019), to name a few, were projects written specifically or developed for her.

Often in Huppert's career, her beauty has been defined by an appearance of naturalness with minimal makeup and affectation, sometimes a defiant display of freckles, a kind of visual statement of the outlier following her own code and individual sensibility. Like Marlene Dietrich, a performer who also appeared in magazine work, Huppert's photographic images later evidence a heightened awareness of fashion and style and ability to bridge a modern minimalism with a timeless elegance, particularly in the 1990s, when Huppert often appeared in a suit and simple white shirt—clothing that defies the assignations of gender. There is also distinct evidence of Huppert's awareness of performance and role-playing for the still camera, and the utilization of clothing as costume. In later photographs, her beauty suggests a defiance of aging and the accepted assumptions of a diminishment of sexual attraction and relevance. An interesting example is Huppert's association with Balenciaga and its publicity campaigns. Although she has been previously associated with fashion houses such as Dior, Armani Privé, or Givenchy, to name a few, her work with Balenciaga and its designer, Demna Gvasalia, is notable in the way it utilizes and endorses Huppert's subversiveness in its campaign.[41] Aside from acknowledging her disregard for aging, confidence to follow her own path, and identity as an outlier, it also addresses a key aspect of her performance style. Fashion is about the gaze, identification and objectification, but Huppert reverses the relationship with her attitude, which conveys her awareness of this process and her refusal to be available for appropriation. Instead of promising that wearing Balenciaga will make one as desirable as her, Huppert's presentation is pointedly a performance that raises questions about women, power, desirability, and aging, in addition to drawing attention to the purse or clothing Balenciaga is selling. Balenciaga uses Huppert to suggest that its products are for women who are self-confident, regardless of age. The Balenciaga campaign evokes Huppert's defiance of the expectations of aging and relevance, suggesting a timelessness that challenges the ephemeral reality of fashion. Huppert appeared on the red carpet at Cannes 2021 in a form-fitting black satin Balenciaga stretch dress, slit to the waist, revealing matching "pantaboots," an outfit almost futuristic, and was admired in the press for "stealing the show," her costume described as the antithesis of the standard "frothy ballgowns."[42] After Cannes, Huppert appeared in a photo by Katy Grannam in the most Dietrich-like image of the Balenciaga campaign, hand on one hip, in an off-the-shoulder trench coat holding a signature Balenciaga bag, facing the camera, returning the gaze, with a look of insouciance, as if saying, "I am the subject in control," recalling Serge Toubiana's comment that "You will know nothing of me, because it is I who am looking at you."[43] Huppert was also dressed in Balenciaga at the Balenciaga autumn/winter 2022 show and was photographed in sunglasses, wearing black leather jeans, her thumbs in her pockets, overtly performing the pose of a "rocker chick," challenging assumptions about the aging woman, inspiring a journalist to report, "Often lauded for her perfect French style, Balenciaga has brought out a more subversive side to the

The Balenciaga campaign 2021: the empowered woman returning the gaze.

30 Introduction

68-year-old that's impossibly cool."[44] In November 2022, Huppert appeared in an ad seated at an executive style office desk overlooking a view of the city, facing the camera, usurping a more typically masculine position, announcing her power. Huppert's description of herself as both actor and spectator communicates a consciousness of acting, performance, and the politics of the gaze and identification.[45] By referencing her persona and performance, Huppert disrupts the fantasy invoked in the image being offered to the viewer, and that self-possession is exactly what Balenciaga knows creates an image of empowerment that is cutting-edge modern. Although, ironically, the Balenciaga campaign exploits Huppert's association with defiance to sell its brand, her performative presentations of Balenciaga create a tension that disturbs the objectifying "to-be-looked-at" essence of the fashion image.[46]

Although I am not including a discussion of Huppert's estimable and diverse photographic and fashion career, the important collection edited by Ronald Chammah and Jean Fouchet, *Isabelle Huppert: La femme aux portraits* (*Woman of Many Faces*) and the 2005 MoMa PS1 photographic exhibition that accompanied it, reveal how elements of her filmic performance style inform her presence in these images. There is the same control of Huppert's availability to the viewer of the photograph—present yet absent, intimate without inviting familiarity, safeguarding her privacy, resisting full access, and, as Toubiana suggests, her own direct gaze, "erasing any ideas of voyeurism."[47] Obstructing expectations of objectification directs the viewer toward a different relationship, one that Huppert, in part, controls. Patrice Chéreau entitles his contribution to the photography collection "The Abyss as Blank Page," arguing that Huppert creates a space "around which she allows us to write," implying an invitation to participate in the production of meaning, a concept as essential to art and fashion photography as it is to her films.[48] Carole Bellaïche's photography monograph *Isabelle Huppert par Carole Bellaïche* (2019) identifies Huppert in relation to many concerns of this project—her naturalness and neutrality, which allows her to be everywoman, as evident in the photographs shot in Paris; her affinity with predecessors like Dietrich and Garbo (which extends beyond the visual to include these stars' attitudes and modernist style); and her placement in foreign locations that speaks of her autonomy and existential pursuits of self-fulfillment beyond the familiar. Even the unusual shots in her childhood home—unusual because Huppert is very private about her personal life, outside of, perhaps, her work with her daughter, Lolita Chammah, who may be exempt because, as a professional actor, she, too, is a public figure—seem to respect the boundaries of personal privacy Huppert is known for, evoking the idea of childhood as a part of identity and subjectivity women tend to suppress and forget. Ultimately, I agree with Patrice Chéreau's observation that we cannot know Huppert from one film or a hundred photographs; we can just, as he suggests, locate "a general topography."[49] That is the point of this book: rather than being exhaustive, it is a guide, a collection of some ideas, and an expression of my profound admiration for Huppert's distinctive achievement.

1

MODERNIST PERFORMANCE

Une modernité de jeu

Dans tous les films que j'ai faits . . . j'ai toujours joué des femmes dont les parcours étaient la métaphore d'une certaine condition des femmes. Je ne sais pas si ça peut changer le monde mais, en tout cas, ça ne peut pas lui faire de mal.[1]

—Isabelle Huppert

Isabelle Huppert's career takes off in the mid-1970s, rises meteorically in the 1980s, and has yet to subside. Concurrent with the impact of the women's and gay liberation movements, as well as the development of the postwar European art film and its articulation of social experience, Huppert's career can be described as one dramatizing the struggles inherent to a woman's place in a culture in transition, where sexual freedom and gender politics are being redefined. Her iconic presence, denoting self-determination, is inherently challenging.

Huppert has built a body of work that can be considered feminist in its interrogation of the position of women and articulation of the contradictions intrinsic to the social times following the explosive second wave of the women's movement and radical feminism. The demand for equality, the freedom to pursue one's desires, the changing perceptions initiated by the women's movement, struggle against a patriarchal culture reluctant to cede women their rights. Huppert's films often pose existential questions about independence, agency, subjectivity, and the pursuit of needs authentic to oneself and take a strong position against their dismissal through the traditional nonresolutions of victimhood, sacrifice, and

34   Chapter 1

renunciation. This thesis—that Huppert's career-defining films are about the woman's desire for self-definition—is iterated through a performance style that supports her autonomy.

The performance style Huppert has developed is modernist in its reconception of characterization, performance, and, by extension, identification and spectatorship. The politics essential to her image—the insistence on self-realization—is underlined by a style of performing that allows her to resist being fully exposed and offered as a fantasy of availability for the viewer's gaze. Typically, one identifies with a character presented as a fully realized individual, psychologically detailed by the actor's ability to exteriorize emotions and account for motivations, creating an adept mimetic impersonation. Instead of creating the illusion of a person embedded in the narrative who can be accessed by the viewer for the duration of the story, Huppert allows a space for the character, without fully masking herself. Rather than striving for a semblance of coherence and clarity, she reveals an interiority (an abstraction of instincts, feelings, states of mind) not always governed by consciousness alone. The exposure of the unconscious reveals desires that are present yet not always acknowledged or visible, necessary for showing an experience in contradiction. Huppert's characters are more abstract and ambiguous, presented through her remarkable ability to concisely dramatize impulses, layers of feelings that are not rational or easily understood, often challenging the mandate of the culture. By intentionally including gaps and lacunae, Huppert's approach directs the viewer to read the character in relation to the social context presented in the narrative. Identification shifts from the individual experience to the overarching ideas explored—for example, agency as a response to oppression. Bovarysme is a locus classicus of the experience of contradiction, as Emma can never achieve a sense of happiness, no matter what she tries. Huppert's interpretation of Emma in Chabrol's *Madame Bovary* (1991), acknowledges Emma's entitlement, prioritizing the strength of the character reacting to the inequities of the society. Huppert states, "I wanted to give Emma Bovary a certain arrogance, a certain understanding of what she was doing. I think that arrogance made her more modern."[2] Her suicide is an act of protest, instead of sacrifice or self-immolation.

Huppert's performance always implies Huppert's presence, which points to the character's relevance in the present. At the same time, Huppert maintains a level of privacy, controlling what is imparted and how one relates to the character. The intention of a more traditional mode of acting is to produce the familiarity of a personal experience where the pleasure in the illusion is that nothing is held back. Rather than inviting identification that will allow for transparency and full disclosure, Huppert challenges the viewer precisely because she retains a part of the character that remains opaque, without becoming and inhabiting another person for the spectator's pleasure, thus never offering a character who can, on some level, be subsumed by the viewer. Instead of contributing to the illusion of availability supporting the fantasy of voyeurism and the invitation of appropriation, Huppert modulates appearance with restraint, maintaining a mystery that counteracts the pretense of familiarity expected as part of the pleasure of spectatorship. This is, in part, what makes her work so radical—Huppert subverts the conditions for voyeurism often endemic to spectatorship and narrative film by refusing to be fully present, defined, and available—hence, not consumable.

Serge Toubiana claims Huppert creates a distinction between "intimacy" and "familiarity," and, Patrice Chéreau states, as an actor "Isabelle Huppert is both intimate and distant": she offers intimacy but maintains her distance and never relinquishes her privacy or autonomy.[3] Similarly, the pleasure of the screen performance is not connected to a fantasy of submission and appropriation, an awareness Huppert communicates by returning the "gaze," as if it is "she who is taking control, she who is watching us."[4] For example, referring to her role in *La Pianiste*, Huppert claims that Haneke empowers the character as well as her status as the actress, reversing the standard of the woman as object of the gaze: "Je n'étais pas regardée. J'étais regardée regardante" (I was watching myself being watched). Huppert is not simply the object being viewed but also the subject viewing—creating a tension that exposes the process.[5] The viewer, too, is invited to maintain a reflective critical regard of what it means to be looked at, foregrounding the contradictions of being both subject and object.

Absence as Resistance

Huppert's performance, for the still photograph and the cinema, is often described in terms of presence and absence—for example, as Serge Toubiana

36   Chapter 1

notes, she is willing to be photographed on the condition that she can be absent.[6] Huppert describes this as intentional: "I am active in producing my absence."[7] She also connects this to the idea of being aware of herself being watched, and it is precisely this awareness that allows her to create what she calls this "alterity," a place of resistance where she can absent herself. "J'ai conscience de me regarder étant regardée. Et j'ai l'impression que c'est parce que j'ai la faculté de regarder celui qui me regarde que je peux créer cette alterité, ce lieu de résistance ou je vais pouvoir m'absenter" (I am aware of watching myself while being watched. And I have the impression that it is because I have the ability to observe the one who is watching me that I can create this alterity, this place of resistance where I will be able to be absent).[8] This strategy of resistance through absence is dramatized, for example, in the scene in *Sauve qui peut (la vie)* where Isabelle, the prostitute, looks out the window and absents herself from the hotel room, and we hear her subjective thoughts and desires in a voiceover as her client, M. Personne, fondles her offscreen. The film presents the idea that one can be, at once, both subject and object, implying an understanding that actively maintaining control of oneself—one's authentic self—counters the surrender and passivity of exploitation and objectification.[9] Godard is using Huppert's presence, her ability to be present and not fully present, still the subject in control, to communicate this idea. This place of resistance that Huppert discusses, created through a constructed absence (the philosophical concept of alterity she mentions suggests an awareness of how the other sees you), a disappearance while present, refers to absenting oneself from the spectator's objectifying gaze, being both subject and object, creating what she calls a place where she can stand back.[10] Huppert challenges the power dynamic intrinsic to the gaze and being its object, foregrounding the underlying implications of the relation it hinges on, setting new terms that qualify what can be seen and known, thus subverting the illusion of submission and availability necessary to the fantasy of mastery involved in spectatorship.

This is essential to Huppert's art: she creates an empowering space of resistance, almost an inaccessibility, and reformulates the process of how one engages with the work, inviting the viewer to enter the narrative differently. It estranges the viewer in the Brechtian sense, as one can no longer use familiar patterns and strategies to respond to the performer, as she is never fully available. Serge Toubiana describes Huppert's acting as "a strange, singular relationship between control, or self-control, on the one hand and the unconscious and impulsive on the other. It is in this limbo, this undefined and blurred area, that she hides and reveals herself, appears and disappears. There lie the foundations of her acting."[11] As Huppert remarks, "S'absenter dans les images—de soi" (To absent oneself among images—of oneself).[12] This is also described as a protective strategy (presumably from exposure and appropriation) in part because the person she is playing draws from her own being.[13] It is by resisting objectification through the retention of control and agency that she returns the gaze, remaining subject and object, "regarder étant regardéé"; like Manet's Olympia, "it is she who is watching us." This is why Huppert is so often described as being "absent" and "present," an elusiveness that contributes to the self-possession and empowerment that characterizes her. Huppert retains something of herself that she controls as she chooses, never fully exposed. This also explains how Huppert can play victims without being victimized. Huppert's characters remain active, retaining a certain agency, and one is invited to identify with the idea—the rejection of victimhood. Huppert has said: "I've played a lot of characters who were victims, but I never was the victim: as an actress, I was the center of the film, so I had the character all to myself—and the movie all to myself. It's not as if I were in a supporting role being dominated by a man. I was a privileged victim who expresses herself. That's my kind of feminism."[14] Huppert's performance style, therefore, supports the feminist content of much of her greatest work—the woman's refusal to be appropriated as an object or rendered a victim—and in the films of a number of directors whose works incorporate modernist strategies (e.g., Chabrol, Haneke, Godard, Jacquot, Schroeter, Sang-soo), the results move close to a form of Brechtian "epic cinema" or modernist theater in the way the "narratives" pose the problem of a woman's struggle for independence and freedom without compromising the content through a form that often encourages availability and submission.

Performance and Abstraction

Huppert has said: "To me the experience of an actress is to go through layers of states of mind." She opposes abstracting states of mind to "pretending

38   Chapter 1

to look like a character, which is by definition arbitrary and fictional, and which does not exist," creating a different kind of reality.[15] Huppert has described acting as a form of dreaming ("We are awake but in a dream"), and the audience, too, as being "in a kind of a dream, watching somebody else's dream that becomes yours."[16] This shifts the value of performance from one intended to re-create a fictional character who can be understood by motivations that account for behavior in an empirically real setting to a form of identification with a state of mind, traces of unconscious urges or ineffable compulsion. Instead of striving for an imitation of reality, truth or authenticity is abstracted in the experience revealed, be it claustration, desire, and so on. In Catherine Breillat's *Abus de faiblesse* (*Abuse of Weakness*, 2013), Huppert's performance recreates the idea of disability and its relation to loss of power, beyond simply mimicking the effects of the stroke suffered by the director. Verhoeven's *Elle* strains the viewer's attempt to read the film as a realist narrative, and stakes out symbolic territory, abstracting an emotional terrain. Huppert invites the viewer to see beneath the surface, following Chabrol's analogy of performance in which the actor's work is compared to an X-ray technician who reveals what is inside as opposed to a therapist who offers a psychological analysis.[17] It also allows for behavior that can't necessarily be rationalized by the conscious mind. The viewer still must produce a reading of what is shown, but the performance itself changes the terms of the reading. Huppert's modernist style of performance abstracts an essence without attempting to recreate a psychologically concrete, rounded character. Huppert claims "that the more abstract the subject and apparently impossible to embody the material becomes, the easier it seems, paradoxically, to do so," in that the absence of limitations gives her the opportunity to throw herself into it and be immersed in different states.[18] It requires the viewer to fill in the gaps, interpret actively, mediate between the character and the world of the film, thereby producing an idea about human life instead of promoting the pleasure of verisimilitude, resolution, and coherence as an end in itself.[19] Huppert explains that "mais être actrice, c'est également un rapport au monde, une façon d'être là et de ne pas y être. On incarne des états, des pulsions" (but being an actress is also about a relation to the world, a way of being there and not being there. We embody states, impulses).[20] Huppert connects the idea of abstraction to that of being present, yet not entirely, creating a different kind of performance that is also conceptual, interrogative, inviting an active, participatory spectator. As Chéreau states, "Isabelle is an abyss around which she allows us to write: Isabelle Huppert, the abyss as blank page."[21]

Performance and Interiority

In describing her conception of performance, Huppert returns often to an idea used by Godard, distinguishing between the terms *exprimer* and *imprimer*.[22] "Je crois que s'il y a une modernité de jeu, c'est justement cette idée qu'il est plus intéressant d'imprimer que d'exprimer" (I believe if there is modernity in acting, it is precisely the idea that it is more interesting to *imprimer*/impress than *exprimer*/express).[23] The idea of acting as pointing inward implies interiority, nuance, and subtlety instead of acting as the effort of emoting and overtly expressing, which is traditionally expected and valued. Godard promotes acting as subtraction, rejecting the creation of psychologically plausible characters through overstatement. Huppert often discusses the importance of a performance that suggests a movement inward, one that incorporates contemplation and silence. Even in her more heightened performances—for example, Jeanne in *La Cérémonie*, a character who displays barely contained, explosive resentment and a degree of madness—Huppert's tendency is toward minimalism, being compressed into body language, nuance, and detail: the various subtle indications of Jeanne's being off-kilter, such as the rhythms of her hurried movements and manner of speech, or her habits of chewing gum or checking her nails, her excessively violent perusing of Mme. Lelièvre's clothing, or the unusual calmness with which she utters her satisfied, final utterance "On a bien fait" (Well done) following the killings. Huppert develops a form of performance that uses the body very precisely, and her movements, silences, or changes of facial expression convey meaning. The idea of resistance might be conveyed in her confident stride, carriage, or look of determination or disconnection. It is a form of acting that is pared down and condensed and that points inward as opposed to one that is emotive or explanatory.

Huppert adds the idea that *imprimer*—to impress—is connected to the unconscious, "en fait l'impression c'est l'inconscient."[24] The acknowledgment

Jeanne's (Isabelle Huppert) striking calmness following the massacre: Jeanne and Sophie (Sandrine Bonnaire) in *La Cérémonie*.

of unconscious motivation characteristic of modernist narrative art allows for actions that are not driven by rational logic or intent. Huppert draws from an intuitive unconscious place (recall her analogy to dreaming) to animate characters whose actions are not uniquely consciously motivated. As Robin Wood notes of the modernist tendencies of Henry James's novels, such as *The Wings of the Dove* (1902) and *The Golden Bowl* (1904), "to arrive at a point where all clarity (of motivation, perception, moral judgment) is no longer possible, and where all certitude dissolves."[25] With regard to *The Golden Bowl* he comments, "The characters are at once agonizingly *self*-conscious and dangerously *un*conscious of their true motivations—an unconsciousness that sets them free to do things they couldn't possibly do consciously. What one witnesses in the late novels is no less than the dissolution of the nineteenth century view of characters as something integrated and definable."[26] Huppert's ability to visualize interiority without full explanation suggests that motivation is both conscious and unconscious, and that the most extreme behavior—Violette Nozière's attempt to murder her parents, Marie Latour's spiraling recklessness and disregard for patriarchal laws in *Une affaire de femmes*, or Erika's compulsive integration of violence with sexual expression and cutting in *La Pianiste*—takes on a complexity that resists the idea that everything has to be seen, expressed, and accounted for to be real. It also reveals a darker side, ideologically considered perverse or amoral, that is both estranging and humanizing. In *La Pianiste*, Erika's comment to Walter ("I disgust you, huh?") indicates an awareness of her difference, that she enacts what others, who are confined by shame or accepted values, repress. Huppert claims that the most extravagant, incomprehensible behaviors are often indetectable, and it is that idea that she would like to restore to characters like Erika or Medea. She is suggesting that normality can also encompass savagery or madness.[27] Huppert develops an idea of performance dependent on restraint, abstraction, and the revelation of interiority over an outwardly expressive performance that enhances the illusion of a psychologically real person embedded in a narrative world. The definitive Huppert films require the viewer to place madness, extreme behavior, or a damaged psyche as responses to the inequities and constraints of the culture, whether the protagonists are fully conscious of this or not. The objective is less to perfect the illusion of embodying a definable character, as it is to create a person whose behavior poses questions about ideas— the responses, for example, to alienation or oppression.

Melodrama and Hysteria

Narratives addressing a woman's alienation from her social place and the desire for the freedom denied her is the terrain of melodrama. While the term "melodrama" has been derided as characterizing narratives that are sentimental, marked by excessive emotion and passivity, the genre also accommodates a modernist strain, one that presents and analyzes excess and hysteria from a position that relies on irony and distance, combined with pathos in its mode of address, as a means of exploring the woman's powerlessness and the cost of her alienation.[28] Melodrama can accommodate a modernist approach, as it is a mode that is generally anti-naturalist, with characters closer to allegorical figures; its tendency toward abstraction and its exploration of interior unspoken desires and feelings also mitigates against expectations of realism. There is a self-reflexive aspect to melodrama, as these films often acknowledge that being a woman involves performance to suit social expectations; the woman searches for an image

42   Chapter 1

that will offer self-validation as she negotiates her status as a woman. Several of Huppert's women-centered melodramas are modernist in the way they explore these ideas, using an actress who complements the concerns of the genre. Huppert connects the idea of hysteria and the search for a meaningful identity—the mainstays of melodrama—to the actress and her performance. Quoting Baudrillard ("La femme hystérique pense qu'elle n'est rien et cherche toujours qui elle est"), Huppert then adds, "Je pense que c'est une bonne définition de l'actrice!" ("The female hysteric thinks that she is nothing and constantly searches for who she is." I think that's a good definition of an actress!).[29] By linking hysteria as a quest for self-definition to her understanding of herself as an actress who uses roles as a means of exploring her own identity as a woman, Huppert interprets hysteria to be a substantive aspect of a women's experience in a patriarchal culture.

Many of the concerns explored in Huppert's films relate to the traditions of the woman's film, melodrama, and the woman's novel from which it draws, demonstrating a revision of the tropes of the genre, such as madness, hysteria, compulsion, the obsolescence of the male, and familial/marital dysfunction. Huppert's rejection of victimization and the ideological compromises of romanticized renunciation, eroticized helplessness or surrender, politicizes the underpinnings of the genre by shifting the implications of the crisis raised by the narrative toward an ending that is nonrecuperable and often beyond negotiation. Huppert's endorsement of the significance of the woman's ego, entitlement, and subjectivity emphasizes the validity of resistance and protest.

One of the most distinctive iterations of the genre is the figure of the madwoman as the embodiment of rage. Several of Huppert's films empathize with the madwoman, placing madness or monstrous behavior alongside the yearning for self-fulfillment and self-realization. At times "madness" is a response to trauma (e.g., *Violette Nozière*, *Malina* [1991], *La Pianiste*, *Elle*, which recognize the family—and, by extension, the culture—as a source of the protagonist's struggle to define herself as a sexually healthy, independent being); class disparity (*La Cérémonie*); or colonialist exploitation and disempowerment, where gender complicates colonialist politics (*Un barrage contre le Pacifique*, *White Material*). The madwoman or outlier alienated from the social order refuses to accept her impotence and concede defeat. By exposing the underside of normative

Modernist Performance   43

patriarchal social demands, these films refuse to mask the consequences of oppression—a mainstay of feminist cinema.

Huppert's magnificent embodiment of the nameless woman in Schroeter's *Malina* is a tour-de-force performance of encroaching madness as an expression of the woman's obliteration under patriarchy, past and present. Ingeborg Bachmann's modernist novel invites one to experience the woman's consciousness directly through her internal voice. *Malina* translates that voice through performance, supported by the musical score, the restless camera, and the details of the mise-en-scène, particularly of the apartment and the fire imagery in the last segment of the film, that combine to dramatize cinematically the madwoman's fury and disintegration, her inevitable self-immolation, and her disappearance into a crack in the wall that contains her. Huppert's performance bodily translates the narrator's urgent agitation and hysteria, in movements that are at times rhythmic, compulsive without seeming excessive, even in extreme moments, such as when she is scratching obsessively at the wood in the guest room she eventually flees, attempting to destroy the place that suffocates her, or exteriorizing the sense of succumbing to what she perceives as a virus, in a performance that seems entirely self-effacing. Within the often operatic extravagance of the mise-en-scène, the active camera, and the disjunctive score, Huppert's performance communicates a purity and authenticity in the woman's experience of negation, resulting in a descent into madness that seems entirely stripped of artifice.

Like Bachmann's alter ego, Huppert is able to inform her performance with her intelligence, communicating a sense of awareness of the woman's experience of being both surveyor and surveyed, evident in details like her repeatedly checking her mirror and reapplying her lipstick or accounting to Malina (her partner or possible incarnation of her own ego) her unwillingness to wear the striped dress he's given her until the end, when she is near dissolution and can no longer represent who she is through her choice of attire. Huppert demonstrates the woman's voice and mind from the outside in instead of inside out, vivifying the existential concerns of the novel through movement and stasis, building a performance that is akin to dance by showing rather than explaining, raising questions about the woman's need for reassurance that she exists, why she is in a process of disappearing, why she can no longer communicate, why her existence is in crisis. Bachmann's novel elaborates and places the woman's trajectory

Isabelle Huppert's tour-de-force presentation of a woman's consciousness in *Malina*.

within a frame of social history and examines how the father and fascism seep into and infect everyday life in Vienna (making it an interesting companion piece to *La Pianiste*)—an important frame that the film touches upon without the details it needs to fully frame the woman's deterioration within the culture. Schroeter's *Malina* remains more cryptic than Bachmann's; however, Huppert's exteriorization of the ineffable through her performance is a remarkable interpretation of the meaning of "madness" and its tradition in women's fiction.

Performance and Being: The Politics of Agency

The search for authenticity in part characterizes what inspires the second wave of feminism (Betty Friedan's "problem that has no name"), but also is rooted more generally in postwar thought and art—for example, in existentialism, the art film (which should be expanded to include Rossellini and neorealism) and absurdist theater. A number of postwar films explore "nothingness," the possibility to rethink and liberate oneself from conventions anchored in an outdated morality and traditional values, and a life lived in bad faith. The resulting alienation, the rejection of conformity and oppression, consciously or otherwise, is explored in postwar art: for example, the radical and highly original Rossellini-Bergman collaborations (which share affinities with Huppert's existentialist journey films, such as *Villa Amalia*) and in theater, of which Jean Genet's *The Maids* (1947) is exemplary. These works are modernist, related to melodrama, politicized and remarkably aware in their articulation of issues of oppression pertaining to women and class. They are self-referential in their presentation of being, role-playing, and performing, and informed by an existential investigation of the imperative of acting (*agir*) or personal agency in response to oppression. This idea is explored in *The Maids*, where two sisters stage their dreams of murder, and in Chabrol's *La Cérémonie*, a cinematic adaptation of Ruth Rendell's *A Judgment in Stone* (1977), which is also informed by the same notorious event as is Genet's play, the sibling maids who reenact the planned murder of their employer. Huppert costars in *La Cérémonie*, in the role of Jeanne, a postal worker who joins forces with a housekeeper to act out their barely repressed frustrations and resentment, and she played the part of Solange in an Australian theater company's production of *The Maids* with Cate Blanchett as Claire. Both of these works explore the theme of characters whose estrangement and inability to account for their powerlessness builds to the point of a dangerous threat of explosion. The final actions in many of Huppert's greatest films are of characters, pushed to the point to act, making a statement, intentionally or otherwise. In the best of these, the directors offer an analysis of the heroine's volatile, pent-up energies, which express her response to ongoing oppression.[30] Huppert comments that, in *La Pianiste*, Haneke does not allow Erika to commit suicide, authorizing her to live, resisting the melodramatic ending of victimhood and suffering as self-destruction, however plausible and familiar that would be as a response.[31] Neither does *La Pianiste* indulge Jelinek's sardonic parody and self-laceration in the novel. There is something heroic and transcendent about Erika's final refusal to perform and her choice to stab herself without committing suicide as she walks away from the concert hall. It is an authentic act of engagement and protest in the Sartrean sense, forcing herself to channel her pain as a reaction to a deadened alienation, the strategy she has chosen to feel alive. The most extreme or violent denouements, Marie Latour's blasphemous "Hail Mary" recited prior to her death by the guillotine, *La Cérémonie's* operatic and convulsive murders, or the brutal murder of the patriarch in *White Material* are less climaxes than are statements of the heroine's

46   Chapter 1

active response to the contradictions and injustices of the social world that fuel the dramatic action. The most flawed, inscrutable characters, even those tinged by madness, can ultimately attain heroic status; it is their agency—the active resistance that is being acknowledged, the extent that they pursue their desire for freedom. Can one condemn a slave who rebels? is a central political question raised in *Une affaire de femmes*. Chabrol claims that what he finds moving about Emma is "the beauty of the battle of trying."[32] Sartre similarly remarks of Claire and Solange in Genet's *The Maids* that "both of them are characterized by the imaginary splendor of their projects and the radical failure of their undertakings."[33] It is the expression of resistance, imagining the possibility of reinvention, that is exhilarating.

Performance and Collaboration

One can say that all performances, even those following the most "method" of acting styles, where one is encouraged to create a character from the inside out, are, to some extent, collaborative, offering a fictional character intermixed with the expectations of a star-actor's image and persona. The characters that Huppert creates are "collaborative" in the sense of creating a distinct character explored through her. She describes acting as a total engagement of herself as a person, distinguished from the act of imitation, of disguise, or the inhabiting of other lives. Huppert describes acting as a movement inward, not becoming someone else but rather "a way of finding out who I was."[34] This is different from creating a fictional character intended to exist wholly apart (actors often talk about "staying in character" throughout a shoot, both on- and offscreen, as if embodying another person for dramatic purposes). Instead, the result is a character anchored in the reality of her being, creating what she describes as "that exact encounter or fusion between me as a person and the character."[35] Huppert has also described her agency: "J'ai le sentiment de creuser mon propre film à l'intérieur de tous ceux que je traverse. Tous ces destins de femmes sont des métaphores de la condition féminine, mais aussi de ma propre vie" (I feel as if I am furrowing my own film inside all those I pass through. All these women's destinies are metaphors for the feminine condition, but also of my own life).[36] Integrating the personal directly with the broader consideration of women's destiny more generally intensifies the political underpinning of this method of performance, particularly in conjunction with directors who encourage the extrapolation of the personal to the social. Many of the directors Huppert has worked with encourage this conception of performance, often choosing her, in part, because of this integration of character and self, and Huppert acknowledges her participation in embodying a character that she, in part, creates. "Après, il faut rencontrer un metteur en scène qui le comprenne, qui n'impose pas de vision pré-établie, qui reste ouvert à ma propre interprétation" (So, one must find a director who understands this and doesn't impose a preconceived vision, remaining open to my interpretation).[37] Directors like Chabrol trusted Huppert, not giving her much verbal direction, signaling to her an emotional moment simply by bringing the camera closer. Chabrol illustrates the significance of performance in determining meaning by citing the moment preceding Emma Bovary's decision to swallow the arsenic: "Mais c'est un moment où le jeu de l'actrice est aussi une chose déterminante. Isabelle occupe tout l'écran" (It's a moment where the performance of the actress is also a determining factor. Isabelle fills the screen).[38] Chabrol also asserts that "casting is 80% of the job of directing actors."[39] Huppert claims Haneke identified with her interpretation of Erika in *La Pianiste*, comparing their relationship to that of Truffaut and Jean-Pierre Léaud: "Le metteur-en-scène greffe une part de lui-même sur l'actrice; c'est ce qui s'est passé entre Haneke et moi dans *La Pianiste*: il s'est reconnue en moi" (The director grafts a part of himself onto the actress; that's what happened between Haneke and myself in *La Pianiste*: he identified with me).[40] Godard encourages the blending of actor and role by naming the characters in *Sauve qui peut (la vie)* and *Passion* "Isabelle." Huppert has spoken of how well he understood her and incorporated aspects of her in her roles.[41] Chabrol's intense concern with the meticulous re-creation of Flaubert's realist novel *Madame Bovary* stops short in his audacious casting of a red-haired actress who makes no attempt to become the iconic dark-haired Emma. It is an adaptation, an interpretation, using an actor that brings herself to the part and modulates the character accordingly. Huppert claims, "Chabrol's concept made me develop the conquering aspect of the character much more, and not play her as a victim from the very beginning"—Huppert's Emma Bovary.[42] This helps contemporize the narrative while acknowledging the actor as

48   Chapter 1

a collaborative artist who creates the character in conjunction with mise-en-scène and the totality of the film, which Huppert uses to interpret the director's intentions and vision. It suggests a consideration of who the actor is and how she informs the role and character, allowing her the freedom to shape meaning, which is why several directors (e.g., Haneke, Verhoeven, Hansen-Løve) acknowledge their films' total dependence on Huppert. Hong Sang-soo, in his whimsical *In Another Country*, pays tribute to her (most lovingly, perhaps, in the lifeguard's "song for Anne"), building the narrative around her presence, recognizing the iconic persona in her characters as a means of exploring issues pertaining to gender roles and freedom. This modernist self-reflexivity, which surfaces in other films where Huppert's characters are actresses—for example, Guillaume Nicloux's *Valley of Love* (2015) or Marco Bellocchio's *Bella addormentata* (*Dormant Beauty*, 2012), which references Huppert's performance in Mauro Bolognini's *La storia vera della signora dalle camelie* (*Lady of the Camelias*, 1981) as belonging to the character—foregrounds the process whereby a performance is presented through an interpretation that is always in part a mediation between the actor and the role.[43]

Modernist Performance: Precedents

Modernist performances have their roots in classical cinema, and one might well include Garbo and Dietrich in this tradition. Robert Wilson's video portrait of Huppert made up and posed to re-create Steichen's famous photograph of Garbo extends beyond making a statement pointing to a physical resemblance of a face (one that Patrice Chéreau notes as well).[44] Garbo's performance style might also be described as contemplative, minimalist, inward, and modern. In fact, Huppert describes Garbo's style in a manner similar to her own: "Garbo a incarné emblématiquement ce moment paradoxal, cette zone opaque entre le retrait et le moment de paraître. Je crois que pour une actrice, tout ce joue là. Comment être à la fois visible et invisible. Idéalement, le visible devrait être invisible, et l'invisible devrait apparaître sur l'écran" (Garbo was the emblematic embodiment of that paradoxical moment, that opaque zone that lies between withdrawing and the moment of appearing. I think that, for an actress, that's what performance is all about. How to be visible and invisible at

Edward Steichen's portrait *Greta Garbo, Hollywood, 1938*.

the same time. Ideally, making the visible invisible and revealing what is invisible onscreen).[45] The latter, making the visible invisible and revealing what is invisible, is precisely how Huppert distinguishes *imprimer* from *exprimer*. Like Huppert, Garbo too retains her privacy and projects an aura of melancholy, and her often-discussed "mystery" might also be attributable to the same strategy of offering intimacy without the familiarity that can accompany an illusion of availability. Toubiana's comments about

Huppert's photographs are equally appropriate for Garbo: "Her cameralike gaze seems like a challenge, erasing any ideas of voyeurism: You want to see my body, but it is my soul that I reveal."[46] Garbo and Dietrich, among other great women stars of the classical period, are so self-contained and self-sufficient that their male romantic love interests rarely match their energies and have been described, by Andrew Britton, as "erased phalluses," because of their notable irrelevance to the women whose identities are not dependent on the male for definition, and who are ultimately unnecessary to their survival.[47] Queen Christina's fluid sexuality and the film's final shot of Garbo in male garb, alone on the ship, emblematic of the outsider who has no place, is an iconic example.

Several of Huppert's films also suggest that the husband risks becoming obsolete—Chabrol's *L'ivresse de pouvoir* (2006), *Une affaire de femmes*, *Coup de foudre*—emasculated, or a hindrance to the protagonist for similar reasons, because the woman's ambitions often far exceed the need of them and their identities are not defined by them, and he becomes symbolic of patriarchal constraint. This independence and self-sufficiency also accompanies an identification or alliance with women, which the narratives suggest with or without the conscious awareness of the protagonist: the mother in *Violette Nozière*; the friend/love object Rachelle, who has tragically disappeared in *Une affaire de femmes*, replaced by Loulou or a visually feminized lover; the partner-in-crime of *La Cérémonie* (which hints at a lesbian relationship between Jeanne and Sophie, dropping Jeanne's husband from Ruth Rendell's *A Judgment in Stone*, on which the film is based); the young female lover in *Villa Amalia*; or the female lover-partner who supplants the husband in *Coup de foudre*.

The woman's film in the 1930s and its generic variations in the 1940s provides a space for the intensely politicized Sternberg/Dietrich collaborations, as well as performances by stars like Garbo, Katharine Hepburn, Barbara Stanwyck, and Bette Davis, who used a variety of performance styles to interrogate women's position in the culture, and the resistance they embodied arguably fueled the audience's commitment to them. Garbo and Dietrich are closest to Huppert in their rejection of a traditional mimetic performance style (attributable, in part, to their roots in European cinema and modernism, however distinct from one another) and an interpretation of characters not dependent upon psychological plausibility. Dietrich's performances in the Sternberg films—for example, X-27 using

Greta Garbo in *Queen Christina* (1933): the impossible ending.

the reflection of the soldier's saber to adjust her veil or her applying her lipstick prior to her execution at the end of *Dishonored* (1931)—has little to do with verisimilitude, and, while the ideas are Sternberg's, it is Dietrich's insouciance and resistance, abstracted and performed in those gestures, that he is relying upon to give meaning to the moment.[48]

Unfortunately, Dietrich's significance to women has been diminished by feminist theory that misconstrues her as an example of the supreme fetish, undermining the agency, awareness, and intelligence intrinsic to the star persona. *The Devil Is a Woman* (1935) offers an analysis of fetishism as a means of masculine control; the irony is that Concha/Dietrich rejects this and uses it to her own ends, illustrating Huppert's idea that the woman can be both subject and object, desiring and desired, being aware of the dynamic inherent in the specularization of a woman's image and taking control of it at the same time. The comparison to Dietrich is more along the lines of a shared defiance and disdain of being anything close to a victim; Huppert's Emma "riding" Léon in bed in *Madame Bovary* is an example of a kind of Dietrich-like sensibility. Carol Bellaïche's portraits of Dietrich, taken in conjunction with a film to have been directed by Louis Malle, starring Huppert as Dietrich, are evocative for the images of Huppert as Dietrich, many in the *Morocco*-era male garb of top hat and

Dietrich's (X-27) gesture of resistance in *Dishonored*.

tails, more so for the affinity with the performer who always, like Huppert, made space for a character alongside herself and her persona.

Huppert can be also aligned with an earlier generation of postwar French stars who evidence aspects of a modernist style. Stéphane Audran, for example, who collaborated extensively with Claude Chabrol, developed a performance style sometimes characterized by blankness and opacity.[49] Catherine Deneuve, Delphine Seyrig, and Jeanne Moreau worked with modernist filmmakers like Alain Resnais, Marguerite Duras, Chantal Akerman, and Luis Buñuel and are described as manifesting a certain restraint, privacy, and minimalism in their acting styles, which can be considered modernist in the same vein as Huppert, though to differing degrees. Ginette Vincendeau describes characteristics that contribute to the New Wave actresses' modernist conception of acting: concentrating on "behaviour, looks and gestures rather than psychology," rejecting a "Tradition of Quality" acting, "underplaying" and "ma[king] performances appear 'modern' and blurr[ing] the distinction between fiction and document," and "not

An image of defiance: Emma usurping the male role, smoking a cigar while straddling her lover in *Madame Bovary*.

being dominant in the mise-en-scène but just one element of it." She lists Jeanne Moreau, Emmanuelle Riva, Anouk Aimée, Stéphane Audran, Delphine Seyrig as actors "whose role was to reflect the sophisticated, intellectual mood of the films," the New Wave ideology of "authenticity" and "modernity," describing their femininity in terms like "anti-conformist" and "cerebral."[50] Moreau is defined as an "anti-star" associated with auteur cinema with "an understated performance style."[51] She also suggests that Moreau's persona communicates "a modern woman" and elaborates: "Her characters' existential boredom, sometimes to the point of anomie, echoed those of contemporary literature. They evoked a latter-day Madame Bovary, especially in the way motherhood (for instance in *Les Amants*, *Moderato Contabile* and *Jules et Jim*) problematized her sexuality"—a description that might have been written of Huppert's Madame Bovary.[52]

Rossellini and Ingrid Bergman's postwar collaborations offer a significant precedent of a modernist style in films that were revelatory in their radical use of Bergman as a person and an iconic presence, combining actor and character, intimacy and distance, deliberately challenging the expectations of her star persona. Bergman is positioned as the central presence of these films about women who feel alienated from their lives and search for authenticity in a heavily male-dominant world that has lost its authority,

54   Chapter 1

experiences that Bergman no doubt well understood, given the public way she pursued her desires and lived her life despite the vocal opposition this elicited and the cost to her career. *Stromboli* (1950), *Europa '51* (1952), and *Viaggio in Italia* (1954) have yet to receive their full due as remarkably groundbreaking in their blend of the personal and political. Bergman's performance style in the Rossellini films is very different from her acting in the films of other directors like Hitchcock or Renoir, which can be highly expressive, inviting a different kind of identification. Although all of Bergman's films use her sexuality and intelligence and draw narrative meaning from the disturbance they generate, her acting in the Rossellini films is far more constrained, and, though less revealing of unconscious layering, it withholds exteriorizing motivations resulting in characters less available for any kind of audience appropriation. These films allow Bergman to be present but distant, and the uncertainty of the narrative endings support the mystery and privacy the actor/character retains, demanding an active critical reading from the viewer, who is asked to place these women-centered narratives within precise social contexts, as evidenced in the Italian title of *Europa '51*. The Rossellini collaborations also draw on Bergman's offscreen identity, foregrounding the idea of a character as a melding of actor and role. Benoît Jacquot's *Villa Amalia* appears, in many ways, to be influenced by and indebted to these films, in its positioning of Huppert in the role of a woman rethinking her identity (including a voyage in Italy) in a way that will include an integration of the body and physical sensation. The description of the Bergman films with Rossellini as "documentaries on a face" is comparable to Huppert's comment on Jacquot's idea that every good film is a documentary about the actor.[53]

Huppert's modernist approach, of representing women's experiences through her person, creates a space, a "blank page," where the viewer is invited to fill in and produce a reading through the confluence of performance, mise-en-scène, identification and social context.[54] The pleasure of this performance style, derived from a cinema of ideas that raises questions about a woman's place in the culture, demands an active, engaged spectator and has been slow to be appreciated, particularly in North America, where traditional ideas of performance and entertainment still dominate. There are important contemporary stars like Juliette Binoche, who is associated with a different style of performance, one that is expressive, demonstrative, and emotionally available, projecting strength and

In *Viaggio in Italia* (1954), Katharine Joyce / Ingrid Bergman's existentialist crisis is revealed through her responses to the antiquities and landscapes of Naples.

sometimes vulnerability, more fully articulated in the sense of explaining the feelings and motivations of the character, who is perhaps more easily assimilable. The distinction to what Huppert offers was utilized in the Australian production of Genet's *The Maids* (2014), where Cate Blanchett plays Claire to Huppert's Solange, using very different performance styles. Although both performances are stylized, Blanchett was more familiar and conventional, though highly expressive, while Huppert played Solange with more Brechtian stylization and overstatement, combining the ritualized aspects of circus art and a flattened delivery. Solange and Claire are characters performing a ritual, not accomplished actors, yet by the time Solange delivers her final soliloquy to the audience following Claire as Madame's "death," declaring their freedom, she becomes Solange/Huppert—resistant, touched by madness, reveling in her notoriety yet empathetic in her articulation of the maids' revolt and liberation. Some critics, like the *New York Times*'s Ben Brantley, valued Blanchett's performance and were more critical of Huppert's overt stylization, even though Genet's intentions were to denaturalize performance, and the play's director authorized the distinction between the two actors and styles.[55] Nevertheless, it suggests a resistance to performance styles that are not accessible or explanatory and raise questions producing lacunae that the audience must grapple with or resolve.

The frequent conflation of Huppert's persona with coldness, blankness, arrogance, impassivity, or perverseness may be derived from a discomfort with the power inherent in the image, the resistance to being fully available, the self-possession and self-valuation that can suggest a narcissistic self-absorption (the antithesis of self-abnegation and victimhood), or the exposure and indulgence of problematic, extreme behavior less often revealed or acknowledged. Even in films where Huppert's character approaches parody and playfully acknowledges the stereotypes associated with the persona—for example, Guillaume Nicloux's *La Religieuse* (*The Nun*, 2013), François Ozon's *8 femmes* (*8 Women*, 2002), and David O. Russell's *I Heart Huckabees* (2004)—Huppert skillfully endows her characters with an integrity that respects the seriousness of the role, however humorous, rejecting parody and thus retaining the film's political significance as a critique of the culture.[56] Other cases, like Neil Jordan's *Greta* (2018), fail

Cate Blanchett and Isabelle Huppert as Claire and Solange in *The Maids*. Huppert's more extreme stylized performance contrasts with Blanchett's.

to evidence an understanding of the star image, resorting to a surface parodic iteration of monstrosity emptied of its political potency. Molly Haskell's rancorous condemnation of both Huppert and *Elle* published in *Film Comment* (cited in "Reading *Elle*") may be attributable to an unwillingness to read Huppert's work in the manner it invites, unlike a classical Hollywood film. Huppert's winning of the Golden Globe's Best Actress Award for her controversial performance in *Elle*, which demands a distinctive level of engagement to be appreciated in a film that does not follow the rules of realism, was an unusual, long overdue acknowledgment in America of Huppert's complex performance style, an achievement long celebrated in France.

2

HUPPERT AND GODARD

Acting Degree Zero

Sauve qui peut (la vie) (1980) was Godard's second return to narrative cinema, and it was followed by *Passion* (1982), also a fictional narrative film, considered the first of his trilogy of the sublime. Both feature Isabelle Huppert in an ensemble cast, and his influence is discernible in the style of performance she continued to develop. Godard's instruction for an approach to acting and characterization that aims for neutrality, revealing an interior reality without the traditional emphasis on psychology and expressiveness, remains significant to Huppert's modernist style. Godard's predilection for integrating elements of the actor's person in his manner of blurring the distinctions between fiction and document is supported by Huppert's ongoing practice of blending a character with herself. As she stated in a press conference for *L'avenir*, "All films I do are personal to me. It reflects the way I am, what I think. It's me. It's her but it's me. It always makes a personal statement. For me as an actress it's always very personal."[1] As Anna Karina noted of her experiences of performance in Godard's films: "It was more like being than acting."[2]

Godard's cinema is highly personal, with the director and his subjectivity at its center. His films are his *essais*—essays/attempts to talk about his ideas and an ideal of integrating the personal with the social and historical through artistic practice. "One can't invent a story until one has lived it," the character of the director claims in *Passion*, and one assumes Godard would agree. The play on the ambiguous meaning of the word *histoire* in *Sauve qui peut (la vie)* to refer to a story or personal drama as well as history summarizes Godard's intent to consider these interdependently, to think of one's life in a broader historical frame, the theme of *Tout va*

60   Chapter 2

bien (1972). Godard has claimed in his *Scénario de Sauve qui peut (la vie)* (1979) that his film offers the viewer a means of analyzing his ideas: "What I'm trying to show you is how I see so that you can then judge . . ." The idea of the caméra-stylo evolves from a preoccupation with writing and rhetoric to one more aligned with the visual and aural elements of representation. "I didn't want to write a scenario. I wanted to see it. You have to go back in time to the Bible. Was the Law written or seen?" (*Scénario du film Passion*, 1982). *Sauve qui peut (la vie)* is credited as being composed by Godard, and its modernist stylistic strategies of slowing images and revealing the influence of music, climaxing by the end with the orchestra fully present on-set, invites the scrutiny of a critically aware viewer. With *Passion* and Godard's increasing absorption in the sublime, Godard no longer is offering the opportunity for analysis (which implies the possibility of critiquing and "judging for yourself") but moves toward something less self-questioning, or less open to debate, as the filmmaker's role as creator is compared to a divine act and the body of the film to the body of Christ, and creation is depicted as a lonely struggle, intensified by Godard's identification with the expatriate as a misunderstood outsider. The conceit of foregrounding the director as a central protagonist at times produces a self-portrait, an autocritique, and, by *Passion*, a quasi-shrine (however humorous) acknowledging the responsibilities of the artist to the elusive perfection of image and light.

Sauve qui peut (la vie)

It is instructive to compare Godard's "second" return to narrative cinema to his "first," *Tout va bien* (1972), as they share similarities. *Tout va bien*, which offers a stand-in for Godard in the lead protagonist Jacques (Yves Montand), investigates the idea that creativity and fulfillment depend on the integration of work (the public) and love (the private); only then can one engage fully with the social world and reach the ideal of living responsibly and historically. Jacques, too, is a director who takes hiatuses, describing himself as "a filmmaker who occasionally makes commercials." In a recorded interview on the set of a commercial, he discusses his reevaluation of his and Suzanne's relationship in the wake of May '68, as well as his filmmaking practice, in a way that addresses the realities of 1972. Suzanne (Jane Fonda), like Denise Rimbaud (Nathalie Baye) in *Sauve qui peut (la vie)*, is a correspondent who no longer corresponds to anything and who discovers that, in order to talk about social politics, she has to look deeper and put herself in the place of another. Denise, too, wants to write about "how things really are," and, like Suzanne at the Salumi factory, she visits an industrial farm and looks for a job at a press to experience firsthand the gestures of work. Like Suzanne's demonstration that sex hived off from work is insufficient, Denise reminds Paul, "Nights should grow out of days, you said." Despite Godard/Gorin's issues with Fonda's liberal politics, raised in *Letter to Jane* (1972), both Montand and Fonda layer their characters with their own personal histories, producing a film that becomes complex and collaborative. Two actor-activists, figures of identification struggling to hold on to their integrity in their personal and professional lives, stand in for Godard but extend beyond him, producing a statement on social agency that is, ultimately, inspiring. By the end of *Tout va bien*, Suzanne is out observing (and, presumably, reporting on) a volatile demonstration in an industrial-sized supermarket, and Jacques is planning a film and photographing locations in the city.

Forty-four years ago, when *Sauve qui peut (la vie)* was released, it was difficult to separate the formal beauty of its imagery and construction from the cynical tone of the film. Reading Marguerite Duras's statement in absentia (against a blackboard inscribed with "Caïn et Abel/Cinéma et Vidéo") Paul Godard (Jacques Dutronc) states, "I make films out of boredom to pass the time. If I could pass the time doing nothing, I'd do nothing. Unable to do nothing, I make films. That's the only reason. That's true for me as well." Unlike *Tout va bien*, *Sauve qui peut (la vie)* is a more introspective film, less optimistic that movement from a position of stasis is possible (at least for the male protagonist), its concerns less related to political revaluation and the integration of one's personal identity with work and political agency than with the male's fears of social change. *Sauve qui peut (la vie)* addresses the problem of sexual politics and the violence that underpins it, borrowing from Lacanian psychoanalysis and the idea of the child's movement from the imaginary stage of maternal plenitude and idealized desire to the symbolic stage of patriarchy, to which the film's sections, such as "The Imaginary," loosely refer. Unlike Jacques, Paul Godard (borrowing the name of both Godard and his father) is both a figure

62   Chapter 2

of fascination and loathing. He is attractive—Dutronc was a rock star, and the opening scene underlines this status with the bellhop who attaches himself like a groupie in an uncomfortably homophobic scene—and alienating; in an intentionally flat performance, Dutronc plays him as slightly anesthetized, disconnected, a character whose sexual desire is most vocally directed to his daughter. Paul Godard's place is in a no-man's-land outside of such recognized social spaces as a home or an apartment. He is imaged in long shot, descending the escalator of an impersonal convention-like hotel, where he renews his lease in six-month increments (annoying his ex-wife, who waits for monthly support payments, asking him if he's still at the "super-luxe" hotel). He is aligned with M. Personne, one of Isabelle Rivière's (Isabelle Huppert) clients, in their shared sexual fantasies for the daughter, and spatially connected to the "boss" who hires Isabelle to come to a hotel similar to the one where Paul resides, to participate in his direction of an assembly-line sex machine, where he orchestrates sound and image. Paul also refers to women, specifically his ex-wife and daughter, with the denigrating term *salopes* (sluts). He is a character with whom it is difficult to identify, and while this is a strategy common to modernist art, the question becomes whether the film intends to use this to encourage identification with the women's positions (as Godard claimed at the time of the film's release), or whether it remains a lament about the male's fears of exclusion and his own superfluousness.[3]

When I first saw *Sauve qui peut (la vie)* in 1980, I thought the film was ultimately narcissistic—a work about male subjectivity and anxiety and the director's fears of female independence and his subsequent loss of power. Despite the participation of Marguerite Duras and the collaborative input of Anne-Marie Miéville (credited as one of the scenarists with Jean-Claude Carrière, and an editor with Godard) whose interests in the woman's position and psychoanalysis are evident in the film, the male voice seemed to be the "enunciating" one.[4] I thought only a male would include a scene where an attractive female farm worker, illustrating an advantage of her work on the farm, drops her pants and bends over, waiting to be licked by a cow. One could argue that the women characters were defined by their sexual function: the intellectual/lover, the sex worker/prostitute, the mother/daughter, a typology one can find as easily in a western. The theme of incest seemed to haunt the film, foregrounding what is repressed in the struggle necessary to take one's place in the

Symbolic order of patriarchy. Paul feels least threatened paying for sex, as the relationship excludes intimacy and its attendant responsibilities. The film seemed a good example of the argument that a deconstructed modernist work does not guarantee that its position would not be patriarchal or phallocentric. To some extent, this reaction was reflective of its time. Feminist critics debated whether the film was pornographic or about pornography, impatient with its obsessions with male fantasies and fears of impotence; their reaction, however understandable, simplifies to some extent what the film accomplishes as a document about the tensions of its time.[5] In retrospect, *Sauve qui peut (la vie)* seems to capture an essence of a social moment, one that felt as contradictory as the film, on the cusp of change and yet resistant to it. Part of the reason for the violence underlying gender relations is the ambivalence about change and a woman's place. The film uses Denise and Isabelle and the offscreen voice and ideas of Marguerite Duras to signal *la parole de femmes*, a woman's perspective on the woman's position in culture and a modernist challenge to the male gaze of fictional narratives, as commentary on the narrative; as Duras says in voice-over against a shot of Denise at work, "If a woman exists—and I'm not sure there is a place for her. . . ." It is, precisely, the male's struggle with the "other" and her place, and its implications for him, that is the subject of the film and perhaps the advice of the title.

After an opening prelude introducing an annoyed Paul Godard at the hotel where he resides—being disturbed by a loudly singing female opera singer and a sexually aggressive bellhop, both of whom follow and haunt him—the film introduces itself formally with the intertitles "Number 1. Sauve Qui Peut" and "0. (La Vie)," followed by a shot of Denise riding her bicycle in the countryside, and the title "The Imaginary." Denise is associated with Lacan's phase of satisfaction and completion (women, Duras tells us, are aligned with *enfance*, childhood, and men with childishness). Denise privileges her need to experience freedom, as expressed in her rides in the country, moving independently and trying to see things differently; she uses Paul's logic that passion, or a mutually creative and satisfying relationship, depends on the interdependence of public and private and the acceptance that women no longer wish to be sequestered exclusively in either place. "La passion, c'est pas ça" (What passion isn't) becomes a refrain in the film. Denise explodes violently over Paul's casual acceptance of Duras's refusal to appear and decision to leave, which denies Denise

64   Chapter 2

the opportunity to interview her; this, and her disregard for the one possibly tender comment Paul makes in the entire film—"Longer than you think"—delivered as a shout as she leaves, echoing her earlier questions and his responses regarding their working and personal relationship ("You'll help me?"; "Yes, I will"; "You'll love me a long time?"; "Longer than you think"), suggests that Denise is no longer listening; Paul's inability to commit to her either personally or professionally confirms her decision to move on. Denise is seen in shots connected to transition; she has left the city and is privileged in a number of decompositional slow motion shots of her cycling in the countryside, at train stations, in moments of contemplation, or while writing. Sometimes an intrusion or a cutaway to a "micro" scene is used as commentary, as when the camera leaves her in the café to catch the gossip of two women; or, at the moment Denise is negotiating her salary, it turns to follow a woman dressed as if she may be a prostitute; or the scene where Denise waits at the train station and sees two men slapping a woman and commanding her to choose (emphasized in slow motion) and her defiant refusal to do so. It is as if these moments are inserted to illustrate what Denise is rejecting in terms of traditional roles pertaining to labor or gender—as she writes, "something in the mind and body that arches against repetition." She is thinking about work as well as the choices available to women, venturing beyond a comfort zone and aligning herself with Duras and new ideas about parole de femmes. She is also demanding equality, as in the distinction she makes to Paul about preferring to rely on each other instead of one relying on the other, and has the strength and determination to move in a new direction. "C'est pas triste" (It isn't sad), she tells Paul, summarizing her decision to leave him. She no longer needs Paul to define herself. The scene in the apartment of Paul reaching across the table to embrace Denise and their crashing to the floor together, slowed down to emphasize the violence that accompanies the attempt, startlingly captures their inability to express affection without inflicting pain. It even manages to surprise Isabelle, who has come to see the apartment, and who is always blasé about the eccentricities she sees in her work.

Isabelle is introduced almost halfway into the story, with the title "3. Commerce." Godard's identification with the figure of the prostitute has a history in his oeuvre—*Vivre sa vie* (*My Life to Live*, 1962), *Deux ou trois choses que je sais d'elle* (*Two or Three Things I Know about Her*, 1967)—and is shared by other intellectuals and artists, including Walter Benjamin and Baudelaire, who saw prostitution as a perfect metaphor for alienated labor and urban capitalist modernity, with the prostitute, like the artist, a figure who commodifies the self for money. The question of whether this metaphoric use of the woman by the male is an idealization reflective of male fantasies and exploitive of the woman has been debated.[6] Although these concerns are valid, I think the treatment of these characters is not only metaphoric or reflective of a masculine investigation but is also complicated by the actors who bring a part of themselves to their roles and present the woman's subjectivity. In *Vivre sa vie* (1962), Anna Karina is more than a victim of fate in a fallen woman's melodrama; her suffering is placed within a social context—the men who control her because of her failing struggles to earn money and the compromises she must make—that contributes to her oppression. She is also more than an artist's muse or an objectified image of beauty. Karina imbues the role with an intelligence and awareness that defines Nana; her attempt to claim responsibility for her actions is complicated and undermined by a social structure where she is exploited and objectified. Marina Vlady's character in *Deux ou trois choses que je sais d'elle* (1967) is similarly supported by the analytical attributes of the actor-intellectual who presents the idea of prostitution as a logical condition of capitalism and the alienated inhabitants of the urban city. Isabelle Huppert demonstrates the character Isabelle's response of resistance and, ultimately, her autonomy. Isabelle's sangfroid, composure, and blasé attitude is often almost dryly humorous and one of her survival strategies. Her natural self-protectiveness mitigates the abuse she often experiences in her work. Instead of reacting and exposing herself to the humiliation she expects, Isabelle deflects her objectification (necessary to the fantasy of power often enacted in the prostitute-client relationship) through her disinterest, lack of responsiveness or expressivity, and ability to detach herself, retaining her subjectivity by absenting herself from a situation, disappearing while present. In *Sauve qui peut (la vie)*, Isabelle is both the actor as prostitute and prostitute as actor who enacts a role because she is paid to do so, without letting the work define or objectify her.

Although, in a traditional narrative, Huppert's late entrance to the narrative and tangential relation to Paul and Denise might suggest that she is a secondary character, in fact she is central to the film; as Godard states, she is one of those "secondary characters which seem to me primary."[7]

66   Chapter 2

Sauve qui peut (la vie) is not a story about the separation of a couple, but of positions and choices available to men and women in a late modern capitalist society. Huppert describes the film as fiction but not quite, as it is also a documentary about the actors drawing from who they were, as distinct from creating a character. Describing herself at the time as being "not so sure of her life yet," Huppert sees the film as a statement about who she was at the time. She is called "Isabelle," which suggests that Godard is using her persona to inform the character. As Godard notes in a Dick Cavett interview, "When she says her name in the film, the way she says it, you know it is her."[8] Huppert was a rising young star, maneuvering a career in a sexist, patriarchal film industry in a hierarchy where she had little power. As Huppert commented: "He showed my fragility and my dependence, as a beginning actress, with respect to the world of men, of power, of money."[9] When Godard approached her with the project, she was shooting *Heaven's Gate*, where she also plays the role of a prostitute-brothel owner, but, more importantly, an independent woman with an identity outside of proscribed divisions of public and private. Huppert describes Godard's brief visit to see her when she was shooting on location in Wyoming, claiming that all he said to her about the role was that he wants it to be "the face of suffering," perhaps an allusion to Karina's Nana in *Vivre sa vie*; however, in *Sauve qui peut (la vie)* Huppert is anything but a suffering or tragic victim.[10] Isabelle seems to be working as a prostitute out of a lack of lucrative employment choices; when offered an alternative, she appears interested, though the mysterious job she considers—to travel and get paid large sums of money—may be another form of prostitution (a comment perhaps on the price demanded of the rising star). Godard equates prostitution with women's lack of independence, a lesson Isabelle learns when she fails to report her earnings, and her pimp spanks her and makes her repeat, "No one is independent. Not the typist, schoolgirl, bourgeoise, farmer, tennis champ . . . only banks are independent." Isabelle adaptively works the system to her benefit; when her sister approaches her for help in becoming a prostitute to make some quick cash, Isabelle calculates 50 percent of the earnings to keep for herself. She is introduced scanning the lineup at a movie theater for potential clients, which is where she finds Paul. A cutaway interlude to another couple at the theater, a woman being berated by her boyfriend for trying to build a meaningful relationship by offering to remove her pants, suggests that exchanging your body is common to women's experience; the scene that follows is of Isabelle faking an orgasm in Paul's hotel room. Isabelle sees her job as performative, and her lack of effort in making this seem credible or personal, and Paul's awareness of it ("Don't work so hard. Stop pretending") is in itself a form of resistance to participating in a fantasy beyond a business transaction.

This is further strengthened by the voice-over of Isabelle, offered as counterpoint to the image of having sex, imagining cleaning her apartment to the extent that she impresses other members of the commune. This strategy of audibly foregrounding Isabelle's inner thoughts as a means of separating herself from fully experiencing her situation is an expression of her autonomy; it is reiterated in a number of other instances in the films, most remarkably with the client M. Personne in a scene that also takes place in a hotel room. Isabelle's warning to her sister about prostitution, delivered with her matter-of-fact detachment ("What they like is to humiliate you"), resonates in most of her scenes with clients, outside of the one with Paul Godard and the older man she sees in her new apartment following her move toward a new kind of independence. She understands that her clients are often buying fantasies that depend on the woman's debasement.

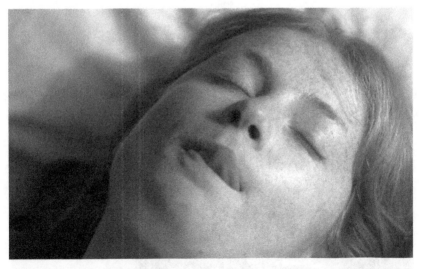

Isabelle's performance as resistance to the male's fantasy of ownership and domination in *Sauve qui peut (la vie)*.

The scene with M. Personne can be read as an illustration of how Isabelle's voice-over, in counterpoint to the image, illustrates John Berger's distinction between nakedness and nudity.[11] To M. Personne, she is nude: an object of exchange rented for the male whose possession she temporarily becomes. M. Personne denigrates her, insisting she add "Monsieur" when addressing him, waving her over to him, bum facing him so he can touch her while he negotiates a business deal over the phone. Isabelle's responses to his proprietary commands, a half-hearted, slightly mocking "Oui, Monsieur," or her derisive question, delivered innocently, as to whether M. Personne is his real name (*personne* can mean "person" or "nobody") immediately signals her detachment from the relationship of control and subservience that he is implementing and announces in few words that she is not agreeing to his terms. As in a number of other shots where she or Denise are framed by a window, the camera focuses on her while she looks outside.

Isabelle's voice-over begins, describing a peaceful spring day at the beach with her friend Cass, picnicking on the sand. M. Personne's haggling voice is at first muted but then disappears, whereas Isabelle's voice-over dominates as she describes holding Cass, sleeping together (which she says was better than making love), later having dinner, and asking Cass

Isabelle's disengagement counters her objectification: *Sauve qui peut (la vie)*.

to live with her, and Cass saying no. The focus returns to M. Personne and his double standard, expressing concern that she is "showing her ass" to the city. The scene is remarkably poignant in the way Isabelle's words usurp and dominate the action, moving away from lived reality to one that she controls, suggesting her subjectivity and resistance to her subordination. Her voice insists that she is naked but not objectified—a distinction that becomes crucial to Huppert's persona.[12] Isabelle's face only reveals the calm of the memory, ignoring M. Personne, as if he weren't there. Godard intercuts the scene with a number of documentary-like images of a busy urban street, perhaps shot from a hidden camera that only one passerby seems to acknowledge or notice; the editing connects inside and out, suggesting they are of a part of "the middle-class middle-classing," as they say in *Tout va bien*. M. Personne acts out his fantasies, worrying about who outside might see, before continuing with the family scenario wherein he instructs Isabelle to pretend she is a daughter returning home and must show her parents her body, which he frames in explicitly sexualized terms. The scene echoes Paul Godard's admission of his desire to "bugger" Cécile, and the film's thematic of Oedipal repression and its iteration as incest and male/paternal desire. In the scene with Cécile, Paul's voice speaks against the slow motion image of Cécile on the sports field, an effect that sexualizes the daughter, who is watched by her father and coach. Cécile, too, is crossing gender lines in her desire to pursue football, an area connected in the film to masculinity. M. Personne is identified with sports, for example, and Paul's aggression is in line with his overall response to women and change; he complains to Denise that he has to pay for Cécile's football lessons, because she wanted them, but this is "just talk." Paul questions the coach as to whether his daughter has breasts yet and whether he has desires to touch his daughter sexually. Although the coach does not admit to any such desire, and Paul's complaint about the way mothers can touch their daughters and sons more easily than men, somewhat undermines the shock effect of his sexually explicit questions to the coach, the scene—along with a later one at the café, where he tosses T-shirts at his daughter for her birthday and urges her to try them on and expose herself, is ambiguous in terms of how it is offered to be read. The scene on the sports field is preceded by the title "2. Fear," a Brechtian announcement of the male anxiety around castration and exclusion, represented by Paul, the father.

70   Chapter 2

Another example of the film's ambivalence with regard to its position on the subject of gender relations is evident in a scene that was singled out for its cleverness and self-reflexivity when the film was released: in the hotel where Isabelle has been summoned by a "boss," along with a male underling, Thierry, and another prostitute, Nicole, to participate in the choreography of an assembly-line sex "machine," first creating the image and then adding sound effects. Isabelle's self-containment and indifference to her surroundings is evident in her request to first use the phone to pursue her interest in the apartment. As in the earlier scenes with clients, Isabelle's voice-over detaches her from her surroundings, as she recalls a conversation about "heroes and losers," ending with "It's all combines and bullshit," perhaps as a response to the boss's staging of power and control. Isabelle is treated respectfully and allowed her dignity, only being asked to apply lipstick to the boss's face while flatteringly framed in the image next to a bouquet of flowers, like a still life in an impressionist painting.[13] A naked Nicole, on the other hand, is humiliated by her placement on all fours, under the desk, referred to as a "fat slob" and forced to repeat a refrain that her "body is not great"; in contrast to the stars Huppert and Baye, she is an average-looking woman. While Godard is presenting an ironic, self-deprecating metaphor for the role of the director and his perception of the treatment of women in the cinema, it is not entirely successful as such, given the distinctions made, and it might be included with the scene at Cécile's practice, or the opening scene of the bellhop begging to have sex with Paul, as moments that arguably evidence an uncomfortable complicity along with the intended critique of the empowered heterosexual male.[14]

Isabelle, like Denise, is seen in the process of transition, initially presented as a private, introspective person who interiorizes her thoughts ("I don't think your sister has friends," a flatmate comments to her sister earlier) to one who openly and genuinely interacts with others. The scene with Denise in the car when they finalize the details of the apartment and the one with the older male client in the kitchen of the new apartment express an unusual aspect of tenderness and ease. She asks Denise sympathetically about her breakup with Paul and tells her she has seen him, and that he is still in town hoping to see Denise again. She compliments the man in her apartment on his performance in a tone that seems, unusually, genuine, and the scene ends with another portrait / still life of Isabelle in a white blouse, softly lit at the window—an image of lightness, contentment, and independence.

From a perspective over forty years later, Paul Godard seems more ambiguous and pathetic. He remains stuck and immobile, unlike the women with whom he interacts, who are motivated toward change. He is alienated from the concept of parole de femmes, and the witticism he makes to the class when Duras refuses to appear—"Every time you see 'un camion' passing, think it's the 'parole de femmes' passing" (referencing Duras's 1977 film, Le camion) is visualized a number of times by cuts to a truck on the road and has more significance than initially suggested. For example, the cut from M. Personne instructing Isabelle to a truck literalizes an idea about women and their voice that eludes Paul or the other male characters. It is Denise who ultimately leaves Paul, and, when he realizes this is a reality and then meets his ex-wife and Cécile on the street, he is more conciliatory, asking his ex-wife if they can meet once a week instead of once a month, an offer precipitated by his fear of abandonment. After being knocked down by a car, Paul comforts himself that he is not dying, articulating a fear that defines him. His ex-wife's indifference—"Ça ne nous regarde plus" (It is no longer our business), she tells Cécile—is supported by the camera that follows the two past the orchestra, as they emerge from a darkened underpass into light, leaving Paul behind. Paul's declaration of "not yet dead" implies his stasis; unlike the women in the film, Paul remains frozen and as alone at the end as he is at the start. Whether the fact that he is left for dead is enough to undermine his credibility and offset his preoccupation with his vulnerability is left up to the viewer; the tone suggests that he is, at least, struggling with the reality of women's autonomy, however much it threatens.

Passion

By Passion, the director's fears of his own irrelevance and demise have subsided and been replaced by its antithesis: the director has regained center stage and, far from being abandoned, becomes close to divine, concerned with the creation of light from darkness. The Godard stand-in, the director Jerzy (Jerzy Radiwilowicz), looks similar to Jacques Dutronc but

72   Chapter 2

not quite as rock-star-handsome and even less expressive. Jerzy's status is heightened by his identity as an expatriate from Poland, a country in turmoil at the time with the imposition of martial law and the emergence of Solidarity, a mass workers' resistance movement struggling for unionization, which gives him political credence and, eventually, purpose. Several women vie for the director as a figure of desire, for reasons never entirely clear. Michel (Michel Piccoli), the owner of the factory, asks at one point, "How does he do it? Each time a different one? I have more money. . . ." He also notes that Jerzy's identity as a Pole, in the wake of the Solidarity movement, casts him as a hero. In part it is because Jerzy, the creative center of a large-scale film production, exercises his freedom to choose his muses. They are split primarily between Isabelle (Isabelle Huppert), a politicized factory worker trying to unionize her coworkers who is sanctified as an emblem of religious suffering, and Hanna (Hanna Schygulla), a feisty owner of the hotel and wife of Michel, whom Jerzy meets and would like to use in his film, with whose face (sometimes shot in close-up, like Falconetti in Carl Dreyer's *The Passion of Joan of Arc*, 1928) both Godard and Jerzy are infatuated. While Jerzy refers to the women in narrative terms of light and dark, open and closed, and sees himself "stuck in the middle, but searching," as characters they exist beyond their relationship with him; the actors' names—Hanna (who retains her Germanness, at times reverting to German), Isabelle, and Michel—allude to the personas and histories that inform their identities in the film.

Like *Sauve qui peut (la vie)*, *Passion* is both a personal film about Godard's concerns with the ideal integration of love and creative work, and a meditation on what constitutes a story (*une histoire*). Where *Sauve qui peut (la vie)* analyzes gender relations, deconstructing its narrative presentation through the techniques of decompositional slow motion, a foregrounding of sound and music, and the editing of voice-overs against the image, *Passion* expands on the question of what characterizes art/commercial cinema, beginning with its rejection of a dominant story. The story, we are told, is open ended, neither truth nor fiction, a consideration of space, the human face as it is in Rembrandt's *The Night Watch*, and, supremely, lighting, as it is manifested in the great works of the Western canon restaged as tableaux vivants that become increasingly cinematic through movement. The "story" ("There are no rules," confirms M. Coutard) moves along a path marked by interruption and digression. Aside from Jerzy and his concerns, the story is about representation, infidelity, a worker protesting being fired because of her activism, a maid who is a practicing gymnast, a husband who has lost his wife, a film production that cannot be produced and producers who fear producing a film lacking a traditional narrative, a father teaching his daughter between takes, a supplier wanting to be paid, and oppression on-set and off. *Une histoire* retains its ambiguity in terms of its meaning as a story, a drama, a fuss. The predicament of Jerzy caught between Isabelle and Hanna is, arguably, the least interesting part of the *histoire*. Like Paul Godard, he is an ambiguous figure of identification. Isabelle's directness and simple honesty counter Jerzy's evasions and interest in her as a working-class virgin/icon that satisfies his romanticized ideas of religiosity and politics. Isabelle is the only person who takes Jerzy to task—for his dishonesty ("I still don't know if you have a wife"), his broken promises regarding supporting her at work ("Is this solidarity?") or inviting her to see his work ("That's where I said you abandoned me"), his equivocation regarding declaring his marital status or leaving with her—"I don't know," he says, and she responds, "It's the first time you're telling the truth." Jerzy's skills at communicating with Hanna are equally troubled. His story about the native Indians who are killed by the white man for their failure with English syntax is met with Hanna's bewildered "I don't understand [*comprendre*]"; finally, giving up, she orders him instead to take her ("*prendre*") in his arms.

More arresting are the breathtaking tableaux realized in splendid detail—attesting to their lavish expense—that raise questions about vision, interpretation, and the relevance of art to the contemporary world. Vivified, the paintings become divested of their aura as immutable art and come alive in their tales of oppression, power, and yearning for the divine. Set against the other threads of the narrative, they comment on the present, joined across time by a still relevant humanism. The oppression, for example, depicted in the tableau of Goya's *The Third of May 1808*, set against Isabelle's story of being oppressed at the factory and being chased by the *patron* or police, or the women who try and flee the set only to be forcibly returned to their place, pinned down as "nudes" while the men on-set stay fully dressed, connects ideas about power and resistance, the image, representation, and ownership. Similarly, the religious tableaux of the Virgin and children relate to Isabelle whose opening words—"Father, why have you forsaken me?"—introduce the character. Just as the Virgin

74   Chapter 2

in a religious painting confirms the religious morality of the artist and the owner, so too the character of Isabelle, who combines working-class authenticity with suffering for others as a sacrificial lamb, becomes a testament to Godard's moral voice and his role as the artist creating something sublime. Godard suggested Isabelle's character as a kind of contemporary reworking of Simone Weil (a model also for Ingrid Bergman's Irene Girard in Rossellini's *Europa '51*, where Irene's suffering becomes redirected to her social commitment and identity as a kind of Christian saint by the end of the film).[15] Isabelle's identity as a working-class person who loves her work as much as she loves Jerzy inspires him finally to move beyond his quandaries regarding light and creation. "Grâce à vous" (Thanks to you), Jerzy tells Isabelle, when he has decided to become reengaged in the social world and return to Poland. The combination of grace and commitment produces passion, a word as multivalent as *histoire* in connoting a deep connection to political agency as well as religious inspiration, and a desire to heal the world. When Jerzy finally decides to take Isabelle, the Virgin, and "do it from behind, so that it leaves no trace," he is preserving her status as a Madonna or lamb of god, as well as his own significance as a modern El Greco producing his own *Assumption of the Virgin*. This is summed up in the cut from the scene of Isabelle, naked on the bed, to the tableau vivant of the woman and child angels.

Both Isabelle and Hanna are active, challenging characters existing beyond their assignation as options for Jerzy. Isabelle is introduced at the opening of the film at work in the factory, pushing a heavy cart and riding her bicycle alongside Jerzy as he drives alongside her in his car demanding, "let me talk to you." She is characterized by a stammer that may be attributed to her lack of empowerment or the language to protest (comparable to the Indians Jerzy mentions), which isn't the same as suggesting that it signifies her vulnerability. On the contrary, Isabelle is the film's directly questioning voice—she does speak for herself, admonishing Hanna not to mock the working class, demanding Jerzy's attention and help in organizing her coworkers, declaring her refusal to accept her dismissal ("I'm going to fight back"), encouraging her coworkers to resist, staging protests to block le patron (the boss) from driving up to the factory, questioning why there are never any workers represented in films. Isabelle's stammers are compensated by her harmonica playing, a form of free expression she uses because she lacks "les mots justes" (the right words). Other times

Isabelle's emblematic identification with the workplace in *Passion*.

she is extremely eloquent, such as when she confronts Jerzy and asks him, "Why didn't you want me to look at your work? That's where you abandoned me." In a lovely digressive moment during the worker's meeting Isabelle has organized, Isabelle looks directly at the camera, almost like Michel Poiccard (Jean-Paul Belmondo) in *Breathless*, and acknowledges the camera, playfully wrinkling her brow, as if confirming her subjectivity and independence with a return of the gaze.

In the latter part of the film, Isabelle is connected to nature, seen alone at the river framed by branches of a tree, set apart from the chaos of the hotel or film set. "What does he see in her?" becomes a recurring question in the film. Hanna responds with "She has no ass," while another man later asks, "What does he like about her? She does have something the others don't," and then proceeds to ask about her stammer. Although idealized as a representative of the working class (someone who actually acts and produces) and a contemporary iteration of a saint or martyr like Simone Weil, Isabelle retains her genuineness, confrontational honesty, independence, and sense of self. Her ideological purity is manifested in her complete rejection of capitalism: she offers to donate her severance

Acknowledging the camera and viewer in *Passion*.

monies to Jerzy's film, whereas he suggests that she buy the factory instead. Isabelle fuses the ideas of suffering and oppression with the characteristics of self-effacement, strength, and dignity.

Hanna is an equally strong presence, though in a different way. "What is the story?" she says. "Just look carefully at the human beings, look at their eyes and lips." Godard films Hanna's face in a series of medium and close shots that suggest his fascination with its strength and subtle expressivity, and Schygulla's history as a cinematic icon of erotic desire and sexual independence developed through her career with Fassbinder. Godard encourages this overlap when, for example, she speaks German intermixed with French. She owns the hotel ("You can't throw me out," she tells her husband) and speaks frankly with him, answering with a sarcastic "Oui, Patron," when he forbids her to speak to his workers. She is the wife—her status visualized in the fur she wears—who betrays her husband and announces it: "I wish I could have loved you passionately." Although Jerzy claims to want to use her in his film in a Rubens tableau and is fascinated with shots of her face in close-up, displayed in a kind of screen test on a video monitor, their attraction seems more related to sexual desire than to work. "The work you ask," Hanna tells him, "is too close to love." Ultimately Jerzy leans toward Isabelle and a Catholicized Solidarity, but is finally committed to neither woman, claiming at the end, "I better keep my eye on those bitches." *Passion* is saved by a sense of humor that makes the film more appealing, lightening and balancing its weightier concerns with the director and his centrality to the world, as when Isabelle tells Jerzy directly that she still doesn't know if he has a wife, and he responds by muttering under his breath in Polish, or in the film's attempt at narrative resolution when everyone leaves to go "home." Hanna meets Isabelle on the road and tells her to get in the car and come with her to Poland. "Arrêtes ton histoire" (Stop your drama), she advises. "It was already over when it started."

Passion is concerned with the rhythms of labor and love, and, as the film proceeds, the rhythms and movements increase in tempo and intensify, building in a manner organized to appear increasingly chaotic. As the reality of completing the film without rules or a story becomes less and less likely, and human nature prevents the possibility of successfully maintaining multiple love relationships, the film moves toward the point of dissolution. Although entirely different in tone and style, *Passion* owes a great deal to Renoir's masterpiece, *La règle du jeu* (*The Rules of the Game*, 1939), both in thematic terms ("If love has wings, is it not to fly?"), and complex handling of mise-en-scène, particularly in the latter part of the film, where the yearning for freedom can no longer be accommodated by cultural mores, and the level of activity becomes increasingly frenetic in a highly choreographed manner. Both films acknowledge the rules that constrain individuals. In Renoir's film, at least two men risk losing their wives, and at La Colinière the play of desire spins out of control, moving toward the point of tragedy. *Passion* alludes to *La règle du jeu* in particular moments—for instance, shots of Hanna in the greenhouse, or Jerzy in the hotel kitchen, where the young woman working there playfully threatens to commit suicide over him while the man demanding his check chases Michel, or in Michel's plaintive comment to his wife, acknowledging his loss, "I, too, wish I could have loved you passionately." Although Godard cuts between the hotel and the film set, paralleling the breakdown in both places (the women on-set increasingly unwilling to be fixed in their place), there are similarities in the way both directors interweave narrative strands that interrupt, disrupt, or digress, each being equally important to the whole. Renoir's film, like Godard's,

78   Chapter 2

foregrounds the question of representation through the use of Beaumarchais's *The Marriage of Figaro* and Mozart's music. *La règle du jeu* is also constructed around a character who stands in for the director, underlined by Renoir's appearance as Octave, an artist who feels impotent and is, in some ways, an outsider to the social group. Jerzy, also a stand-in for Godard, identifies himself as an outsider as well, but is idealized to the point where one at times wonders, like Michel, why he attracts the attention he does. Renoir's generosity to all of the characters complicates identification and refers the viewer to the broader social culture, the film's real subject. *Passion* is less distanced from the male protagonist who remains at its center, and, while neither Isabelle nor Hanna are presented as traditional characters and identification has to be modified accordingly, the film remains focused on the male lead and can still be read as a tribute to his desirability, despite his admitted imperfections. At the same time, Godard's concerns in *Passion* are not limited to its protagonists, and the larger questions about what constitutes a story, how to represent life, how the cinema, like a painting, mediates between truth, desire, and the imagination, are interesting in themselves. Ultimately, both films share the conviction that art is central to lived experience.

Isabelle Huppert has remarked on Godard's precision and control as a director, despite the impression of improvisation his films sometimes give.[16] At the same time, Godard's use of the personas of Isabelle, Hanna, or Michel invites a reading that allows for the overlay of the actors that enriches the characters and sometimes contradicts or creates tensions in dialogue with the director's position, illustrating Godard's understanding of the cinema's potential as a crossroads between documentary and fiction and a collaborative art form. Although Godard hoped for the actors' input in creating the narratives of these films, the reality of the director's position of power inhibited the freedom necessary for this kind of fully collaborative work.[17] The result is a textured approach to the film's subject that retains the strain of relations never entirely equitable, in a process of struggle and contradiction.

Godard's idea of performance is modernist and specific; he did not want the actors to be overtly expressive or interpretative, inviting an emblematic use of characters over one that is psychologically defined. Huppert's performance achieves the neutrality Godard sought. Ideas are demonstrated and affirmed instead of embodied in a person with whom one identifies; Isabelle can both present an empathetic character and an idea that the character represents—a commodified *civilization du cul* or a saintly idealization of the working class.[18] Instead of offering motivations for her character, one sees the gestures of Isabelle at work, in her businesslike relationship to her clients in *Sauve qui peut (la vie)* or organizing, resisting, protesting in *Passion*, illustrating without outwardly expressing or projecting a rationalization of her character. Huppert demonstrates Godard's ideas of a performance style of "impressing" over "expressing," or acting as subtraction, to which she frequently returned to in interviews when describing her performance style. Shots communicate her introspective absences, silences, and protection of self, which heightens the sense of privacy that is central to Huppert's persona. However distinct, both *Sauve qui peut (la vie)* and *Passion* use Isabelle Huppert to inform the characters of Isabelle in both films, astutely using the actor's intelligence and strength to present women who are confident, forthright, and resistant through a style of performance that is subtle, understated and minimalist. Huppert humanizes the blasé, aloof prostitute as well as the factory agitator and religious martyr by interpreting these characters through her being and identity as an independent working woman in an industry dominated by men. While this supports Godard's claims to encourage identification with the position of the prostitute who insists on maintaining her autonomy or the worker in *Passion* who loves her work as much as her lover, she still remains the other to the male protagonist-director at the films' center. It is a struggle that is foregrounded without resolution. The problem of sanctification in *Passion* and its attendant notions of sacrifice, submission, and adoration complicate the presentation of independence, and the full endorsement of the woman's position that Godard is never completely able to make. It refers one back to the artist as the creator who has the final word. With Godard, the personal is anchored firmly in the self.

3

A WOMAN'S FILM

Une affaire de femmes

Une affaire de femmes, Chabrol's second collaboration with Isabelle Huppert, may well be their greatest achievement. Conceived for Huppert, who starred in the role of Marie Latour, the screenplay of this distinctly feminist project is credited to Chabrol and Colo Tavernier O'Hagan. It is a film not only about the politics of abortion and women's right to make decisions about their bodies and identities but also about a xenophobic society and the lengths taken to secure a masculinist, nationalist agenda, pointing to the interdependence of sexual and racial oppression. The story is based on the life and death of Marie Giraud, the last woman to be guillotined in France, who was charged with committing crimes against the state in her role as practicing abortion and abetting prostitution. The film portrays Vichy France as a site of heightened patriarchal authoritarianism and racial discrimination, representing an intensification of the norm, as opposed to an anomalous moment in France's history. As Chabrol's compilation documentary *L'Oeil de Vichy* (*The Eye of Vichy*, 1993) demonstrates, Vichy France shared the values of its occupiers: the Nazis' promotion of family and fatherland and their discriminatory politics. Fascism won its support through publicized policies stated with unambiguous clarity, flourishing in a culture where hierarchies of domination/ submission and intolerance were already firmly embedded. Because Marie Latour was tried for crimes against the state—those that threaten the structural basis of a self-protective patriarchal society—and delivered the extreme judgment of capital punishment, her story lends itself to a commentary upon women's oppression more generally, a subject the film investigates. *Une affaire de femmes* uses Marie emblematically as a platform for opening up an interrogation into the power dynamics ensuring the perpetuation of the

82   Chapter 3

state that serves the interests of men. As the title suggests, the film is a story of women; it uses the individual as a means of investigating central feminist concerns regarding women's prerogative to exercise autonomy over their bodies and define themselves independently outside of their domestic identities. Abortions offer women the possibility to determine and thus control the terms of motherhood and acknowledge their sexuality and autonomy. "I've been a slave since I was fourteen and I don't see how it can change," Marie complains to her husband, who responds, "Like most women." Angered by this complacency, she replies, "I don't care about 'most' women. I can't take it any longer." Abortion becomes a service for women that potentially frees Marie and those who seek her out from the constraints of domestic slavery. Marie Latour's death sentence serves as a warning, to deter women from pursuing their right to freedom and self-determination.

Une affaire de femmes draws from the genre of the woman's film, a subsection of the melodrama, and can be read as a variation of *Madame Bovary*. Chabrol's interest in Bovarysme threads through his oeuvre, and with Huppert he finds a perfect collaborator to realize its prototypical aspects and emphasize its potential feminist underpinnings. Unlike Emma Bovary, Marie is not a petite bourgeoise suffering from ennui, but a member of an underclass who must be resourceful in meeting the basic challenges of feeding the family, particularly with husbands called away for duty. Nevertheless, their crimes are a refusal to accept a subordinated place and relinquish what is readily available to men: the access to money and economic betterment, and the pursuit of an identity not connected to the family. Marie is selfish, ambitious, and committed to her desires. The narcissism and self-indulgence that characterizes the Bovary prototype is inherently transgressive in women, as it is self-directed toward the fulfillment of personal needs. The traditional role of the homemaker fails to satiate Marie, and an intense dissatisfaction fueled by a sense of entitlement drives her toward a trajectory that undoes her, instigating a crisis she can't fully comprehend. Rather than merely the historical figure of the last woman guillotined, she becomes an archetype of resistance and dissatisfaction and it is precisely her typicality that is emphasized.[1] The subversiveness of Huppert's persona is, in part, attributable to a "narcissism" and self-valuation that propels the characters she often plays to please themselves, usurping a course of action acceptable only to men.[2] Marie Latour is not recuperated as a "fallen woman" or a self-sacrificing heroine, as is often the trajectory of the melodrama, though her tragedy is in part attributable to her increasing inability to read the determination of the culture; she is, instead, a woman who resists a naturalized place of oppression, leading the viewer to question why the obligatory acceptance of inequity and sacrifice is the right response in the first place. Rather than delineating a rationale of causality that accounts for her notoriety as the last woman guillotined (an approach Chabrol takes with Violette, undermining her designation as an exotic criminal by connecting her desires to a journey of maturation familiar to women), Chabrol emphasizes Marie's ordinariness and lack of distinction, using her character to interrogate the patriarchal society she threatens. *Une affaire de femmes* depends on Huppert to emphasize Marie's reckless indulgence of her own needs and unconscious protest against the treatment of women within the culture. Huppert's interpretation registers contradiction and sustains the complexity necessary to the character so that, by the end of the film, she inspires great pathos.

Huppert's Marie is a character whose motivations are never fully explained or psychologically analyzed, which maintains ambiguity. Instead of offering a figure with whom the viewer can identify unreservedly, there is an elusiveness to Huppert's Marie, as she is not idealized. As Huppert describes her: "Sur *Une affaire de femmes*, en revanche, nous étions bien d'accord qu'il s'aggissait d'un personnage à la fois parfaitement pathétique, parfaitement déguellasse, et parfaitement émouvant" (In the case of *Une affaire de femmes*, however, we were in complete agreement that it was a character perfectly pathetic, perfectly disgusting, and perfectly moving).[3] Chabrol's notion that the performance should reveal an interiority as an X-ray does implies a dramatization of motivations both conscious and unconscious, sometimes in contradiction. The film demands a reading of the character based on what Huppert shows in conjunction with her placement in the context of the narrative. Chabrol's trust in Huppert's ability to reveal a layered interiority without accounting for motivations is evident in the film's use of the close-up and the medium close-up, which avoids imposing the identification that the close-up often invites. Instead of encouraging the viewer to "become" Marie and follow the narrative through an identification with her perspective, one is invited to observe Marie's responses to the social world around her, registering emotions of which she herself may not be fully aware.

84   Chapter 3

Like other heroines of the melodrama, Marie's motivations are neither fully conscious nor always justifiable. Politically disinterested, she gravitates toward her profession as an abortionist through her practical wherewithal and business skills that will provide food and improvements for her family, who are impoverished by the conditions of wartime (having never performed an abortion, she comments that "it can't be harder than anything else") while also enjoying her newfound status, as evidenced in her look of satisfaction when Ginette, her neighbor and first "patient," thanks her, calling her "Doctor." Marie has no commitment to any ideology, despite a vague, unconvincing claim to be "for" the resistance. Although everyone is "for" the resistance in theory, in practice Marie, like most citizens, lives with the occupation easily and is attracted to the strength and power embodied in fascist showmanship. She finds a lover, Lucien (Nils Tavernier), who manifests the macho posturing of the collaborationist Vichy regime: "mopping up" for the Germans, unconcerned with questions of morality. Lucien exploits his links to the German occupying forces and, like Marie, enjoys the privileges offered by collaboration, similarly describing his work as rendering "services." When the Germans sponsor a public contest inviting a male to demonstrate his masculine prowess and behead a goose with a clean sweep of a blade, adorned in a headpiece caricaturing an elderly woman, Marie tells her son that participation is open to anyone, French or German; her son then asks, "Jews, too?," demonstrating his awareness of their status as outsiders. Marie's light response—"No, silly"—suggests that she is untroubled by the contradiction, adapting to the realities of the occupation and its discriminatory racist ideology until it affects her personally, with the loss of a female friend whose disappearance she mourns. She is indifferent to politics, instinctive and calculating rather than thoughtful or instinctive, cognizant of an opportunity in the circumstances created in wartime. Her industriousness and new wealth afford her unimagined opportunities—social mobility, comforts for herself and family, music lessons in preparation of a career she anticipates. Marie's actions are largely anchored in a practical, businesslike approach to life based on exchange, a response to a demand created by the prohibition against any type of birth control. The payment (in extra soap, the gift of a phonograph, and, later, hard cash paid in advance) dramatically improves the standards and living conditions for herself and her family.

Huppert's restrained interpretation presents an interiority of underlying impulses and contempt that impel her to cross boundaries that become intolerable to the heavily masculinist society of Vichy France, belying a manner that appears ordinary and almost unobtrusive. Marie's actions are often impulsive, and her defiance deepens and intensifies as she samples an alternate lifestyle that offers her the possibility of discarding the traditional structure of the male-centered family and pursuing her desires of becoming a singer, having a lover and freeing herself of marital obligations. The film implies a profound affinity for women of which Marie is unlikely fully aware. For example, she aligns herself with a prostitute, Lulu (Marie Trintignant), in whom she confides almost boastfully that she too partakes of unauthorized, unlawful activities. Although payment for services is the only criteria Marie demands, the film indicates an identification with women generally—with their needs, like her own, to define and control their lives beyond the intervention of male proprietary sanctions. Her business, a service she believes is exclusive to the women's domain, helps women free themselves from the burden of unwanted pregnancies, which compound impoverishment and the curtailment of the personal.

This in itself is a radical idea; Marie is acknowledging women's right to private decision-making over their bodies. Abortion is, in fact, a service for women—unlike prostitution, which services men. It allows women the freedom to control and determine the terms and conditions of motherhood, reproduction, and sexuality, thus providing recourse to what binds them to their prescribed roles. In the moment she describes herself as someone who challenges the law, she is expressing pride in what she does for herself and for other women. The women she helps openly state why they require her services: Ginette needs help aborting a baby she can't support alone, women are enjoying sexual encounters while their husbands are away, a woman wishes to have a sexual relationship with her husband without the concern of an unwanted pregnancy. The most striking example of Marie's subtle identification with her clients is in the scene where a railway worker's wife, Jasmine, comes to her home, seeking an abortion. The scene prior to her visit establishes the situation: Jasmine and her husband, a railway crossing guard, live with their numerous children in an overcrowded, one-room home near the train tracks. Jasmine's husband finds her alone in the shed, attempting to abort her fetus by swallowing poison, and convinces her to seek out an abortionist. Jasmine's visit begins with a medium-close shot of Marie looking out the window, followed by a cut to a long take of Jasmine in the foreground, with Marie in the background, listening to her describe her intensely personal reasons for refusing to have another child she does not want. Jasmine declares that she doesn't love her children and never has experienced maternal love, and that she regrets the loss of her body and independence through her series of pregnancies. By this point in the narrative, one is aware that Marie doesn't require an explanation for what is to her a business venture, and thus Jasmine's monologue is unnecessary. Yet the camera movement from Jasmine toward Marie connects them, ending in a close shot of Marie's glistening, reddened eyes suggesting that she is touched by Jasmine's admissions and that she identifies with her—not by way of any overtly articulated politics but by a mutual rejection of the imposition of the demands of motherhood and its attendant pressures and frustrations when it is not wanted.

When Jasmine lies in her marital bed with her husband, burning with fever (metaphorically with rage), she rejects her husband's pleas to call a doctor and chooses to die, a political choice of escape from an oppressive, unhappy life. The scene is intercut with Marie's waking from a nightmare, as if experiencing a premonition of her death. The film never clarifies

Marie's identification with Jasmine's (Dominique Blanc) conflicted feelings in *Une affaire de femmes*.

A Woman's Film   87

whether Marie and her assistant are negligent and therefore responsible for Jasmine's death, or whether it is attributable to Jasmine's prior attempts to induce an abortion. When Jasmine's sister-in-law comes to inform Marie of and implicate her in Jasmine's death, Marie's steadfast, vehement denial of wrongdoing and genuine distress, captured in a long-take close-up, is complicated by her almost blasé willingness to accept the offer of outstanding payment ("If you insist . . .") before offering the children of the deceased a drink. Huppert presents this as a natural, instinctive response, never imposing or offering an explanation or justification, as if refusing to account for behavior that is not always admirable—it just is. It supports the film's contention that Marie not be heroized as a crusader for women's rights; she enjoys the freedom and prosperity her business brings and sees the service she offers as women's business—their choice to control their bodies and, by extension, their lives.

Une affaire de femmes begins by debunking a variety of myths regarding motherhood and romance used to co-opt women into acquiescing to their own oppression. What if mothers don't love their children equally, or are happier without their husbands, or have dreams to be something other than a homemaker? Part of the pleasures of the woman's film is in the acknowledgment of the ambivalence women experience between their place in society and their fantasies of independence.[4] The narrative immediately establishes Marie Latour's preference for her daughter and women in general: she openly favors her daughter and is nonchalant about expressing this in front of "le canard" (the ugly duckling), her endearment for her son Pierrot. For example, within his earshot, she tells her neighbor, "I got it right with this little one"—referring to her daughter, whom she is carrying up the stairs. When Pierrot confronts her as to whether she was happy when he was born, she replies evasively, "It's always right to have a boy." This doesn't serve to negate her love for him, as evident in scenes such as the one where she lies next to him, comforting him with soft caresses when he is crying, promising to snuggle with him after checking on Ginette. Rather, her response expresses her conflict between what she desires (a preference for her daughter or more generally for women) and duty—what is deemed "right." In an early scene, Marie tells her young son she is leaving him alone in charge of his little sister and is going out for a night of fun with her friend Rachelle, rationalizing matter-of-factly, without apology or excuses, that she has a right to her pleasure—because

88   Chapter 3

she needs the distraction, and "I'm still young, after all." In a scene where the two women are dancing in a pub, a cut to a point-of-view shot of Rachelle from Marie's vantage point presents her as an object of Marie's gaze and desire. The interjected shot interrupts continuity: Marie looks at Rachelle and tells her, "Tu as beaux yeux tu sais" (subtitled, "You've got angel eyes") in the romantic tone of a lover. After the two leave at curfew, Marie sings outside the pub for Rachelle, who tells her admiringly, "It's beautiful when you sing," and Marie responds by confiding her desire to sing onstage and her certainty that she will. The moment is privileged in a close two-shot of the women, and, despite the brevity of the scene, it is a defining one, and the relationship remains a motivating force for Marie's trajectory, with Rachelle's sudden absence haunting the rest of the narrative. When Marie later returns to the pub asking for news of Rachelle, she learns that the Germans have taken her away because of her status as a Jew. The scene is first shot from behind, with Marie listening to the pub owner, and is followed by a cut to a close-up, registering her inability to comprehend; Marie protests that Rachelle was not Jewish, that she would have told her. The problem is not the disappearance of a Jewish citizen, but of a friendship/love that is central to her life. Marie is never presented as particularly sentimental, yet the scene where Rachelle's absence is confirmed is followed by one where the camera moves laterally to find Marie sitting on the steps in a dimly lit hall outside of her apartment, softly crying. It is a distinctive moment of Marie quietly grieving the disappearance of Rachelle. The genuine expression of profound loss is notably different from Marie's usual obliviousness, practicality, and restraint. It is one of a few significant shots where the depth of Marie's emotions is registered in a close-up, emphasizing an unusual expressiveness. In the stairwell, she meets her neighbor Ginette, who tells Marie of her lover Bernard's departure. Marie responds that Rachelle was taken away because they said she was Jewish, as if the two were equivalent. Marie's open indifference to her husband Paul's (François Cluzet) return is antithetical to her response to Rachelle's disappearance, from which she never fully recovers. Marie discards her husband, with his reappearance an unwelcome intrusion to the idyll created by his absence; when Jasmine asks her how she handles birth control, Marie tells her that she hardly ever sleeps with her husband. The children have replaced him in the matrimonial bed, while Rachelle displaces him romantically and emotionally.

Marie's expression of genuine sorrow at the loss of Rachelle in *Une affaire de femmes*.

The loss of Rachelle, exacerbated by her husband's unannounced and unwelcome return, are subtly related to Marie's increasing illegal activities, which are, consciously and unconsciously, an expression of her protest. Shortly after Paul reappears, Marie befriends Lucie (Marie Trintignant), who is professionally called "Lulu." They go to a bar, where Lulu tells Marie that she is a prostitute. Marie's disclosure of intimacy in return, offered as a sign of friendship, is that she had a friend who was taken away because she was Jewish, a comment that on the surface has little to do with their discussion of prostitution and the way men treat women. Dark-haired Lucie, who resembles Rachelle, proceeds to call Marie "my little angel" throughout their friendship, recalling Marie's endearment for Rachelle. When Lulu steps away momentarily, there is a shot of Marie looking off into the distance as if daydreaming; when Lulu returns, Marie announces that she and Lulu have a lot in common because she is not a "simple housewife"—in fact, she does things that are against the law. Lucie prods her to confess: "Like what, angel?" Marie replies, "That's just it...," referring to her identity as an abortionist, as the French slang for a "backstreet" abortionist is *faiseuse d'anges*, "the maker of angels," aligning Marie's identity as an abortionist to the loss of Rachelle ("angel eyes"). The narrative connects Marie's increasingly emboldened rejection of her place to a suppressed desire or affinity for women and her usurping a male

90   Chapter 3

position. Later, when Marie is particularly pleased with her situation, her success as a businesswoman and newly acquired, upscale home (she now has extra income from the rooms she rents to Lulu), she is shown singing aloud and then sitting down in her kitchen and daydreaming of dancing with Rachelle, as conveyed in the repeated point-of-view shot of her gaze when they danced in the pub, telling her, "You've got angel eyes." The moment is emphasized in a close-up; the faraway look on her face echoes the one in the café, following her disclosure about her friend who was taken away. The inserted flashback supports Rachelle's centrality to Marie's desire, presented as romantic. Later, following a carefree outing with Lucien, Lulu, Marcelle and her children, a man is shot in front of Marie in the street and confronts her silently before dying; Marie is troubled only by the manner in which he looked at her, as if he knew her. This scene is followed by one where Marie again stops in at the pub asking of news of Rachelle; the owner replies, "Ever heard of Jews coming back?," to which she defiantly and angrily replies, "*Rachelle, oui!* She will return!" The political persecution of the times, interjected obliquely, is significant to Marie only in terms of personal loss, as if she and her companions filter out the unpleasantness of the occupation by continuing to pursue their pleasure regardless. Ironically, Marie becomes a victim of a society whose values she largely shares, which intensifies her bewilderment when she hears the gravity of the charges against her. At the same time, her escalating transgressions are connected to a not-altogether-conscious affinity for the position of women and her loss of Rachelle.

As in many women's films, the fantasy the narrative explores involves the erasure of the husband, or what he represents, and the assumption of his position as a figure of power. In *Une affaire de femmes*, the act of performing an abortion is coded as the woman's appropriation of the male's role through the image of the insertion of a phallic tube into the vagina. The act is often shot as a metaphor of lovemaking, where the woman lies prone, feet spread. Ginette verbalizes the connection when, lying on the floor, she comments ironically that people often make love on the ground. The shot of the act (as when Pierrot peers through the keyhole) isolates the limited view of the spread legs and inserted tube. Marie usurps the phallus visually and metaphorically, even in her newfound ability to buy and smoke cigarettes and toss a pack to her husband, expressing a new sense of power, while her husband reverses roles, staying home and caring for the children, feeling increasingly useless, calling himself a cuckold, emasculated by his war wounds and his wife's rejection. Marie augments her revenue by renting another room in her home to another prostitute, Marcelle—Lulu's refusal to rent her child's bedroom offered at a discount indicates that she has scruples that Marie lacks—and enlists her house-keeper, Fernande, to sleep with her husband, even offering her a raise as an incentive, not comprehending Fernande's objection, in addition to training her as an apprentice abortionist.

Increasingly, Marie's defiance and reorganization of her position is more openly proclaimed and less disguised; boundaries break down, and the implications of her actions become less and less manageable. The scene following Marie's proposal to Fernande, where she brings Lucien home for afternoon sex, is a case in point. She and Lucien chase each other around the living room, almost cartoon-like, bottles in hand, to the sound of the popular hit "Alla en el Rancho Grande," to which Marie sings along, on the phonograph. Their relationship is characterized as more playful than sexual; Lucien is visually feminized (or, at least, androgenized) through Nils Tavernier's delicate beauty, and his name, a variation of "Lucie," subtly complicates the reasons for Marie's attraction. At one point the doorbell rings; a client has arrived for an appointment. Marie, having forgotten, exclaims, "Ah, merde!" (Oh, shit!) then yells out "J'arrive!" (Coming!), leaving Lucien to tend to the woman in the kitchen. In the interim, Pierrot comes home from school and proceeds to spy on his mother's activities from the adjacent room. When Lucien admonishes him for peeping at "le sale cuisine de bonne femme" (a woman's dirty business), he soberly responds, "You are not my dad," disregarding the lover's attempt at moral education. Meanwhile, Marie begins the abortion, has Fernande finish up ("I'm running late"), admonishes her son for spying, and sends him to the bedroom to do his homework so she can pick up where she left off with her lover. Having erased the father from the home, Marie revels in her new sense of power. Huppert emphasizes Marie's actions with-out accounting for any intention; instead, she presents them in a manner that prioritizes her experience of fun and pleasure, contained in her own subjectivity, without a hint of anxiety or discomfort or thought given to the coexistence of lover/child/illegal procedure within the familial home. Emboldened by her success and the freedom it brings, Marie disconnects from the reality of social toleration, satiating herself, like Emma Bovary,

92   Chapter 3

with a spiraling recklessness and indiscretion that destroys any semblance of propriety.[5]

Marie's final transgression, which precipitates the trajectory toward her death sentence, occurs when she invites Lulu, Marcelle, and Lucien back to her home and is discovered by her husband with her lover entwined and asleep in the conjugal bed, the others strewn about the apartment. It is unclear what precisely has taken place or was witnessed by her children (the image of Lulu asleep near a child's stuffed toy suggests the incongruity); however, Marie knows that her husband would return eventually and no longer seems to care. The scene directly follows Marie's final inquiry into Rachelle's departure, connecting her now permanent loss of Rachelle ("Did you ever hear of Jews returning?") with the flagrant rebellion that seals her fate. Paul retreats to his castrated space in the children's bedroom and begins his decoupage to the police commissioner—his chosen form of release and self-expression that he claims makes him feel less useless—by stating the crimes that will lead to his wife's arrest. The husband's emasculation is also that of the state's under occupation, and Marie becomes the scapegoat, sacrificed as a warning to all women who claim their independence. The narrator's reading of Paul's indictment extends over a cut to Marie setting off alone for her singing lesson with a look of complete satisfaction and contentment. She enters an exclusive, upscale building and begins the lesson while the camera at first hesitates to follow and remains outside, circling the building as from a child's height, peering in from a distance, before dissolving into a closer shot from inside. Chabrol comments that Marie is filmed from outside, like Alice through the looking glass, in the universe of her desires cut off from the world around her. The idea is emphasized in the reflection of the street life on the window glass, before the camera moves indoors. Enclosed in the tight framing of the camera, Marie is cut off in her own world, where she can imagine her reality as a singer.[6] Unlike the renditions of popular tunes sung earlier, Marie sings here with a plaintive expression, intense concentration and effort, insensible to what her activities have unleashed. Her singing is remarkably haunting and moving, as if emanating from a source of profound feeling for which she herself cannot fully account. The scene is pivotal to the narrative; the juxtaposition of Marie's single-minded determination to fulfill a destiny she has chosen and the terrible consequences that the pursuit of her own desires engenders create the pathos of the film. Marie is self-absorbed in an increasingly insular world and often heedless of the repercussions of her actions but undeserving of the shocking severity of the charges against her. The scene of Marie's arrest that follows acts as a caesura that will introduce the final movement—the unrelenting, quick enactment of Marie's punishment—and is almost abstract in its concision. Buoyed by the encouragement of her singing teacher, Marie rushes excitedly into the courtyard outside her home and stops to first dance with her daughter and then Pierrot ("You're so light, even though you eat! Mommy's going to be a singer!") before being confronted by her arresting officers, who only pronounce her name. Framed between their darkened silhouettes, she follows them wordlessly, as if she had been expecting their arrival one day. The son's adult voice as narrator claims that he was seven when his mother was arrested, "and she was probably not much older than me in her heart. Her fate would be played out in a world more foreign to us than the one that greeted Alice on the other side of the looking glass." His voice counterposes the father's voice-over of the indictment and the male institutions that condemn Marie Latour, providing a touching defense of his mother and her almost childlike indulgence of pleasure and desire that will take her on a journey she no longer can control.

Marie never thinks analytically about her social world until she is incarcerated and becomes more aware of the exigencies of male privilege. The battle lines are clearly drawn in terms of gender and class, heightened by the country's humiliation through its quick capitulation to Germany, becoming a passive, feminized, occupied state. Paul's identification as a cuckold is also that of France, as represented by the political institution of the state tribunal; Marie becomes a victim of both, the private supported publicly through the judiciary and the church, who, under the guise of moral rectitude, will do whatever is necessary to guarantee their power. Ironically, the excuse of Marie's abject obstruction of motherhood is used to rationalize the judgment of capital punishment, executing a mother and depriving her children of her existence. Marie does not comprehend her lawyer's explanation that the excessive charge against her, on the grounds of morality, is a reflection of the social climate of defeat through the conditions of occupation and counters simply that she has promised the magistrate not to resume her activities. Her admission to her lawyer, captured in the camera's slow movement forward into a close-up, that she still has

94   Chapter 3

her plans—"I want to be a chanteuse"—accompanied by a self-deprecating smile, evokes a naivete affecting in its innocent directness.

Marie begins to attain a prise de conscience—a gradual awakening to the tightly enforced system securing male privilege that she is up against. Incarcerated in a cell with other women, Marie articulates what she has learned: that men, particularly those privileged and empowered by their class and status, will never offer women equitable justice. The lengthy statement Marie recounts is privileged with a close-up of Marie's half-lit face at its start, the camera then moving back to include the cellmates, as if speaking for all of them, before there is a cut back to Marie; set within the bleak, stylized confines of the cell the monologue can be abstracted and read as a political feminist awakening: "It's true. They spend the war sitting on their ass, then pick a woman out of the blue—not one born with a silver spoon in her mouth. They throw her in prison just to set an example but who will take care of Mouche and Pierrot? They don't care . . . they have maids to take care of their kids. It's easy to keep your hands clean if you're rich . . . and it's all men. How could men understand anyway?" Though Marie is not presented in a manner that encourages empathy before her arrest, she elicits great pathos in the last movement of the film that is, in part, attributable to the limited perspective she attains. The scene ends with her cellmate urging her to sleep and Marie's answer that she can't anymore is registered in a medium close-up with a tear falling down her face. Her clear-sighted analysis of the confluence of gender and class in securing the oppression of women is devastating.

An example of Huppert's restrained, minimalist performance style is her response, rendered in close-up, to the judge proclaiming her sentence of execution. The almost imperceptible flare of her nostrils, followed by a very slight dropping of her jaw, registers her shock at the severity of the sentence. She understands that the law not only protects men and rich men in particular but also collaborates with organized religion in maintaining women's oppression through the myth of maternal adoration. Marie's realization is dramatized when she is moved to her solitary cell prior to her execution. The sinister nuns in the prison, an extension of the male-privileged church, are uniformly uncompassionate. The scene begins with a close-up of Marie's chained feet, tilting up to her hands reaching for the communion necklace and then to her tear-stained face. Marie begins to put on the first communion necklace given to her by her cellmate as a

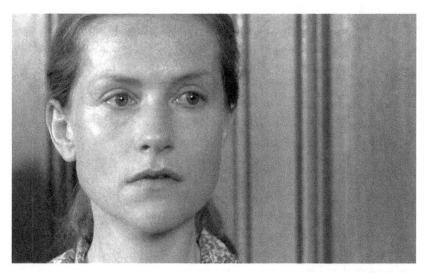

The subtle registration of shock upon the hearing of the verdict: *Une affaire de femmes*.

token of comfort. She then rips it off and tosses it, substituting her own version of supplication: "Hail Mary, full of shit (*plein de merde*), rotten is the fruit of thy womb," indicting a male-controlled church that exploits maternity through a desexualized symbol of a mother to keep women subjugated. It is a startling and provocative moment that articulates Marie's awareness of the system that accuses her. The rejection of the prayer to the mother of Christ prior to her execution summarizes the film's clear identification of the collusion between church and state. It is Marie's gesture, fueled by Huppert's determination, clear-sightedness, and resistance, that gives the moment such force and resonance. The scene was highly contentious when the film was released; it was cut from some prints and may be a contributing reason (along with the film's position on abortion and capital punishment) to tear-gassing the theater in Paris at which it premiered. Huppert's articulation of the scene, delivered with a purity almost reminiscent of Falconetti's Joan of Arc, is the apotheosis of the narrative; rendered in close-up, she proclaims her curse with an expression of both trepidation and anger and then, with a few minimal gestures, rips off the necklace, discards it, and touches her neck, summarizing the injustice she awaits. The scene in the cell is intercut with a shot of Marie's daughter Mouche screaming in her bed and Pierrot knocking his head against the

96   Chapter 3

wall, validating Marie's fears for them. Despite the narrative's complex rendering of its central protagonist, the film supports Marie Latour's identity as a loving mother who genuinely believed she was caring for her children by bettering their lives while refusing to sacrifice her own, without sentimentality. Scenes like the one where she delights in indulging the children with treats of cookies, jam, and cocoa or new clothes evidence a genuine commitment to their welfare. The privileging of Pierrot as the film's narrative voice and witness supports the mother-child bond and corroborates Marie's commitment to her children through his love for her, as he recalls in an adult voice her gaiety and singing, against the images of her walk to the guillotine. His words serve as an epitaph—"It feels like there's a big black hole inside"—lending the film an overwhelming sense of melancholy and personal loss to that of anger at the injustice of her execution, which was exploited as a warning to other women.

In a scene toward the end of the film, Marie's lawyer and another man of his social standing sit in a lush park, peopled with other bourgeois members of their class, and discuss the "monstrous" hypocrisy of the sentence and the refusal of a pardon. They identify France and every citizen's collusive participation in the crimes enacted by Nazi Germany, including agreeing to send Jewish children to Germany. Despite their articulated awareness of their guilt and complicity with the system they condemn, Marie's lawyer demonstrates his ongoing complacency and cowardice by sending an articling student to visit Marie prior to the execution.[7] The scene with the junior lawyer is structured around the close-up of Marie, eyes red from crying, asking whether he has children, before recounting having confessed to the priest; she states uncertainly that Maréchal Pétain was right, inquires if her death by the guillotine will be painful, and repeats that she has been told that asking for forgiveness may ensure that she may not go to hell.[8] The moment is almost unbearable in its conveyance of Marie's fears and complete loss of control over her world.

Une affaire de femmes remains a remarkably contemporary film in its courageous analysis of abortion, capital punishment, and the still-tarnished history of France's betrayal of its citizens during this era. Abortion laws were only legalized in France in 1975, and even then only in situations of distress up to the tenth week of a pregnancy; the laws were further liberalized and amended in 1979, less than a decade prior to the film's release. The implications are evident in the controversial reception the film elicited in France and abroad. At the time of its release, debates regarding women's rights and access to state-supported abortions were still inflamed and intensified in a largely Catholic country; many distributors refused to pick up the film, despite the awards it garnered. One theater owner cut Marie's sacrilegious "Hail Mary" curse toward the end of the film. The film's producer, Marin Karmitz, claims he started his own company, mk2 films, to distribute the film in the United States, arguing that the issue of capital punishment in addition to abortion complicated its reception abroad.[9] When *Une affaire de femmes* was released in 1988, France had taken few steps toward addressing a shameful period of its history; it wasn't until 1995 that Jacques Chirac officially apologized for France's eager participation in the roundup of its citizens (zealously including thousands of Jewish women and children who weren't demanded by the German occupying government and who wouldn't have been found without their assistance). Marcel Ophüls's groundbreaking *Le chagrin et la pitié* (*The Sorrow and the Pity*, 1969) forced a discussion of the suppressed crimes of Vichy France and challenged the inflated myths of national resistance, opening up a space for the profound humiliation and betrayal it papered over. Given the continued struggles with abortion laws, fears of the outsider, and resurgence of authoritarian right-wing governments around the world supporting duty, family, and fatherland, *Une affaire de femmes* remains a prescient analysis of the interdependence of gender and racial oppression used to enforce patriarchal empowerment and perpetuate masculinist, conservative regimes.

The casting of Huppert is critical to the film's politics. Marie is mostly unreflective and seemingly incognizant of why she acts as she does, beyond wanting the freedom not typically experienced by women; by the time she does achieve a limited prise de conscience of the interconnected institutions that protect male privilege, it is Huppert's emphasis of Marie's instinctive understanding, finally, of why she is being sacrificed and the injustice of her sentence that makes the film so poignant.[10] Huppert's ability to reveal an interiority of drives, along with a minimalist style of expression, leaves a space for the viewer to read her actions within a precise social context. Her interpretation of Marie—her fearless insistence on prioritizing her desires—underlines the feminist intentions of *Une affaire de femmes*, raising questions about a woman's place.

4

HUPPERT AND BOVARYSME

"Archetypes of Dissatisfaction"

Following his first two collaborations with Isabelle Huppert, *Violette Nozière* and *Une affaire de femmes*, Chabrol felt he had found the ideal actor to play Emma Bovary. Both Violette Nozière and Marie Latour are prototypes of the idea of "Bovarysme": women dissatisfied with their place who believe themselves worthy of something better. Like Emma, they cannot reconcile their ambitions with their perceived mediocre lives. Discontent fuels their resistance, resulting in an escalating series of transgressions that is finally devastating. The characters' bold attempts to direct their lives, despite the misogyny they are up against, distinguish them from passive victims of destiny, and it is precisely their perseverance and defiance that fascinates; one identifies with their attempts to assuage a persistent discontent. Although Chabrol claimed he was faithful to Flaubert (acknowledged in the film's subtitle, *de Gustave Flaubert*) and maintains the modernist aspects of the realist narrative that distinguished the novel, his film is an adaptation and a collaboration that emphasizes the social context of its time. Huppert's Emma significantly reorients the viewer toward a feminist reading that acknowledges Emma's disquiet and unhappiness, placing it within the inequities of a society that prohibits her from taking control of her life. The emptiness that Emma desperately tries to fill is not unlike Betty Friedan's "problem that has no name": the condition of the housewife who can't account for her alienation and detachment from her identity as a woman. Emma too pursues an idea of happiness that is always elusive. Huppert describes the despair that results from a sense of emptiness as one of the most moving aspects of Emma's character.[1] Like *Violette Nozière* and *Une affaire de femmes*, *Madame Bovary* explicitly sets

100   Chapter 4

Emma's ennui and restlessness within the patriarchal culture that dooms her beyond simply critiquing the banalities of the upwardly striving bourgeoisie and the complacent selfishness of the aristocracy. The feminist analysis of the interdependence of patriarchy, class and women's oppression contemporizes Flaubert's novel, insisting on its continuing relevance.

Chabrol significantly shifts viewer identification from Charles to Emma, omitting the framing chapters, which emphasize Charles's experience for the male reader to whom Flaubert was directing the narrative.[2] Huppert maintains what she calls a "double regard," or dual perspective, identifying with both Flaubert and the character she plays, creating a narrative layering that combines irony and pathos and balances the social critique with qualified empathy.[3] While Chabrol's irony invites an intellectual response, his version supports Emma through its star—as Vincente Minnelli's *Madame Bovary* (1949) did with Jennifer Jones—and is less caustic and contemptuous than Flaubert's, and more humanist in its endorsement of a feminist commitment to Emma over the novel's derisive tone, which too often includes her. In a novel where scorn at times threatens to overtake pathos, the casting of Emma in Chabrol's film is critical to maintaining a careful modulation that privileges empathy, balancing the critique of Emma's choices with the pathos of what drives her. One of the celebrated modernist aspects of the novel is that it recognizes the unconscious, producing a heroine driven by impulses and desires that elude her understanding.[4] Chabrol's adaptation with Huppert is a post-second-wave, late twentieth-century rendition that fully acknowledges the nascent Freudian and feminist potential of the original text and its identification of hysteria, which Emma perceives as nerves and then madness, attributing the *brouillard*, or fog, from which she suffers to a distinctly hierarchical society that excludes her. Huppert imbues Emma's experience of this indefinable fog with a certain ironic awareness that her persona brings to the role; it becomes a manifestation of her sense of her own powerlessness—the unsettled turmoil that she feels when she fails to direct her life as she imagines it. Aggravated by her feelings of confinement, this turmoil becomes a void that she can never satiate. Whereas Minnelli palpably and viscerally exteriorizes Emma's hysteria through mise-en-scène and Jennifer Jones's performance, as suppressed energies boiling over, Chabrol and Huppert's expression of hysteria and madness is more akin to a deep sense of unconscious alienation and ennui that is expressed bodily, through performance.[5] Huppert reveals this surfacing of conflicted feelings without suggesting that Emma is fully aware of them, creating for the viewer the novel's "double regard," a perspective that Emma lacks. Whereas Flaubert can present Emma's interior thoughts, Chabrol relies on the tension between the intermittent, detached male narrator and, more significantly, Emma's responses, to visualize Emma's states of mind and distill them in small gestures that, although Emma may not be cognizant of them, confer meaning to the viewer. Chabrol claimed that Huppert was an ideal Emma because she can "express common, everyday emotions, things that her character doesn't analyze. And she does it automatically; without analyzing them, they come out"—in this way bringing the invisible to the surface without analyzing or accounting for the reasons Emma acts as she does.[6] As described in Chabrol's approach to characterization, Emma demonstrates the analogy of an X-ray technician offering an internal image as opposed to a therapist's explanation.[7] In this way, Chabrol recedes as an authorial presence and offers the viewer greater latitude of interpretation, allowing them to question and interpret the character within a detailed social milieu. It also abstracts Emma's dilemma beyond her as a character: she becomes an archetype, and her dissatisfaction is universalized, not reduced to the causality of a particular narrative.[8] For example, in a scene where Félicité admires Emma's floral *bouquet de mariage*, traditionally kept as a sentimental token, Emma picks it up inattentively, pricks her finger on the base of the bouquet, and licks the blood, and then tosses the bouquet into the fire, to Félicité's surprise ("You're burning it, Madame?"). Emma justifies the bouquet's lack of significance with her offhand comment: "We're off to a new life." The gesture and Huppert's expression of indifference not only reveal Emma's disregard for her marriage but also echo the scene where she first meets Charles (Jean-François Balmer). There, too, she pricks her finger while needlepointing and sucks it, exposing needlepointing as a performance of feminine domesticity that is inauthentic to Emma. When Léon comes to call, she jumps up and grabs her needlepoint to create an image of feminine propriety. Emma uses marriage and the pretense of domesticity to escape her boredom, without any commitment or attachment to normative gender roles and their meanings. The film demands that the viewer actively read Emma through a distillation of gestures or actions that are often beyond her understanding or conscious intention.

102   Chapter 4

Emma's existence is expressed via costume, staging, and performance. She acts out roles, not always convincingly—the eligible young woman, the newlywed wife, the happy mother—as a substitute for any intense feeling or satisfaction she derives from these identities. When Emma decides to retrieve Berthe from the care of the wet-nurse Mère Rolet and take care of her herself, she stages her conception of maternal adoration for a crowd of neighbors, as the narrator recounts: "Madame Bovary undressed the child to show off her limbs. She'd say she adored children. They were her comfort, joy and weakness and she'd give herself over to poetic outbursts." The scene is counterpointed to one shortly following; Emma's attempts to be a model wife and mother soon give way to intense melancholy. She attempts to secure help from the priest, suggesting to him that her suffering might be specifically related to women's lives, but the priest refuses to comfort her, demeaning the problems of a woman of the bourgeois class, and suggests a cup of tea instead. It is a scene of intense pathos as Emma is for once not performing, and her pain is evident in her touching her brow and soft crying. Her response to the priest's final indifferent "You asked me something? What was it?" ("Nothing . . . nothing") is at once ironic and moving as she realizes he cannot accept that her suffering is profound, and she herself cannot connect what she feels to her sense of nothingness and alienation. When Emma returns home, Berthe's attempts to gain her mother's attention by pulling on her skirt annoys her. "Laisses moi!" (Leave me alone!), she complains, still visibly upset. "It is strange how ugly she is." Berthe's persistence escalates Emma's anger—"Will you stop it already?"—which in turn intensifies Berthe's cries. Emma then pushes Berthe away, which causes the child to fall and injure herself. Emma's actions are immediately followed by her regret and shock at what she has done; "I'm going mad . . . *pauvre chérie*," she murmurs. Huppert plays this scene with an authenticity that naturalizes the chain of reactions and humanizes Emma, encouraging empathy despite the critique the shocking behavior invites. Without the structure of performing a role, Emma reveals her conflicted feelings about motherhood, showing what is concealed by myth, thus inviting identification with elemental emotions that are a suppressed part of maternal experience. In *Une affaire de femmes*, Marie Latour's favoring of her daughter over her son or privileging her night out with her girlfriend Rachelle above tending to her children similarly reveals the woman's rejection of standardized expectations and behavior. Huppert expresses these instinctive reactions naturally in a way that reveals what is suppressed, questioning the value judgments that support them.

Emma's increasing disengagement from who she is and what she wants is expressed via the intensification of the props and accoutrements of haute bourgeois femininity, including, in the latter part of the narrative, elaborate attention-getting costumes, on which she relies to make a statement. At the same time, the film suggests that her desires are more significantly aligned with the masculine world of power and freedom, particularly that of the aristocracy. Even her increasingly reckless consumption reveal a sublimated desire to taste the freedom that accompanies wealth, and that Rodolphe (Christophe Malavoy) or the nobility at the ball for example, enjoy. Like other melodramatic heroines, the lover as object of desire is often attractive because of the fantasy he embodies and the lifestyle the female protagonist covets, rather than who he is. Lisa's romantic obsession with Stefan in Ophüls's adaptation of Stefan Zweig's *Letter from an Unknown Woman* (1948) similarly suggests that it is the idea that Stefan and his music conjures, of privilege, art, freedom, travel, multiple lovers, that fascinates Lisa. Like Rodolphe, he is the antithesis of the constraints and obligations of domesticity. Emma states this directly to Rodolphe when he glibly bemoans provincial life: "You have no cause to complain, after all, you are free, rich," and, later, "We poor women have no such distractions." Emma articulates her awareness and understanding that men, particularly those of a certain class, enjoy privileges to which women have no access. These words describing Rodolphe as "rich, happy, free" are poignantly repeated during her final visit to beg him for help, summing up what has always eluded her. Charles's lack of ambition and inability to secure the status or success Emma hopes for enrages her, because his failure becomes hers. When Charles tells Emma of being berated professionally by a colleague over his choice of treatment (foreshadowing his misjudged surgery on Hippolyte) and failing to respond or defend his reputation, she begins by establishing that he was humiliated, which she experiences personally, hence her volatile response: "How dare he judge you, it's shameful." When Charles tries to calm Emma she explodes in anger, "No, I won't stand for it!" and violently gets up from her chair, knocking it over, and leaves the room, slamming the door behind her and exclaiming to herself, "What a pitiful man!" The scene follows the occasion of the ball and precedes Emma's attendant hope that the Marquis might invite

104   Chapter 4

them again. Emma's experience of the ball is not focused on the discovery of her own status as a desirable object of the gaze, but is an education in self-indulgence and freedom from the binds of bourgeois convention, as is evident in the rendezvous notes she sees passed around surreptitiously, the talk of travel and betting on horses, or the windows that are smashed to satisfy a woman's whim when feeling warm. Charles's overriding characteristics—sacrifice, self-abnegation, submissiveness, humility—are typically aligned with women and the bourgeois values designed to disempower them, which Emma rejects as oppressive and constraining.

Rodolphe first meets Madame Bovary when he comes to the house seeking medical help for an employee who needs bloodletting and astutely notices her unusual composure and attendance, describing her as "a woman among fainting men." Charles often relies on Emma, seeking her help and advice in situations that are typically his to resolve. He will often defer to her, ceding responsibility to her to control and manage their financial affairs, signing a proxy permitting her to continue borrowing money despite their mounting debt, in part because he respects her strength and ability, and in part because he is desperate to make her happy. When his mother protests, Emma stands and proclaims dramatically, "Enough, Madame, enough! I'll tear the order up." Charles's mother identifies Emma's histrionics as empty gestures, which only serves to upset Charles who, eager to please Emma, defends her to his mother: "You're causing trouble." His question to Emma—"Are you happy?"—repeats throughout the film like a leitmotif; he senses Emma's chronic lack of contentment as well as his inability to help her. Ironically, Charles's solicitousness and reliance on Emma only minimizes her desire. When Hippolyte develops a painful, raging infection following the surgery Charles has performed, he turns to Emma, befuddled, and says, "I don't understand it, he's getting worse. Will you come look?," to which she answers calmly, with detachment, "Yes, gladly, but I can't cure him." Emma visits Hippolyte at the inn and hears the callous comments of the locals—"He stinks"; "It's bad for business"—which not only reflects their bourgeois indifference but also the pointed critique of her husband's failure. Finally, the woman who runs the inn says within Emma's earshot that another doctor, a celebrity, needs to be called in, and Emma departs, humiliated. When Hippolyte's condition deteriorates, and the doctor recommends amputation, Charles's panic builds at the thought that if Hippolyte should die, he will be responsible: "I'll

Huppert and Bovarysme 105

have murdered him, everyone will know, I'll be dishonored." At this point, Emma orders him contemptuously to sit down ("You're getting on my nerves"), and Charles quietly complies. The next shot privileges Emma's expression of disdain with a slow movement into a close-up, accompanied by the narrator, who describes how Emma remembers her "lost dreams," her "useless privations." As the camera moves in closer to Emma's face, we are told of her regret in religious terms, that "she repented her past virtue as if it were a crime," inverting the moral standards of marriage and monogamy, and "the thought of her lover came back to charm her." When Charles rises, the narrator describes him "as alien and distant as ever," then returns to Emma, who, without uttering a word, expresses her remorse for having uselessly denied herself and makes the decision to resume her affair. The scene ends with Charles terrified, asking for a kiss, to which she answers, "Laisses moi!" (Leave me alone!) Surprised at her anger, Charles declares his love for her, desperate for a sign of support or affection. Emma responds angrily ("Enough!") and leaves the room, slamming the door with such vehemence that an object hanging on the wall comes crashing down. Huppert's Emma expresses the depths of her resentment, disgust, finally rage in minimalist terms, in a few succinct shots, illustrating the narrator's commentary with subtlety and a restrained outward expression, yet communicating clearly that Emma's decision to return to her lover is, in her view, a just response to Charles's latest disgrace and the dishonor that she experiences directly as her own.

Ironically, Emma deepens her debts with Lheureux by buying Rodolphe gifts like a riding crop as tokens of her love, which he finds humiliating and inappropriate. "It's embarrassing for a man," he complains, precisely because Emma is usurping a standard male position. Emma's boldness in seeking Rodolphe out for her pleasure, running alone across the damp fields in the early morning and breathlessly entering his home and racing to his bedroom, is similarly discouraged under the guise of concern that Emma risks compromising herself by being seen. More profoundly, she is seizing the male's role in pursuing her desire, and Rodolphe is securing his right to control the affair. Huppert's Emma is a woman who openly expresses her sexuality and enjoys sexual pleasure. She is direct and frank with Charles on their wedding night that, rather than see his office in their new home, she wants to go to bed, and the next morning Charles's appetite and delight suggest a night of sexual activity that Emma initiated. When

Rodolphe seduces Emma in the forest, she is fully aware of his intentions, particularly when the horses disappear. "I must be mad to listen to you," she murmurs, but then allows him to proceed. The shot that follows, implying the sex they had, privileges Emma, capturing her flushed cheeks and expression of complete satisfaction and unusual contentment. The camera cranes up to follow her gaze, showing the trees and the sky from below, an illustration of Emma's authentic physical and almost spiritual pleasure presented as a force of nature, recalling in contrast Rodolphe's disingenuous proposal of ascribing to "an eternal morality around and above us like the landscape and the clear blue sky" before finding Rodolphe in long shot tending to the horses. Chabrol relies on Huppert to "show" Emma's reveries following sex, an emphasis that is far more radical than Flaubert's description of Rodolphe casually repairing the horse's bridle as an indication of his indifference after the fact.

As the seasoned seducer that he is, Rodolphe exploits Emma, sensing her boredom and repressed sexual desire, but Emma is an apt pupil, and she later also assumes the dominant role in the seduction of "l'enfant" (the child) Léon (Lucas Belvaux). In the hotel in Rouen where they meet and make love in a gondola-shaped bed, parodying Emma's dreams of

The emphasis on Emma's gratification privileges her pleasure over Rodolfe's exploitation in *Madame Bovary*.

escape and travel with Rodolphe, she straddles him seated atop his back, dressed in a corset and smoking a cigar, parodying a man of the world. Emma explains that, as a result of Charles's inheritance, she is rich, and the narrator notes dryly that "he was more her mistress than she his. Where had she learned such corruption . . ." The camera accompanies this with a medium close-up of Huppert's face, registering her expression of experience and triumph. At moments like this, the narrative commentary counterpointed by Emma's complete self-indulgence creates a wry tone in its acknowledgment of and tribute to Emma's insolence and her active disdain for bourgeois mores. Emma has been described as incarnating the virtues of the dandy as outlined by Baudelaire,[9] a comparison that Flaubert invokes in the way he at times describes her, "a cigarette in her mouth, *as though flouting the whole world*," and "her waist tightly buttoned up in a vest, like a man," but more importantly in Emma's pursuit of her desire.[10] Emma's Bovarysme, the ideal self of her imagination that she esteems as the dandy, manifests in her striving to emulate an aristocratic lifestyle rooted in a belief in her superiority to bourgeois society, her self-preoccupation and the statement she creates of her importance and originality through clothing. Flaubert's claim "Madame Bovary, c'est moi" is perhaps an identification not only with the female but also with the artist/dandy. This ideal, combined with Emma's not-fully-conscious rejection of bourgeois morality and its imposition of gender inequality, exacerbates her increasing sense of her own entitlement and social alienation. Her intensified disregard for communal standards, and pleasure in shocking the bourgeoisie (*épater le bourgeoisie*) is validated by Rodolphe's encouragement to follow one's duty to oneself ("Cherish what is beautiful and not accept society's rules") during the sequence of the agricultural fair, which edits the trading of manure and prize pigs against Rodolphe's seduction of Emma. Perfectly understanding what Emma wants to hear, Rodolphe allies passion with "heroism, music, poetry, art" instead of the mundane vulgarities of the "loud-mouthed" and "petty." Emma is fascinated by Rodolphe's language of romance novels and the way he frees her of the constraints of bourgeois propriety in the name of romanticism, nature, art and passion. Initially, Rodolphe's manure, intercut with mooing cows, reinforces the rationale of the small protests Emma stages out of boredom, like asking Léon to accompany her to visit Berthe at Mère Rolet's, an indiscretion that spreads around the town by nightfall. Emma's initial naivete—"One must

108   Chapter 4

follow the opinions of the world and its morality"—is quickly supplanted by a dedication to her own needs, just as Rodolphe is committed to his. Ironically, however, the woman's usurpation of this philosophy becomes intolerable in a patriarchal social world that she has underestimated in its power to destroy her.

Huppert has claimed she emphasized the "conquering" aspects of Emma's character, calling her a "heroine of desire."[11] Emma enjoys her sexuality and indulges her own pleasure in increasingly reckless ways. In *Une affaire de femmes*, Marie Latour similarly experiences sexual pleasure with her lover as a form of play and distraction with abandon and complete disregard for the intensely patriarchal world around her. There too Marie's usurpation of male power and privilege and reconception of gender roles and the family is what finally condemns her. The idea of Bovarysme, the woman's unusual insistence on exercising the freedom to change her identity and destiny, supported by an arrogance and sense of entitlement, is at the core of its subversiveness. She actively pursues what she wants as men do, in order to please herself. "I have a lover!" Emma announces to her mirror reflection, just like Violette Nozière. It is an acknowledgment of power for her own pleasure, one not subservient to the pleasure of others. When Emma performs alone in her garden, she plays the roles of both lovers. Narcissism distinguishes these characters while making them intriguing, because their belief in their entitlement opens up a space to ask, "Why not?" Emma Bovary, like Violette Nozière and Marie Latour, rewrites the rules of her domestic life to suit herself, with a brazenness that Huppert has perfected. When Emma openly challenges bourgeois propriety by agreeing to "take exercise" with Rodolphe (summed up in Monsieur Homais's fully aware warning, "Be careful, accidents happen!"), she simultaneously naturalizes her identity as a mother. Before setting off, Emma smiles and waves to Berthe, a small moment that unproblematically blends her insouciance (agreeing to the ride under the flimsy guise of improving her delicate health) with her acknowledgment of herself as a mother.

Emma challenges social conventions out of boredom, a sense of emptiness, a pursuit of an ineffable idea of happiness, and a desire to experience the pleasures that bourgeois women are denied, but remains disappointed and unable to account for her discontent. In a scene following one of her trysts with Léon in Rouen, Emma passes the convent of her childhood and, despite her insistence that she loves Léon, the narrator states, "She wasn't

Huppert and Bovarysme   109

happy. She never had been happy. . . . Nothing was worth this quest. Every-one lied." The scene dramatizes the surfacing of her nagging unconscious, insisting that she still lacks contentment. The moment significantly pre-cedes the denouement beginning with Emma's discovery of the foreclosure and is a moment of clarity, where Emma admits that a sense of emptiness persists, and that she has yet to achieve any real satisfaction. Except for Charles, who is distinguished by his self-abnegation and genuine concern for Emma, Emma discovers that all her relationships with men are based on objectification and exploitation, and that, when they are done with her, they move on unaffected by her devastation. Lheureux squeezes Emma, per his established pattern of destroying people for money, finally reveal-ing his contempt; the notary will only consider helping Emma in exchange for sex, to which she incisively responds, "You're playing with my distress. I'm to be pitied, not bought." Even the priest, in discounting Emma's suf-fering, refuses to recognize her pain and thus negates her significance and humanity. Finally, both Rodolphe and Léon abandon her with no remorse. The outsiders with whom Emma is ultimately aligned, like dark mirrors, negligible in the estimation of patriarchal bourgeois society, are Hippolyte, whose oozing black bile reappears in Emma like stigmata following her arsenic poisoning, and in the blind beggar, dressed as a parody of a man of the world, like Emma in earlier scenes. In her final scene with Rodolphe, she contrasts her commitment and love in the language she uses: "I would have begged. . . ." Emma at first is frightened by the beggar's appearance at the window of the Hirondelle—she screams and he echoes her cry—but later gives him the remainder of her money, as if empathizing and identify-ing with him when she, too, is reduced to begging for help and has a vision of him when she is ill and hallucinating prior to her death. Hippolyte and the beggar are both destroyed by a social hierarchy that leaves human detritus in its wake. Driven by self-aggrandizement, Homais ruins Hip-polyte and smugly advises the beggar, with complete disingenuousness, to cure his skin disease through a better diet before demanding a show.

Emma's comfort comes from other women: her maid Félicité, who gen-uinely cares for Emma and encourages her to act and speak to the notary to save herself, and Mère Rolet, the wet-nurse with whom she finds tempo-rary refuge. When Emma rushes in begging her "for pity . . . I can't breathe, I'm suffocating," Mère Rolet offers to unlace her, and Emma rests there, expecting Léon to soon arrive with the money. The motif of airlessness and the need for release begins with the signal of the open shutter that Père Rouault gives Charles, as the sign that Emma has agreed to marry, or the breaking of windows at the ball, which become images of potential liberation. When Rodolphe sends her his heartless note of his abrupt change of plans, Emma, in medium closeup, appears excited in anticipation of a confirmation of their rendezvous. She walks up the stairs to her attic, reading, and the camera lingers behind, moving in closer to her silhouette, her response registered in the silhouette's shaking hands and the dramatic score that accompanies it. There is a cut to a frontal shot of Emma's hands and a tilt up from the letter to Emma's face, her shock manifested in her tears, dropped jaw, hand briefly touching her neck. She moves toward the camera, registering her visible pain in terms of a sense of suffocation. She then turns away, races up the remaining stairs before proceeding to open the window, teetering on the ledge. There is a cut to another closeup of Emma looking upward, attempting to breathe in air. Emma's defeat and powerlessness is also described to Mère Rolet as suffocation, which will intensify following the poisoning, when Emma requests, "Open the window . . . I'm stifling," as if her confined energies, experienced as airlessness, are slowly killing her. As the narrative progresses to the "final act," Emma gains some conscious insight into the misogyny she is up against and becomes a heroic figure. Although this development is central to the novel and all of its adaptations, Huppert's incisive intelligence contradicts an Emma who is naive, banal, and superficial. The fog in her head, the recurring sense of suffocation and alienation, is given clarity by Huppert's interpretation, which connects Emma's feeling of airlessness with powerlessness and suppression, and a hierarchy oppressive to women. Huppert states that she endows Emma with a certain arrogance and an understanding of what she is doing.[12] Her transition from a moody, self-centered, bored housewife to a tragic heroine is particularly credible because of the awareness imbued in the interpretation of the role, which blends Huppert's intelligence with an intuitive perceptiveness.

Emma's final scene with Rodolphe is a tour de force in the way it begins with Emma's naive hope that, based on the strength of their past love, Rodolphe will "save" her, in the unique way she conflates her relationships with lovers and with God; the incisive clarity of her argument, however, suggests that Emma finally has gained a perspective of what underlies the myth of romantic love in which she was so heavily invested.[13] Emma

Emma's feeling of breathlessness expresses her entrapment in *Madame Bovary*.

differentiates between her genuineness ("I loved you so . . . I almost died of desperation") and Rodolphe's routine, meaningless seductions ("You charmed them just like me. You're a man . . . You make women love you"). Nonetheless, Emma wants to believe in the possibility of happiness and, given Rodolphe's claims to love her, allows Rodolphe to kiss her. Rodolphe, characterized by his loquaciousness when he wants something, is oddly silent. When Emma implores him to speak, he comments briefly that she has been crying, which opens the way for Emma to make her plea for three thousand francs to pay the bailiff and save her from ruin. When Rodolphe curtly refuses with the excuse "I don't have it, chère Madame," Emma is enraged by his flagrant exploitation, realizes that he is typical of all men, and accuses him of never having loved her and "being as bad as the others"; he lacks nothing, she claims, listing his leisure pursuits, assets, and possessions that belie his denial of wealth. She then distinguishes her genuine commitment and generosity ("I'd have given up everything for you, I'd have begged") from his selfishness, ending with the poignant question "Why did you do it?," recalling his false declarations of love; and her admonishment ("You should have sent me away") implicates Rodolphe in her disaster. Emma then rises from the bed and expresses her disappointment in the terms that made Rodolphe attractive to her all along: "And I come to the rich, happy, free man to ask help anyone would give. I

112   Chapter 4

beg, bring back all tenderness, and he turns me away for three thousand francs!" to which Rodolphe, disengaged and unmoved, reiterates, "I don't have it." In stark directness, the encounter reveals the demystification of Emma's intransigent delusions in light of the brutal understanding that she is a replaceable object to be used and disposed. It also confirms the social hierarchy that will never offer her anything, let alone a place of recognition and mutual respect.

Emma's decision to kill herself is an act of resistance by a cognizant subject, not the expression of sacrifice by an object and a victim. When Emma fails to direct her destiny, she chooses instead to take control by way of her death. Far from indulging her helplessness and victimization, Huppert plays these scenes with a studied determination and conviction. Her demand for the key to the room where the drugs are stored ("We have rats at home, I must kill them, they keep me from sleeping") is delivered with the full irony of her painful disillusionment. She is no longer staging her identity for any kind of public statement—in fact, after she swallows the poison, Emma warns the pharmacist's assistance against "saying anything to anyone . . . they'd blame your master," and she smiles as if the thought amuses her. Emma's only miscalculation is that her death will be easy: "I'll fall asleep. It will be over." Instead, Emma's suffering is long and protracted, and her blackened mouth and her vision of the singing blind beggar, which elicits a smile, as if she understands the irony of his appearance, speaks of her identification with an exploited underclass.

Ironically, even the act of dying is overseen by empowered men like the priest and Monsieur Homais. One of the final shots of the film, set against the narrator's dispassionate recounting of Berthe's fate following her parents' death, that as a result of her poverty she has been sent to work in a cotton mill, is a long shot of the village street on market day, where Léon can be seen shaking hands with Lheureux and introducing him to a woman he is with. It is a subtle but startling detail that illustrates a male system of complicity, ruthlessness, and profound indifference. Besides Berthe's fate, Emma's death has no effect on the system of male privilege. The final news, of Homais's success and honors ("Authorities respect him, and public opinion protects him") seals the image of a handshake that is far from benign. Rather than an indulgence in a romantic notion of self-destruction, Emma's suicide in the Chabrol/Huppert adaptation serves as a protest against a hierarchy of gender and class that denies women the wealth, freedom, and

Emma's ironic awareness of her affinity with the beggar as she lays dying in *Madame Bovary*.

power available to men, particularly those of a certain social position. Huppert's conquering, anti-victim approach to Emma creates a tension that the original does not and cannot fully have, distinguishing Emma from the oppressive mediocrity of her milieu. Huppert's dramatization of Emma's experience—the boredom, suffocation, and attempts to subdue the lingering sense of alienation and emptiness—speaks clearly and profoundly to women, humanizing Emma despite her shortcomings. Huppert's vision of Emma Bovary as the first great feminist heroine waging a battle prefiguring those to come brings Flaubert into the modern world.[14]

5

LA PIANISTE AND THE
MODERNIST MELODRAMA

La Pianiste is an incisive, razor-sharp analysis of the pathology of a culture and the resultant oppression of women. It is a film by Michael Haneke, and, as such, it eschews entertainment cinema and its tendency toward commodified sentimentalism in place of intellectual analysis. Haneke's films can be described as auteurist in the sense that his work is highly personal and humanist in its concern with the crisis of values engendered in the postwar world, exacerbated by a commodity-based, technology-centered culture.[1] Haneke's films are also modernist in their subtle self-reflexivity and awareness of how style—mise-en-scène, framing, the relation of sound and image, performance, the centrality of voyeurism to spectatorship—invites interpretation. A number of them can be described as melodramas in their preoccupation with family politics and social inequities. Although melodramas are generally associated with emotional excess and hyperbole, Haneke's are modernist in the way they present an analysis of the intense emotionalism that characterizes the genre, as the films of Douglas Sirk, Fritz Lang, or Otto Preminger often demonstrate. *La Pianiste* is a variant of the melodrama—it evidences an affinity with the Gothic and the Freudian-feminist melodrama in its analysis of the threat of romantic love—but may be more precisely identified as a woman's film, in its interrogation of a woman's struggle to achieve a healthy sexual identity and fit into a social place from which she feels alienated. Like a number of women's films, *La Pianiste* presents a woman-centered narrative in which men have become either irrelevant or dangerous to the protagonist, exploring the cost of the ideal of romantic love to the woman and the violence that underlies it; like George Cukor's *Gaslight*

116   Chapter 5

(1944), Hitchcock's *Rebecca* (1940), and *Marnie* (1964), among a host of other variations, the attractive male will intrude, enter the home, supplant and separate the daughter from the "mother," bringing pain and suffering. Haneke uses these tropes to explore the broader network of power and domination that characterizes the culture.

Although Haneke casts French actors, who speak in French, Haneke's Vienna evidences its fascist history and carefully places the personal within the social, suggesting that the ethos of the culture permeates private life. The film is based on Elfriede Jelinek's novel *The Piano Teacher* (1983), though it is distinctly different in tone and in its rendering of key characters and detailing of a divided culture.[2] Jelinek's novel serves as an indictment of Viennese culture and society, and, around the time of her being awarded a Nobel Prize in Literature, she was quoted as calling Austria a "criminal nation," in reference to its participation in the crimes of the Third Reich.[3] In many ways, Jelinek's and Haneke's Vienna (like Bachmann's in *Malina*) is an updated, contemporary extension of its identity during the fascist era; its past is evident in the present (and Austria shares these affinities with other European countries), with the film's setting in Vienna but its dialogue delivered in French serving to underline the similarities. The connection to a fascist history is inherent to a number of European democratic societies that retain their gender, class, and racial distinctions and biases. The rise and popular support of extreme right-wing parties in both Austria and France beginning in the 1980s and 1990s, and their continued underlying fear of the "other," attests to this. Vienna remains a society characterized by relationships of power and domination (parents and children, men and women, teachers and students, native-born citizens and immigrants, high and low culture) and repression (of freedom, equality, sexuality). This social structure insists upon containment, violence, and submission, and boundaries are valued and maintained; everyone has their place. In her novel, Jelinek emphasizes the extremes, clearly pointing to the demarcations between the white Viennese bourgeoisie and the Turkish male underclass who emerge at night, lining up to seek sexual gratification after a long day's work at the peep show arcades of the city or in its parks, which are abandoned after dark. Haneke's Vienna is more subtly drawn, but it still functions in the rigid polarities and gaps between the Viennese conservatory and the upper-middle-class world of high culture and privilege, where power and oppression is masked by taste and manners, and the sex shops and drive-ins, where sex is commodified and banalized for a predominantly alienated working class male clientele or a youth market who have no other place to go, and no pretense is made of the dynamics underlying what's being sold. The world of *La Pianiste* is part of a cinematic tradition that is exemplified in Hitchcock and can be traced back to German expressionism; underlying respectable, civilized culture is a condoned, unacknowledged violence that keeps everyone in their assigned place and the boundaries drawn and distinct.[4]

Erika is a complicated heroine who resists a traditional solicitation of viewer identification. Highly intelligent and emotionally incapacitated, she responds to the contradictions she experiences with a combination of extreme control and irrational impulse. Erika doesn't explain her motivations or direct the viewer to understand her. Instead, she acts with a matter-of-factness that normalizes the violence or pain that often underlies her actions. Erika's lack of self-awareness and inability to navigate the expectations of the culture forces the audience to comprehend her without the usual explicatory signposts offered by a central protagonist. Haneke wrote *La Pianiste* with Huppert in mind, and the film is a symbiotic collaboration much dependent on her performance style and persona.[5] In terms of acting, Huppert's approach of revealing interiority, minimizing emotional expression and psychological explanation, retaining a mystery regarding motivation perfectly aligns with Haneke's rejection of traditional characterization that overly accounts for and explains, reducing the work of reading, interpretation, and analysis assigned to the viewer. Huppert's characters are not available for this kind of consumption or pleasure, retaining a mystery that problematizes identification and soliciting a critically active spectator.[6] *La Pianiste* further subverts traditional expectations by centering on a female character who usurps the gaze, attempts to control and direct her sexual relationship with her student Walter Klemmer (Benoît Magimel), indulges in voyeurism (foregrounding the process and its attendant objectification), and, as Huppert claims, sees herself as both subject and object, like a metteur en scène, directing the male's desire.[7] Most importantly, Huppert can humanize Erika and solicit empathy (Huppert's Erika is scarred and poignantly aware of her difference) and estrange the viewer, maintaining a level of inscrutability that doesn't direct the viewer as to what to think of her. She can dramatize the contradictions of the subconscious without accounting for its active intrusion

118   Chapter 5

into conscious life; as a composite of a child/adolescent and adult, like Hitchcock's Marnie, Erika demonstrates a kind of timelessness character-istic of the subconscious and its ongoing presence. The film suggests this allusively at times, in long takes of Erika looking, where a slight movement of her eye or a lick of her lips, betrays the complexity of what she feels or is thinking.[8] Huppert's persona also challenges some of the mainstays of the genre that elicit an emotional response: the dramatization of suffering, sac-rifice, self-immolation (modernized as self-laceration) victimhood, and the near-descent into madness. Instead of these being ends in themselves, integral to the pleasure of identification offered, Huppert distances the viewer in a way that puts these issues in "citations," as Julia Kristeva has noted, deflecting a response of fascination to one that questions, analyzes and interrogates the presentation of the woman's position in relation to the culture.[9] It complements what the director provides with the handling of mise-en-scène, framing, structure, and staging; Haneke solicits a tempered involvement with hyperloaded material that insists on a critical distance. The first scene is a case in point; it is literally a battle scene, but the inten-tion is to introduce the pattern of suspicion, humiliation, and violence that is the mother's response to Erika's attempts to express her sexuality.[10]

Mothers and Daughters

Erika's story begins at home, and the precredits sequence of Erika's explo-sive fight with her mother (Annie Girardot) directly sets up the narrative. Erika is fighting for her autonomy, and her mother is insisting on her right to dominate Erika's life and repress her sexual identity. This touches a primal chord: every person must establish independence, usually in adolescence, and detach from parents. Part of this individuation occurs during puberty and comes with the development of a healthy sexual identity. Erika, in her late thirties, is still trying to balance being a good, obedient daughter/child with becoming an independent adult. As sex is banished from the home, Erika seeks release surreptitiously, after work, shopping for clothes that symbolize the desire for a more sexual, adult image or frequenting porn shops or drive-ins. (Not coincidentally, Erika meets one of her students, Fritz Naprawnik, in the porn emporium—an adolescent who, like Erika, is partaking of an illicit sexual experience.) Mrs. Kohut interrogates her daughter and knows Erika is lying (i.e., when she responds, "I went for a walk"), grabs her bag and pulls out the proof—the purchase. This scenario is repeated later in the film, when Erika returns from her night of voyeurism at the drive-in, an activity that is clearly part of a pattern or ritual; Erika's unaccounted-for time and the discovery of purchased clothing that she will likely never wear is met with her mother's violence, expressed in her grabbing for the dress or, in later scenes, attacking the clothes in her closet, fetish symbols of sex and independence. Erika's struggle for the dress results in its tearing (a form of "cutting," linked to what the novel calls Erika's "hobby": Erika's practice of self-harm) which then leads to a physical fight between mother and daughter so violent that Erika rips clumps of hair from her mother's head. The physical struggle is underlined by verbal images even more savage; Erika's mother claims that Erika should have her hands cut off for beating her own mother (a pointed comment, given Erika's identity as a pianist, that conveys an image of castration), which pushes Erika to say, "I wish . . ." Her mother finishes the thought, that Erika wishes her mother would have a heart attack so that she can be free. Seeing the damage both physical and emotional, Erika capitulates and denies the expression of desire for her mother's death and her own release, smiles at her mother's lighthearted comment about her missing clumps of her hair, and begins to cry, expressing her deeply felt remorse, as they examine the fallout from the battle. Erika's plaintive, tearful "Arrêtes, Maman" (Stop, Mama) is touching in the way she reverts seamlessly from the adult back to the child.[11] Huppert's range and depth of emotions of fury, love and regret, deftly compacted into a few moments, illustrates the profound complexity of their bond. Home life is saturated in patterns of violence blended into the intense closeness of familial relations.

The film's opening scene, which significantly precedes the credits, frames the narrative. The fear of the daughter's sexuality is a motif repeated in a number of woman's films (e.g., Hitchcock's *Marnie*) and is one with which women can identify; the signs of sexual development— menstruation, a changing body, and the development of sexual desire—are often warning signs that elicit the mother's ambivalence and trepidation about the consequences of the daughter's developing sexuality, and shame is summoned in defense of the mother's agitation and overwrought

Isabelle Huppert's rendering of Erika's complex emotional and physical response to her mother in *La Pianiste*.

hysteria. The mother's response is related to the danger of the daughter attracting a male who will intrude and displace her, usurping Erika's attentions with the promise of romantic love; the second part of the equation, in the tradition of classical romantic fiction, is the fear that he will seduce, exploit, and abandon her.

The battle over the dress and the body is also connected to a bank book. Erika is the breadwinner who works to save money for the payments on the new apartment. She is also encouraged to maintain her career and standing as a professional, both as a pianist and a teacher. Mrs. Kohut needs Erika for her aspirations for upward mobility to be realized. Erika is encouraged to be aggressive and ambitious so as to remain valued; she is cast as both a child and an alternate, desexualized husband. (Mrs. Kohut's disparaging comment upon ascertaining the cost of the dress—"Have you lost your mind?"—directly aligns Erika with the absent husband, reiterated later when Erika physically touches her in bed: "You're mad, you're completely mad.") The obliteration of men in the Kohut household is pointedly dramatized at the end of the scene when the two lie down, side by side, in their shared matrimonial bed. If the physical fight is overtly shocking, the image of mother and daughter in bed is only slightly less so. The scene introduces the subplot of Anna Schober, Erika's student, who will accompany the Schubert singer and is later perceived as a rival. As they lie together in bed, Mrs. Kohut asks about Anna, and when she hears that she

La Pianiste and the Modernist Melodrama   121

has an affinity for Schubert, warns her that Schubert is Erika's department and to be wary of talented young female students who risk threatening her position and career ("No one must surpass you"). Mrs. Kohut also discourages Erika from pursuing frivolous feminine pursuits that she perceives as demeaning ("Why someone of your standing slaps makeup on like a clown and fritters money on a dress soon out of style . . ."). Erika is groomed to replace the impotent husband; the father, institutionalized in an asylum (according to Erika) and in a later scene pronounced dead, has been effectively expelled from the home. On a psychoanalytic level, Erika retains the mother as love object, never following through the pattern of socialization whereby a girl child relinquishes this love and substitutes the father; as such, Erika fails the Oedipal rite of acquiring a passive feminine identity. Mrs. Kohut encourages this dependence, with the exception of acting out this intense bond in a sexual way. She will share her bed but deny the implications of her behavior. Erika's comment "I saw your pubic hair" during her failed attempt to express physical love for her mother encapsulates the contradiction.

Mrs. Kohut, trapped at home, passes time relentlessly watching TV, drinking to assuage her unhappiness, and tracking her daughter by phone. The only times she is seen emerging from the apartment are to escort Erika to a recital or concert. (In the novel it is clearer that Erika is past the age where a career as a concert pianist and the promise of success and class mobility is still viable; instead, she teaches and plays the odd recital.) Otherwise, Mrs. Kohut is only seen within the confines of the home. The mother appropriates her daughter's destiny as a way of compensating for her own misery. Her excessive concern for Erika's reputation and achievement is, to an extent, her own ambition displaced onto Erika. Her usurpation of her daughter's identity is placed as a response to her own disempowerment. Mrs. Kohut's warning not to let anyone surpass Erika is the final comment that ends the prelude before the main body of the film begins, signaled by the roll of the credits and a montage of Erika outside of the home, in her identity as a teacher. Haneke is commenting on the way a social problem, women's inequality and oppression, reverberates at home. Mrs. Kohut is not simply monstrous; she is encouraging her daughter to escape her own meager destiny. The use of Mrs. Schober as a mirror to Mrs. Kohut—a parallel character who diverts and displaces her own drive and ambition under the guise of sacrifice, and her understanding

122   Chapter 5

of how the world operates (she claims that her daughter is not attractive, and that her talent is her potential ticket to achievement)—reinforces the idea that Mrs. Kohut is not an anomaly, however extreme she may be. Both mothers disrespect boundaries, appropriate their daughters' destiny for their own ends, and favor the same punishment of cutting off the perpetrator's hands; Mrs. Schober, unwittingly, is also referring to Erika. In the scene where she visits Erika in her office following her daughter's assault, she explains her position by saying, "That's why we sacrificed." Erika, otherwise distracted and detached from the conversation, immediately corrects her: "You said 'we.' It's Anna." Mrs. Kohut reiterates this perception in a later scene, when she and Erika are lying in bed following Walter's visit: "All those sacrifices for this." When both women finally meet up in the final sequence on the night of the concert when Erika is to perform in Anna's stead, Mrs. Schober comments to Mrs. Kohut, "You must be proud," and, in one of the film's most sardonic moments, the latter replies, "Why? It's only a school concert." This throwaway line is revealing; mothers are ultimately rarely satisfied, because the achievement they push for can never eliminate or alleviate their source of pain or dissatisfaction. Mrs. Kohut is well aware of women's oppression. When Walter locks her up during the devastating rape scene that is both the climax of the film and an explicit dramatization of the violence and masculine brutality that underlies romantic "love," Mrs. Kohut yells out, "Just because we're women doesn't mean you'll get away with it." In fact, it does, particularly as Walter is additionally empowered by the protection and confidence nurtured by his social class. Despite the mother's attempts to rectify and sidestep inequality by accessing the daughter as a substitute phallus, the system overwhelms. The desire that drives the mother is the fantasy that she and Erika (or Mrs. Schober and Anna) will enjoy some of the privilege that eludes them. Mrs. Kohut, disappointed, more experienced, and protective (if overprotective) of Erika, rejects the accoutrements of sexuality, such as costume and makeup, that contribute to the objectification and degradation of women and to their oppression. She promotes instead a culturally ascribed traditional masculine ethic: hard work, self-promotion, ambition, discipline and ruthlessness. The pattern established at home—repression of sexuality, the triumph of the will, the drive toward power and domination, the use of violence as a means of asserting control when all else fails—is the social and familial model Erika learns and appropriates for herself. Even her choice of sexual pleasure in voyeurism evidences an affinity with a masculine ethos. Erika can have the phallus as long as her mother calls the shots.

The Phallic Woman

Erika internalizes what she learns at home and adapts the standard to the classroom and other relationships. She is stern, uncompromising, aloof, and almost mechanical in her instruction. She has banished sentiment, punishes without mercy, and is not passive. The credit sequence contrasts the prologue of Erika at home and, in a series of short vignettes, introduces Erika at work. An overhead shot of an anonymous student's small hands is accompanied by Erika's off-screen voice, instructing. The credits follow each vignette, acting like silent caesuras between them. The first visible student is Anna, who is playing the Schubert song that will accompany the singer, the refrain of which will be repeated a number of times in the film, like a leitmotif: "Dogs are barking, rattling their chains. People are sleeping in their beds." The words introduce the film's agenda: a wakeup call to a complacent, obstinate privileged class, unaware and asleep; Erika's comment to Anna, to pay attention to the notation and meaning of *froideur* (coldness) and the tone of Schubert's *Winterreisse* (Winter Journey), expresses the alienation that characterizes Erika, one that she well understands. The shots that accompany the credits also include Erika alone in her office and Erika with her student, Fritz Naprawnik, whom she later berates for being in the porn arcade that she herself patronizes. In some ways, both Anna and the young male student are foils to Erika, reflecting aspects of herself that remain unacknowledged, which may be why they are introduced in the opening credit montage and return, symmetrically, at the film's end. In a later scene, after Erika spots Naprawnik perusing porn magazines, she interrogates him mercilessly (as would her mother) in her classroom, crossing the boundaries of propriety. She questions whether his inability to play well is a result of "the images lodged in his head" and continues the barrage over his silence, asking if he thinks "women are bitches (*salopes*) for making men behave like *salauds* (pigs)" (her use of the word *salaud* is one her mother later uses with reference to

Walter). Unsatisfied with an apology—"Sorry for what exactly?"—she dismisses him with the threat of his having to bring *his* mother to the next class ("Maybe she can shed light on this"), intensifying his humiliation. Erika's moments of excess, as in the incident with her student or when she deposits shards of glass in Anna's coat pocket, are eruptions of explosive anger regarding sexuality or sexual rivalry, acted out more nakedly at home. As a teacher, she adapts her mother's role as inquisitor; like Professor Rath in Josef von Sternberg's *The Blue Angel* (1930), Erika will chastise and punish her students for what she refuses or is unable to identify in herself.[12]

The recital scene that follows the credits introduces the problem that precipitates the narrative: a male outsider intrudes into the family by presenting himself as an ideal romantic suitor. Erika and Walter will fall in love over reciprocal performances at a recital, an event that will threaten the mother's supremacy as primary love object and authority. This is brilliantly visualized at the beginning of the scene with Mrs. Kohut and Erika in the cage-like elevator on their way up to the apartment where the soiree is being held. Walter rushes into the building, and Mrs. Kohut moves quickly to shut the elevator door, pointedly excluding him. The gesture safeguards their privacy while visualizing their isolation and entrapment. The two women alone, encaged, are lifted up while Walter bounds up the stairs. He arrives at the apartment as they emerge from the elevator and is about to introduce himself but the two women ignore him and enter. While Erika plays, Walter watches, mesmerized (and a cut to Mrs. Kohut notes her concern), and when he tries to impress her during the intermission, Erika rebuffs him, sternly commenting on his precocity and immaturity. She then proceeds to talk about Schumann, and, as if warning Walter to keep his distance, speaks of the composer's awareness of losing his mind. Walter comments on her understanding of this as if it were her own self, and she attributes her authority on the subject by citing her father as an example of madness that is close to her. Mrs. Kohut, already threatened by Walter, denigrates him at the intermission with the comment "He's a bit of a leech, isn't he." These remarks make an impression, as is the intention, and Erika will later echo it back to Walter, admonishing him for "being such a leech." As the concert continues Walter pays tribute to Erika (and announces his interest in her) by switching his choice of music to a work by Schubert, and again there is a cut to Mrs. Kohut, who senses the threat intensifying

La Pianiste and the Modernist Melodrama 125

Erika's manifestation of attraction and displeasure at the concert: *La Pianiste*.

and looks over at Erika. While Walter plays, Erika, in a medium-close long take, registers the reciprocation of feelings for Walter (the pleasure magnified via her affinity with Schubert) mixed with her annoyance for having these feelings for him. This complex response is dramatized concisely by the look on her face, her almost-smile, and a slight, almost imperceptible blink of her eye and slight pursing of her lips; when Erika feels she is losing control, she feels threatened.

Pleasure and Punishment

Erika's arousal of feelings of desire is typically followed by punishment. It triggers a loss of control, a loosening of repression that demands containment. This is what Erika has internalized through behavior learned at home: desire is inextricably linked to punishment. Erika's affinity for masochism and sadism—pleasure in punishment—takes various forms. It is the model exemplified in her relationship with her mother (one surmises that Erika expects to be found out and chastised for her purchases, a familiar ritual played out in the opening sequence), who teaches her that sex is an expression of defilement and weakness. It is demonstrated in her fantasy of sex as extreme S&M, where enslavement and power relations are rehearsed and eroticized, the staging reenacting the relationship with her

126   Chapter 5

primary love object, her mother. She will substitute Walter for her mother and spells this out for him as a gesture of love, telling him that he will now give her orders and decide what she will wear. Erika's long-standing desire to be beaten, she explains, is a desire to dramatize her lack of autonomy and powerlessness. She reenacts her experiences of domination and submission by giving orders or receiving them. Reciprocation and love aren't part of Erika's understanding of pleasure and desire, just as equality and independence are not part of her experience; she is not familiar with it. Relationships are structured by power: master/slave, dominator/dominated, those with the phallus/those without.

In place of a healthy, integrated, lived sexuality, Erika indulges in acts of autoeroticism, cut off from human contact. She visits porn emporiums, where she can be a voyeur in the safety of her cubicle, or drive-ins that have an added element of danger, as her voyeurism is outside of a socially designated site and is illicit; drive-ins, like porn sites, are also frequented by youths, who, like Erika, have nowhere else to have sex. Tellingly, Erika's fascination in terms of porn imagery is with the penis; she switches channels until she finds an act of fellatio, and this, coupled with the scent of semen on used tissue papers, particularly arouses her. Haneke uses the Schubert song in part as ironic counterpoint of high with low culture, but in part as commentary on Erika's alienation. The image of her sniffing discarded tissues is accompanied with the tenor's verse "Bark me away, you waking dogs! Don't let me rest in the sleeping hours," which segues from the porn scene into one that follows in the conservatory, fluidly crossing boundaries, as Erika does. Erika's gloved hands reaching for the soiled tissue makes the same point. This obsession is replayed during her first physical encounter, or "love scene," with Walter in the ladies room in the conservatory. Erika's fixation is with controlling the phallus quite literally; she is intrigued by the act of manipulating a penis until it's at its largest, fullest size. She doesn't allow Walter to touch it or release himself; instead, she instructs him to contain and overcome his natural impulses that are connected to pleasure and to be disciplined and endure pain, conjoining pain and pleasure, as is her experience. Walter, at first annoyed, is soon fascinated with the phallic woman. Her commands ("Face me. Don't put it away. Now you can put it away. Facing me! You will receive my instructions") augment her stature as an authority figure, an accomplished pianist, a teacher, an intellectual, as she teaches him the basics of the culture:

La Pianiste and the Modernist Melodrama   127

denial, endurance, and deferral, the triumph of the will, enhance the final glory. He ultimately appreciates the lesson in what Susan Sontag calls "the heroic repression of the sexual impulse" that underscores fascism.[13] He bounds out of the washroom happier and more energized than ever.

Erika's practice of cutting or self-harm (a practice, along with anorexia and other variations expressive of self-discipline and punishment, that remains popular with female adolescents and was particularly rampant in the 1970s in Austria) is another form of displacing uncontrolled emotion and unlived sexuality into a disciplined experience of punishment and controlled pain. The scene of Erika's self-mutilation in the family bathroom illustrates how cutting blends an experience of punishment, pain, and endurance with an expression of sexuality. The scene directly follows the one where Walter has gained entrance to the conservatory and Erika's master class, despite her having voiced her opposition to him following his audition. While he plays, there is a long shot of Erika, her contradictory feelings hinted at in the way she first looks away from him and then, despite her display of disinterest, turns to look more closely. A closer shot reveals her being drawn into Walter's performance, regardless of her preferred indifference: she adjusts her hands, loosens her shoulders, and licks her lip, seeming annoyed and impressed at once. Details of her performance in this scene, like her uncomfortable snicker when she claims she feels unable to nurture Walter's artistic temperament or virtuosity, subtly evidence her anger at his intrusion as well as her attraction to him. Erika's cutting, therefore, becomes her means of reestablishing control for herself, as punishment for losing the battle with Walter and for her emerging desire; it allows her a means of directing her pain, rage, and desire at once. Erika pulls out her carefully wrapped razor blade from her purse, spreads her legs, and ritualistically cuts her labia. The allusion to menstruation, the staging of a girl's entry into puberty, a sign of the desire to separate and form one's own sexual identity, is made when she reenters the dining room. Erika's mother interrupts even this moment of privacy in the bathroom by calling her to dinner, and Erika complies like an obedient daughter, carefully rinsing her blood off the bathtub and reaching for a menstrual pad to soak up her blood. Mrs. Kohut, first mentioning that she is going to get the sauce for dinner (an example of the film's sardonic humor) notices a trail of blood running down Erika's leg that she has failed to clean off and admonishes Erika for coming to the dinner table with

128   Chapter 5

menstrual blood visible on her body, attributing her moodiness to her having her period. Jelinek describes the sensation of cutting in the novel in quasi-sexual terms: "spreading her legs," the blood oozing down the leg.[14] Erika assures herself of her aliveness by cutting—it is a private act, like her nocturnal forays, an assertion of independence. Erika withholds this ritual from her mother even though it takes place at home, and, like her excursions, it is an expression and response of anger and control, that conjoins punishment, sexuality, and pleasure.

When Erika feels threatened or is losing control, she cuts—herself or others. In the scene of the Schubert rehearsal, Walter's attentions to Anna Schober (captured in a long take of Erika watching) anger her, and she abruptly leaves the auditorium, enters the coatroom area, and, in a long take from behind her back, rubs her ear and adjusts her shoulders as she thinks of a response and then acts by leaving cut glass in Anna's coat pocket. The song's refrain—"Why do I avoid the roads where other travelers go?"—that aurally accompanies her act is almost Brechtian or operatic, as it points, musically, to Erika. The police will attribute the violence to a student acting out of jealousy (which is what it is), as it will eliminate Anna as a romantic competitor; it also responds to her mother's instruction to be on guard and not let anyone surpass her. Erika's comment to Walter ("Be her brave protector, go to her") is a declaration of the extent of her feelings for him articulated in Erika's anachronistic conception of romantic love preceded by her equally anachronistic, ironic comment "The sight of blood makes me ill . . . ," which is then followed by her rushing off to the washroom. The other scene where Erika feels compelled to urinate is when she is aroused watching the young couple having sex in their car at the drive-in. Erika's compulsion to urinate when sexually aroused (combined with the element of danger, having transgressed social bounds) suggests that the cutting, and her confronting Walter with an admission of her desire, is part of a pattern of behavior related to Erika's experience of sexual pleasure and regaining control.

Erika's attraction to Walter is also rooted in a desire for normalcy and inclusion in a social world from which she knows she is alienated. After rejecting Walter's offer in her classroom to skip the lesson and enjoy the lovely day together, Walter leaves, and Erika follows him surreptitiously as he exits the conservatory; as always, she takes the male position, as detached voyeur. She watches almost tenderly as he pulls out his hockey

La Pianiste and the Modernist Melodrama   129

bag from his car on the way to his practice. Erika watches bemusedly as he charms two figure skaters who have been knocked aside by a pack of hockey players, attracted to his vitality and social ease, which seem to come effortlessly. Erika is shot behind the bars of a door, visually entrapped, admiring his youth and energy. Walter is one of the sleeping villagers of Schubert's song, satisfied and oblivious. She advises him during one of their classes to forget Schubert: "Anarchy hardly seems your forte. Schubert was quite ugly, did you know? With your looks, nothing can hurt you." Erika speaks about her own experience of suffering and exclusion and is drawn to the idea of freedom and autonomy that he represents. At the same time, Erika cannot express intimacy or love and doesn't seem able or interested in partaking of a reciprocated physical relationship with Walter. When he approaches her, she loses her composure and coughs, conjures migraines, or uses the excuse of being busy with her mother, later chastising him for being a leech and following her home. "Never hound the woman you claim to love," she advises him in terms that are never colloquial, underlining her exclusion from the culture, as do the details of her attire—her hat, gloves, handbag and 1940s-like coat, which serve as references to her mother's generation. In part Erika explains this rejection as a means of self-protection, of safeguarding her need to be in control: "I have no feelings, Walter—get that into your head. If I ever do, they won't defeat my intelligence." As Susan Sontag notes, in S&M sex becomes detached, "severed from personhood, from relationships, from love."[15] When Erika decides to proceed with a relationship, she writes her instructions as a means of controlling her emotional and sexual relationship with Walter, by listing her desires. In this way Erika remains empowered, even while authorizing her idea of sexual pleasure in a complex, detailed list of masochistic punishments that are all self-centered ("Punch me, sit on my face"), an extension of her proclivity for autoeroticism and pleasure in punishment. Erika's instructions are tellingly framed within her relationship to her mother ("Don't worry about Mother, she's my problem"; "Ask why I don't call out to Mother"). The scene where Erika is sequestered in her bedroom with Walter and lays out her proposition is punctuated by cutaway shots to Mrs. Kohut locked out, drinking and demanding that they emerge from the room. Ultimately Erika's idea of love is to replace her mother with Walter and manipulate him to usurp her mother's role, repeating "From now on you give the orders." Erika reenacts the relationship of submission,

130   Chapter 5

powerlessness, and punishment with her mother that is deeply embedded in her psyche, as evidenced in her cache of S&M paraphernalia hidden under the bed, ready for use. When Walter touches her body she sits frozen, legs crossed, and her response is to jump up and eagerly pull out her box of equipment, which includes an executioner's mask.

Erika's vulnerability is laid bare in this scene, and it is a credit to both Haneke and Huppert's performance that Erika remains touchingly empathetic. Erika responds to Walter's shocked silence following her astonishingly graphic list of degradation with her perceptive comment "I disgust you, huh?," articulating her acute awareness of her estrangement from the norm. Her unusually frank admission, attempting to explain her long-standing urge to be beaten, and the remark "I've waited for you, you know," is genuine and moving. The tears in her eyes and her final offer to Walter to hit her is the closest Erika comes to openly acknowledging her needs, which she knows are aberrant and thus elicit great pathos for her character. Erika's answer to why she doesn't cry out to mother—"So that I realize just how powerless I am"—is remarkably telling and aware, summarizing her desire to enact her powerlessness. Walter's initial sympathy ("Erika, you're sick, you need treatment") is soon followed by repulsion; Erika's visible expression of suffering does not move him. Walter is attracted to the phallic teacher—tough, disciplined, authoritative, and empowered who will enhance his experience of sex. He is fascinated with Erika's command of Schubert, her cultured rhetoric, and her unavailability. Walter is also narcissistic and aroused by the ethical line Erika crosses on his behalf, the extreme measures she takes that announce her feelings for him. He understands that the sadistic gesture against Anna is a staking of territory, and he is emboldened by it to follow her into the ladies' room and claim his victory. The act of violence against an innocent bystander not only fails to offend him; it also excites him. Erika's initial assessment of Walter, that he exploits music as a means to self-promotion and glorification, is accurate. Walter is satisfying his ego. When Erika lists her predilection for abuse that only services her, he is disappointed. "What will all this open up for me?" he asks. Walter wants immediate gratification and is impatient. His earlier comment, "I don't know how much longer I want to play this game," is revealing. In the novel his character is far less ambiguous. His sport is seducing and conquering his prey, which he intends to discard. Walter understands life in terms of sports metaphors, how games are played, what the rules are and how to win. A lost play provokes anger. Haneke provides hints of this but seduces the viewer with a charming, handsome young man playing on the expectations of the boy-meets-girl narrative, where the romantic lover saves the woman from her spinster fate, integrates her into the social world and makes her normal (a trajectory analyzed in *Marnie*). Walter's comment following Erika's painful offer to hit her ("I swear I loved you. . . . You don't even know what it is") makes him sympathetic, a figure of identification in this scene. The viewer is inclined to forgive him because he is *bien élevé* (well educated) and has been, if not deceived, then misled. Walter's idea of love will be revealed in the scene where he brutalizes and rapes Erika with the kind of abandon of which only an extreme narcissist, protected by his class, is capable.

It is significant that Erika's attempt to express her love for her mother in their "matrimonial" bed is sandwiched between two failed attempts to engage with Walter, romantically or sexually. The scene where Erika attempts to embrace her mother sexually is both pathetic (a sign that Erika cannot negotiate the norms and demands of the culture, and her mother will fail to help her, despite being the one who, on some level, cares most for her) and touching—Erika is demanding what her mother can never acknowledge, which is the full extent of her need to be loved, touched, embraced, and comforted. After Walter has left, disappointed with Erika's proposition that he consider her scripted demands, Mrs. Kohut rails against Erika's revealed sexual identity ("You might as well set up a bordello here") while Erika lies supine and silent beside her, as if in her coffin. She then demands to be embraced with the proclamation "*Maman, je t'aime.*" Huppert describes the moment as an expression of the character's desire to crawl back into the mother's belly and be safe and protected there, as does Jelinek in her novel: "As if she wanted to crawl back in and hide inside it."[16] Lying next to her mother in the bed she has been encouraged to share, following the failure to agree on terms with Walter, inspires Erika to express her need for a physical expression of love to her primary love object; it is a moment that stages a subconscious reality intruding into consciousness. She is berated and punished for these feelings, as is the pattern ("Don't be so filthy"). Erika cries out with a wail of pain and anguish as her mother pushes her off her body, repeating, "You're mad," completing her identification with the husband, and ends by moving into denial mode, constructing the substitute phallus: "Now go to sleep. You're going to need all your energy. Even if you're just standing in, you must be well prepared; you never know who might be in the audience." Erika tries again to embrace her mother, uncovering her body, and comments on seeing her pubic hair, acknowledging her mother's sexuality. In the novel, Erika's mother warns her against sexual touching (e.g., keeping hands above the covers); Erika is announcing that, despite her mother's demand to repress and deny any hint of sexuality, Erika is also a sexual being who needs the comforts of touch and affection. Mrs. Kohut's advice to suppress her feelings and "go to sleep" is the subject of Schubert's song. The scene ends touchingly, with Erika snuggling up against her as if retreating to a primal stage of infancy and dependence. Huppert's performance in this difficult scene is crucial to one's understanding of Erika as the injured adult/child, trying desperately to be loved and comforted by the person she most loves and trusts.

The failure of the mother, and, by extension, the culture, to acknowledge Erika's sexuality as a part of her identity is also the lament of the outsider in the song that is reiterated throughout the narrative. Instead of functioning, Erika is paralyzed by the contradictions of her socialization and estranged from a social group described as asleep and thus complicit. Erika needs to feel alive in the body as well the mind and can only achieve this in dysfunctional practices like cutting. Her profound

Erika's intense need to be held and loved: mother (Annie Girardot) and daughter in *La Pianiste*.

La Pianiste and the Modernist Melodrama   133

desire is to reactivate the plenitude of infancy: the integration of sexual touch with love and nurturing. Tellingly, the scene in the bedroom is the only instance where Erika experiences physical desire for another person and wishes to act on it, and it is the closest she comes to an expression of love. When this fails, she makes her last desperate attempt to resume a conventional relationship with Walter, to apologize for her drastic miscalculation in announcing her needs and to acquiesce to his terms—that is, offering him immediate sexual gratification. Erika finds Walter at the arena following a hockey game, and her attempt at a "normal" relationship takes on a very different tone. Erika is dressed to please a male in a contemporary soft, sensuous dress that is overtly feminine. The gender politics are visualized in the setting as well as the costumes. Erika intrudes into a male testosterone-laden group of sweaty hockey players just as she does in the porn emporium and, as earlier, remains unintimidated by the male-dominated space, emphasized in the long take that, significantly, situates the scene. Nevertheless, Erika's approach is almost antithetical to the earlier scene in the conservatory washroom, where she conducts the episode in a manner not unlike a sergeant commanding troops toward victory. Now Erika wants to convince Walter that she can be normal and passively feminine. Erika, who begs for forgiveness, is at her most vulnerable. She offers what she assumes is conventional sex, lying down and offering Walter to get on top of her. Walter's initial response mirrors her mother's ("You're mad"), but, seeing an opportunity, he quickly changes direction, tosses out a glib "I love you, too," and takes it. They move into the privacy of the locker room, and he undresses to the point where he can shove his penis in Erika's mouth for a blowjob, the scene playing itself out as the kind of sex adolescents might have. Erika vomits, and Walter, angered by this affront, says, "I must really disgust you. No woman ever puked it back." Erika, undiscouraged and desperate to be accepted, rinses her mouth and claims happily to be clean as a baby "inside and out, thanks to you, darling," but Walter, like an offended adolescent, furiously lashes out at her: "Sorry, you stink so much no one will ever come close to you. Rinse your mouth more often . . . not just when my cock makes you puke." Ironically, Walter's vicious response to Erika's desperate attempt at heteronormative sex and gender relations make her physically sick, her disequilibrium captured in her staggering away shakily on the ice.

134   Chapter 5

Failed love scenes with Walter alternate with scenes of Erika lying in bed near her mother, reiterating the parallels. Walter returns that night, following the incident at the rink, completely enraged for having lost his position of rakish confidence and control through his obsession with Erika that he claims has compelled him to come to their apartment building. His entry into the Kohut apartment after Erika and her mother are asleep marks the beginning of the rape scene that builds in increments of brutality and violence. Walter has crossed a boundary of propriety and has lost all semblance of the smooth, social charmer. Beneath the veneer of manners, civility, and bourgeois politesse emerges an uncontrolled monstrousness. Rape is an act of domination, violence and egocentrism, and Walter returns to claim what he has failed to achieve, to punish the woman who has witnessed and demonstrated his humiliation and who has caused him to lose control. He cites his self-disgust at masturbating under her window, resorting to age-old patriarchal excuses for masculine violence against women: "You're a witch, a pervert, you want to give everyone your illness." Walter's second justification is equally time worn, that he is giving Erika what she desired. He quotes her written instructions ("As for my mother, pay no attention to her") and begins to beat Erika, rationalizing that this is what she wanted. The fascinating aspect of Walter's psychotic brutality in this scene is that he stops only to refresh himself—it follows the moment when he has punched her in the face, causing her nose to bleed, and when he asks for water, there is a faint hope that it is to help her. Walter calls out from the kitchen that although he realizes "this isn't very nice," he adds, "Admit you're partly responsible." When he returns and sees that Erika has moved to help herself, he becomes enraged again and resumes his violence, ignoring her pleas to avoid hitting her face and hands. As is typical, Walter continues his use of sports metaphors and explains that he'd be happy to learn to play, but not if it is exclusively by her rules. He makes a similar comment earlier in the washroom scene—that the playing field has to be level, indicating that Walter remains consistent; it is the viewer who must finally adjust and move past the tendency to forgive handsome men of their selfishness and excessive abuse. Ignoring her plea to stop, Walter finishes himself off on top of Erika, essentially having had sex alone, and moves to leave. After warning her of the uselessness of telling anyone of the assault, Walter continues rationalizing his behavior, saying that "you can't humiliate a man like that. It's not possible." Relieved of his rage, emerging as the victor, Walter resumes his disingenuous social face ("Will you be all right? Do you need anything?"), oblivious of Erika lying prostrate, corpse-like, as good as dead, completely unresponsive. His final ironic comment to her is "You know love isn't everything. See you, then," and trots off. When Mrs. Kohut emerges from the bedroom, she speaks with experience: "Oh my God, child, what did the bastard do to you?" Schubert's song about feeling completely abandoned reverberates.

The final sequence of the film begins with a close-up of a large knife being removed from a drawer in the kitchen and placed carefully in Erika's purse. Erika's mother is calling her off-screen, telling her to hurry, and Erika's comment that she is just getting some water recalls Walter, linking the knife to the rape scene. (Her mother assumes she is nervous because of the concert and comments that she's only replacing someone.) Erika's gesture visually speaks of appropriating the phallus—arming herself with a symbol of power—and it is unclear at this point whether she will use it to punish Walter or herself. Erika's bruised face evidences her status as a survivor of a violent assault, and her demeanor is back to inscrutable detachment. Erika's deadened numbness illustrates her estrangement from the world around her. It is the night of the concert, and Erika is to replace Anna as the accompanist to the singer. There is a cut from the kitchen to a long shot of the impressive conservatory, a bastion of culture with its implications of civilization, tradition, and morality, lit up for the evening's performance, an imposing edifice that represents a world of privilege and entitlement. Erika meets her two adolescent alter egos, Fritz and Anna, as well as Mrs. Schober, Anna's mother, and is inattentive to their conversation. Mrs. Schober finally meets her mirror image, Mrs. Kohut, and together they go to their seats. Erika is left alone in the lobby, which is almost empty, as it is close to showtime. She finally spots the group she is looking for, in a long shot from Erika's point of view. Walter, a young woman, and his relatives, who hosted the recital, enter. Seeing them, Erika smiles slightly and walks toward them, her expectation at this point enigmatic. The final scene thus brings the story symmetrically back to the start, the concert echoing the recital where Erika and Walter meet and fall in love. Erika waits in the lobby, expectantly looking toward the entry. At last Walter enters behind his relatives, his glibly delivered greeting ("My respects, Professor. I can't wait to hear you play") recalls the earlier performance. This time, Walter delivers

136   Chapter 5

this line as he rushes by, willfully oblivious of Erika's battered face, and leaves her standing alone; there is a long take on Erika's look of disappointment as her eyes fill with tears. At this point Erika summons her strength, clenches her face with bared teeth, at once expressing fortitude, profound pain, and determination, pulls the knife out of her purse, and, carefully and quickly, plunges it in and out of her shoulder, a premeditative act that asserts her reclaiming control and expressing her protest. She covers the wound quickly and looks around to see if anyone is there. There is a cut to an exterior shot of the imposing building, and Erika is seen in long shot, briskly walking away from the conservatory. Although stabbing Walter might have been more satisfying for the viewer, Erika is aware of the limitations of the world in which she lives. Walter advised her not to tell anyone ("Anyhow, it's for your own good") and is protected by his gender and class. The long shot of the conservatory, with a bar motif visible in its lighting and architecture, visually reiterates its identity as a jail for Erika, recalling the film's opening scene, where Erika explains her desire to go for a walk as a response to having spent eight hours in "the cage," which is how she refers to the conservatory—a place that entraps her. Erika's walking away from the building is hopeful. In response to Walter's "I can't wait to hear you play," Erika will not play tonight. She leaves her mother, her students, and Walter behind and makes a bold statement by walking away from the building, possibly toward her autonomy. Erika is not committing suicide, which she could have done had she so desired, as would many a heroine in her position of having been seduced and abandoned; she stabs herself in a manner that creates a superficial wound, as is her practice.[17] Her cutting on a grander scale is her means of exteriorizing what she feels but cannot express; it is a familiar form of expression in a manner that she can control. In the novel Erika walks home, and although she is bleeding, passersby pretend not to notice. Jelinek is commenting on the national habit of willful obliviousness, endemic to a hierarchical society that cares little for another's suffering. The film's final shot of the bastion of Viennese culture visualizes the lyrics of Schubert's song ("I've reached the end of dreams / What will I do among the sleepers? / Why do I avoid the roads where other travelers go? . . . / And yet I've done nothing to flee my fellow man / What is this foolish desire driving me to the wilderness?"). In a society where violence against women is rationalized, there is little that Erika can do but walk away; her leaving the shot that lingers on one of the institutions, representative of a system that validates and condones her oppression, is as positive and uplifting an ending as one could hope for.

Huppert's performance is a remarkable tour de force, at once nuanced, elusive, and touching, as she humanizes Erika without ironing out her complexities or soliciting direct identification with her. Huppert's ability to reveal the layers of the character without explanation is precisely in line with Haneke's insistence that the spectator produce an interpretation. It is a performance that privileges the spaces between what is shown and what is not, referencing the demands of the social structure that contain and almost destroy her. Erika's ability to walk away and resist becoming a victim makes an important statement about women and survival.

6

READING *ELLE*

I've played a lot of characters who were victims, but I never was the victim: as an actress I was the center of the film, so I had the character all to myself—and the movie all to myself. It's not as if I were in a supporting role being dominated by a man. I was a privileged victim who expresses herself. That's my kind of feminism.

—Isabelle Huppert

Paul Verhoeven's film *Elle* (2016), starring Isabelle Huppert, draws from cinematic conventions—the thriller, the horror film and its close counterpart, the Gothic melodrama—while resisting categorization and interpretation. Its expository scene, a brutal rape curiously witnessed solely by a house cat, is its opening volley. The rape acts as a leitmotif, structuring the narrative like an obsession; it will be replayed as a traumatic memory, a fantasy where the victim reclaims her power and avenges the assault, as a repeated encounter where she does, in fact, stab and unmask her assailant, and as a performance or ritual that sets the terms for two consensual sexual encounters in which desire, punishment, and guilt are key components. Because of this, some critics have focused on the film's attitude toward rape and violence, and its problematic association with pleasure (the pleasure of punishment, vengeance, voyeurism, and satire).

Elle also shares a strong affinity with the European art film (Verhoeven has mentioned Buñuel's *The Discreet Charm of the Bourgeoisie* and Renoir's social realist *La règle du jeu* while others have evoked Haneke and Huppert's *La Pianiste*) that colors how one reads it.[1] Its casting of Isabelle Huppert, whose long career has been associated with postwar European cinema and a performance style that can be considered modernist, establishes

140   Chapter 6

a character who is neither fully accessible nor psychologically defined, resisting a certain kind of appropriation on the part of the viewer that is expected of traditional identification. Instead, Huppert's Michèle invites a more active form of viewer participation and interpretation as her character leaves spaces that defy a full explanation of motivation. Her insistence on maintaining a level of ambiguity and withholding full disclosure of the character's subjectivity creates a mystery, obstructing the viewer's expected pleasure of becoming someone else for the duration of the narrative. Huppert's self-possession and resistance to being fully available or inviting a pretense of familiarity with the viewer, contributes to her iconic image as a cold, impassive, perverse ice queen, which may be an expression of discomfort with a persona not open to being fully explained, exposed, and revealed. Molly Haskell's visceral response to *Elle* and its casting choice of Huppert as its central protagonist reveals a profound animus toward the persona, which is, in part, attributable to Huppert's unwillingness to project a heroine who is fully likable and definable.[2] Huppert's ability to reveal subconscious strata produces a character who defies a rational reading; she is not afraid to discourage the emotional empathy traditionally afforded the victim. Identification shifts from the individual to her position as a woman in a particular culture, inviting a critical distance that implies an intellectual involvement that qualifies an emotional one. Rather than a film about a woman and her rapist, *Elle* presents a hypothesis about the sanctioning of masculine violence and its legitimization through a culture still dominated by the Father. When Michèle confronts her assailant, the paradigmatic guy next door, to account for the assault, he states simply, "It was necessary." As a woman who challenges the power relations of a culture (her identity as the complicit "ash girl," "killing" the father, questioning the nature of maternal love, helming a company of young men who resent her power over them) the assault is, symbolically, a response of necessity.

In interviews, Huppert has cautioned against reading the film too literally and suggested that Michèle's relationship with her attacker should be approached as a fantasy or fable (which one reviewer rejects by claiming that "there is nothing in Verhoeven's direction to suggest that we should not read the film as a cohesive and realistic—if exaggerated—whole").[3] In fact, the film does invite an ambiguous representation of reality, and as *Elle* is as much an art film as it is genre-based, it is staking out symbolic territory and less concerned with privileging realism. Scenes like the one where Michèle and her neighbor Patrick (Laurent Lafitte) secure the shutters of her house from the gales that threaten to shatter the glass, or where Michèle follows Patrick down to the basement to observe the "inverted flame combustion" of his furnace (a moment that the same reviewer derides based on evaluative standards of logic and reality) are similar to the moments in melodrama and the Gothic of an intensity that belies rational interpretation.

Huppert's suggestion, that the narrative may be better approached as a fable or an allegory over a story about the daughter of a serial killer who pursues her rapist, is useful, as it opens up a wider discussion about a woman's unsafe place in a progressive world that remains resistant to her equality and freedom. The film's structure conflates Michele's identity as a victim of masculine violence privately within a dysfunctional family and in her home, and then publicly in the workplace. Michèle's trajectory will be to confront and free herself from this status of and, in so doing, becomes a heroine. This is integral to Huppert's persona; she has noted that, even when playing a victim, she is a "privileged victim who expresses herself."[4]

Huppert has refined a style of restrained, minimalist performance that points inward. Rather than a fully realized, mimetic re-creation, Huppert presents a character whose motivations are both conscious and unconscious, without ironing out her complexities and contradictions. This invites a different kind of viewer identification: one cannot always account for actions or motivations that are not necessarily rational or even

The Gothic trope of the gales as an expression of the tenderness between Michèle and Patrick (Laurent Lafitte) that is suppressed: *Elle*.

142   Chapter 6

ethical, but one can identify with the contradiction of sometimes behaving in ways that are contrary to the set of values to which one may ascribe. The film places Michèle in a context that asks one to piece together elements of the narrative that may lie beyond resolution or the character's comprehension—a characteristic of both modernist art and melodrama. Michèle is not particularly emotionally available to the viewer, or even, for that matter, to herself or to those close to her. She rejects intimacy, and, at times, streaks of cruelty and indifference surface in her behavior that the narrative leaves open to interpretation, suggesting a complexity that the film is reluctant to resolve. Michèle's detachment from her experiences, her sangfroid, feeds the strange tone of humor and absurdity that characterizes the film's understanding of bourgeois life. Having inherited public scrutiny as the child-accomplice of a murderer and a dissolute mother who isn't bound to bourgeois mores, Michèle wants, above all, absolution—the veneer of normalcy and a scandal-free existence, because, on some level, what lies beneath bourgeois propriety and religious repression is an unspeakable violence that threatens. Michèle's tendency is to routinize, tidy up, and thus deny what has taken place. Following the assault, Michèle carefully gathers up the broken china and glass, bathes and orders sushi, even asking for clarification of what a "holiday roll" is, as if unwilling to allow the magnitude of the assault (subtly evident in the blood that colors the bath water) to sidetrack her. She avoids calling the police and when her son asks about her bruises, she lies, claiming to have fallen off her bicycle. Without protest, Michèle quietly accepts the abuse she receives in a cafeteria when a woman, recognizing her as the "ash girl" amid the resurfacing of attention regarding her father's murder spree as he comes up for parole, dumps a tray of garbage on her. Her mother's comment, that Michèle wants a "sanitized version of life," appears accurate. Michèle seems to accept some level of guilt for her participation in her father's night of terror. Despite her complete disavowal of her father, whom she considers a monster and psychopath, she confesses to Patrick: "It was exciting. You get caught up in it." Her major bone of contention with her mother is her refusal to acknowledge her father and visit him in jail, as her mother requests repeatedly, including after her collapse. Ironically, her mother's fatal heart failure follows Michèle's narcissistic monologue in the hospital room where she announces that she won't see her father, that her mother's attempts to manipulate her with her aneurysm ("an abject stunt") won't change that. Michèle refuses her mother's pleas to let go of her hatred and humanize her father, saying that "he's sick," and "he's only a man."

In her commitment to propriety, the rigid standards Michèle imposes on her family members are not necessarily those she applies to herself. Her desires and actions are often contradictory to her bourgeois standards. She is offended by her mother's openly sexualized demeanor, commenting to Anna (Anne Consigny) at her Christmas party, "If I ever show up like that, kill me," and, following the public announcement at dinner that her mother is engaged to be married to her young gigolo boyfriend, Michèle loses her composure, derides her mother with a loud awkward snigger, and publicly berates her: "How do you manage to be so grotesque?" Yet at the same party she has no problem flirting with her neighbor, despite the presence of his wife, responding to his touching her hand by putting her foot on his crotch underneath the table. She has similarly few scruples when agreeing to sleep with Robert, her close friend and business associate's partner, engaging in a form of athletic, military-style sex devoid of intimacy or attachment. (In a film attentive to detail, the shot of her moving the trashcan closer to catch Robert's effluvium is a case in point.) Although on amicable terms with her ex-husband, Richard (Charles Berling), she nonchalantly and intentionally damages his car while parking her own and enjoys informing him casually of the extent of the damage: "Somebody trashed your fender"—the same character who carefully collects the broken china after an assault that leaves her injured. She pepper-sprays Richard impulsively, imagining he may be her stalker, and plants a toothpick in his young girlfriend's hors d'oeuvre as an expression of her resentment for being displaced.[5] Michèle is disdainful of her son, Vincent, who, like his father, she judges to be a failure at staying employed or finding a suitable partner, settling on a classless young harridan who cons Vincent into believing that he is the father of her brown-skinned son, yet she also blithely confides to a staff member in the maternity unit where her grandson was born that she never bonded with her son as mothers do. She surmises that his closeness to Anna may be attributable to her having allowed Anna to breastfeed the baby before her, thus imprinting her in his brain as his mother. She is aware that, emotionally, she lost him from the time of his birth, and she labels him a "big lout with nothing special about him," adding: "I have to admit that I don't know him."

Michèle appears part of a network of social relationships but she never relates fully to or engages profoundly with anyone. Even her matter-of-fact

144   Chapter 6

account of the assault is disconcerting to her closest friends, as she appears indifferent and removed (though Robert's gesturing to the waiter to delay the popping of the champagne in a sign of deference suggests his own detachment). One of the most remarkable examples of disconnection occurs at the hospital after her mother's collapse, when Michèle calmly questions the nurse as to the veracity of her mother's stroke ("Is it for real?"; "There's no way she's faking it or pretending?"), questions so out of place that it momentarily surprises the nurse. The same lack of concern sets the tone for the scene where she attempts to dispose of her mother's ashes, finally scattering them thoughtlessly after a heated argument with Vincent over the paternity of his son. When Michèle sleeps with Robert for the last time, he commends her for the idea of playing dead, an apt description at times of her demeanor.

Ironically, Michèle seems more genuinely alive and sexually aroused when she is alone; she surreptitiously watches her neighbor Patrick unloading oversized religious icons from a van and assembling the crèche, masturbating from the safe distance of her window. Her erotic desire for Patrick is heightened by religious repression, demonstrating sexual energy sublimated in its fetish objects. (Many of Buñuel's films—*Viridiana* [1961], for example—similarly suggest that desire is a manifestation of contradiction, created, in part, through prohibition.) The other scene where Michèle experiences sexual pleasure is in Patrick's cellar, following his inability to perform without his costume and necessary conditions of domination. Having stymied Patrick by ordering him to proceed with his violence, Michèle reaches orgasm alone, writhing and crying out in a manner that appears to conjoin pleasure and pain, and Huppert's ability to so precisely communicate a response of contradiction becomes key to reading the character.[6] Michèle's association of her father with religious practice and fanaticism connects him to Patrick's overwrought crèche figures and his wife's visit to see the pope, the ultimate father figure. At another point Michèle changes the channel on her television from news of the pope's visit in Spain to the refusal of George Leblanc's parole. At the Christmas party, the significance of the pope conducting mass, emphasized in the full screen Verhoeven allots it, is the trigger that initiates Michèle's confession to Patrick about the crimes of her father, his excommunication, and her place in that history. Her admission of her excitement—getting "caught up in it"—suggests a visceral fascination that links her to her father, "the little girl as psychopath next to her father the psychopath." Delivered as a monologue, this intense and deeply personal admission of her father's atrocities and her dubious involvement in them is remarkable for its understated, almost casual, intimacy. Michèle's sexual proclivities are placed within the contradictions of a social world dominated by the law of the father, of which her father and Patrick, both practicing Catholics and serial violators, serve as extreme examples. Pleasure inevitably becomes associated with dirt, shame, and punishment, resulting in a sense of alienation and disconnection from others.

Michèle's egoism and the moral vacuity around her can be attributed to her class as well as to the culture at large. Though Michèle's assaults (at home and, virtually, at work) put her in the position of the victim of sexualized violence and awaken her desire for self-protection and retribution, she is hardly a feminist. In fact, she is an executive partner of a successful company that produces video games whose profits are generated from primitive medieval scenarios of domination and brutality against women, characterized by levels of extreme sexualized cruelty about which she and her partner Anna seem unconcerned. Michèle is astutely aware of the dynamics of the game's fantasies, recommending at one point an intensification of the need to feel the blood, noting that "the orgasmic convulsions are way too timid," or that they are "missing the 'boner' moment." It is only when her face is superimposed over the image of a woman being anally assaulted in the game as a statement to demean her, after the attack in her home, that she is jarred into a course of action. The game world is the id world that discards ethics, responsibility, shame, guilt, and the intimacy of human relationships, replacing it with a dehumanized objectification and disengagement from moral considerations, a world of misogyny and obscenity acceptable within the confines of the game and its identity as a highly successful profit-making consumer product. (Ironically, Patrick's violent identity is dependent on his donning of a mask and garb that he himself describes, identifying the "intruder" he claims he chased, as something one would see on television.) Like many successful women, Michèle is both complicit with and a victim of a misogyny integral to the system of power relations that underpins the contemporary world of technology and capitalism. She is representative of the result: a culture of alienation where her position as a woman leaves her fair game, vulnerable to attack. As Georg Simmel theorized, the quantification and objectification

146   Chapter 6

of relationships in modern urban society produces "the blasé attitude": a detachment that characterizes Michèle and her social milieu.[7]

In some ways, *Elle*'s affinity with the concerns of the Gothic—acknowledging the "horror" of normality and all its contradictions—connects it to Hitchcock (and his influence on Chabrol and Haneke) through the examination of the traumatized child-adult. The adult marked by the child's experience of trauma, often violence with a sexual component, and familial dysfunction is a thematic trope in Hitchcock's work, and one might include Marnie, Norman Bates in *Psycho*, and even Uncle Charlie in *Shadow of a Doubt* (1943) as prime examples of alienated outsiders who are frozen in time, emotionally isolated and unable to achieve a healthy identity as adults who can integrate into their social worlds. Marnie, like Michèle, harbors a trauma she can't fully access in memory, but it is ever present, surfacing in terrifying nightmares and symptoms she can't make legible. Both films use blood as a recurring visual motif to signal sexual violence and the repressed. Marnie develops a self-sufficient independence from men and from intimacy, as a means of self-protection. Vincent's visceral response to his perception of his mother's sexual assault, to smash the assailant's skull with a bat, a variation of Michèle's revenge fantasy of hitting the rapist repeatedly and the blood spraying, is the same as Marnie's memory of "I hit him with a stick." Michèle's comforting response to Vincent, "It's over, it's over," recalls Marnie's "There, there, now"—words probably spoken by her mother. Michèle's identity in the photograph as the notorious "ash girl," revived regularly in the public imagination, reminds her of her participation in a spree of violence that she, too, cannot fully access, except to say that in its latter stages her father returned home, covered in blood and, with her participation, proceeded to burn everything in the house. Although she does recall a feeling of complicity ("I helped feed the fire"), her later comment that "shame isn't a strong enough emotion to stop us doing anything at all, believe me" is an admission of her recruitment and involvement, however ambiguous, in unspeakable crimes beyond the imagination. Michèle's journey in *Elle*, like Marnie's, is consciously or not, to liberate herself from the ever-present past through the process of acknowledging her fears and vulnerability; "I gave the bastard too much power over me" is her rationalization for finally agreeing to visit her father in prison, and when she does finally see her father's body, she whispers to him with a smile, "I killed you by coming here."

Michèle's admission of desiring to kill the father: *Elle*.

Like Norman Bates, Michèle's version of burying secrets is by tidying up her messes, clearing the debris from her assault the way Norman mops up after his "mother's" rampages or hides evidence in the swamp. Both want to recover a semblance of propriety and normalcy through the bourgeois strategy of denial; both enjoy sexual pleasure from a safe voyeuristic distance, or sublimated through the experience of punishment and violence. The culprit in the workplace who creates the degrading image of Michèle being raped is the one Anna thinks is her admirer, who calls out "I love you" after Michèle's firm rebuttal to Kurt, the employee who challenges her authority, suggesting the recurring alignment of desire, power, and punishment. The closest Marnie comes to expressing pleasure (that is also in part sexual) is through her rides on her horse, Forio ("If you want to bite somebody, bite me"), which might shed some light on Michèle's tenderness with an injured bird and house cat (the film's publicity poster is summed up by a profile of Michèle holding her cat) instead of people.

Hitchcock, like Verhoeven, uses the topography of the Gothic to emphasize an emotional landscape and layers of reality that can't be expressed otherwise. The empty train station in *Marnie* marked by a yellow line and yellow handbag, her spillage of the pecans in her mother's kitchen, along with the location of the Bates Motel in *Psycho*, an indication of having gotten lost off the main highway, have a dreamlike force that demand a different kind of reading. The aforementioned scene where Patrick comes over to help Michèle secure the shutters of the many-windowed house so the glass won't shatter from the strength of the winds is a tour de force that has little to do with logic, and everything to do with expressing a mutual, unspoken

148   Chapter 6

tenderness, attraction, and understanding that is touching; beneath the formalities of good neighborliness, Patrick's compassion and gentle protectiveness, and Michèle's vulnerability to what threatens her, expressed through their holding each other in her gated, well-appointed, but potentially fragile home, is breathtaking in its intensity. At this point in the film, Michèle has not unmasked Patrick as her assailant. The scene's significance lies in its establishment of a profound rapport that is essential to the narrative and to understanding Michèle's commitment to Patrick, even after his unmasking. After the road accident, failing to reach either Richard or Anna, Michèle calls her practical Good Samaritan neighbor Patrick, who comes to her rescue. It is also central to the denouement, where she and Vincent agree to join Patrick for a casual dinner, and later when Michèle follows him to the basement. Verhoeven, like Hitchcock in *Marnie* and *Psycho*, rejects offering a full, simplified explanation of its leading protagonist as the avenger of a rape; by this point, theirs is a complex relationship that isn't easily reducible and explained. *Psycho* in particular points to this at its end, countering the psychiatrist's perfectly rational explanation of Norman with the enigmatic final scene of Norman's mother in the jail cell, illustrating a refusal to individuate and limit the farther reaching implications of the narrative. Michèle is aware of the dark side of human nature and understands its attraction, its unbridled force, and what it unleashes; her response to the detective's final question, whether she suspected the rapist might be her neighbor is an elusive "Who could imagine such a thing?" The relationship she and Patrick establish is both protective and predatory, complicating a reading that suggests Michèle is simply in pursuit of vengeance or is erotically aroused by violence. At various points, each ask the other, "Pourquoi?," seeking an explanation for violence for which neither can account.

The repeated reference to the image of the dazed "ash girl" implies its significance in the narrative. The film's editing and structuration suggest that Michèle is a victim of patterns and cycles of patriarchal violence that keep her immobilized. For example, her fantasy of revenge, where she fights and injures her assailant, is positioned between the lunch where her mother requests she see her father and the television documentary on the Legave street murders and her appearance as the ash girl. The assault where she unmasks her assailant is followed by her decision to confront her father in prison. In some ways, breaking free of these patterns implies what Andrew Britton calls in reference to the woman's film and melodrama "an erasure of the phallus" as "something the woman's film does but to which it seldom refers."[8] As a fantasy or fable, one can read the scene where Michèle, in pursuit of her attacker, whom she remembers as being circumcised, demands her employee drop his pants, as dramatizing symbolically the woman reclaiming power by exposing the phallus, draining it of its fascination, strength, and authority—which is what the film does. It is a far more effective strategy than the hatchets, pepper spray, or even the gun that Michèle learns to shoot to protect herself. Michèle's decision to finally face her father, as her mother requests, is a necessary step in rejecting a victimhood that is dependent on fear. Rather than a statement about familial bonds and forgiveness (she claims she has come to spit in her father's face), it is a means of taking charge through a diminution of his status as monster and an acknowledgment of his mortality. The fact that he commits suicide prior to her visit implies the effect it has.

In the final scenes of the film, Michèle similarly recovers her power and reverses her status as a passive, dominated victim by directing Patrick to recreate the scene of the crime under her guidance. Understanding his reliance on the repetition of conditions to perform, she begins by taunting him, smiling as she says, "I'll go to the police and tell them everything," knowing how to arouse him while rewriting the scenario according to her terms. She walks directly in front of his car, boldly announcing her fearlessness and control. In their final sexual encounters in the basement of his house and, then, finally in hers, Michèle makes eye contact with Patrick and smiles, acknowledging his humanity, indicating a reversal of power that momentarily confounds him, prior to proceeding with their ritualized performance of sex.[9]

Michèle's smile acknowledges her awareness of the rules of the game: *Elle*.

150   Chapter 6

Michèle's mother and Patrick's wife condone their husbands' violence by rationalizing their status as sick men without understanding how they are endemic in the culture. "Patrick was a good man who had a tortured soul," his wife explains, sincerely thanking Michèle. "I'm glad you could give him what he needed for a time, at least." The revelation points to her willful complicity; fully aware of her husband's crimes, she supports him under the Christian guise of forgiveness. Ironically, the office party near the end of the narrative is to celebrate the game's success that is also Michèle and Anna's success, and although there is a brief shot of the game's warrior woman marching alone, presumably at the game's end, the sum of its contents is hardly a victory for women. Nevertheless, the film manages a lovely, woman-centered, forgiving ending that suggests "the erasure of the phallus" as an objective or a wish close to its heart. Michèle's world appears visually lighter and warmer through her reconciliation and reconnection to those closest to her. She decides to help Richard by offering him a semblance of employment and, most importantly, reclaims Vincent after the killing through a tender embrace and words of comfort, possibly to both Vincent and herself. At the end of the film, Vincent's family come to accompany her, en famille, on a visit to her parents' memorial site bearing flowers. It is as if she has finally made peace with all of her ambivalence and blockages with regard to familial relations. Finally, Anna arrives and announces that she has thrown Robert out but calls Michèle on her behavior, which she describes as inexcusable and "shabby"; Michèle acknowledges her feelings ("Worse than that, even"). Though Michèle is not entirely changed—she is, for example, still tidying up, approving the new color for the blood-spattered wall she is having repainted, and answers Anna's comment that she wasn't sure Michèle was there with an enigmatic "Physically, anyway"—Anna's offer as they walk away together into the sunlight to move in with her for a bit is a happy, life-affirming conclusion that goes beyond what Hitchcock (or possibly Haneke) might ever have imagined.

Elle is Huppert's film and would have been an entirely different project had the initial idea to cast an American star been realized. Huppert's ability to allow one to see beneath the surface, without self-consciousness, is critical to the film's project of examining the patriarchal, bourgeois Weltanschauung. Huppert can both humanize and estrange simultaneously, which is key to Verhoeven's approach to the material, particularly in the

Reading *Elle* 151

use of irony and dry humor in the details that portray bourgeois behavior as both absurd and familiar. The emphasis, for example, placed on cleanliness—be it a rapist taking the time to wipe himself off with a cloth, or Michèle cleaning herself after masturbating, or the repeated concerns with stained bedsheets or clothing—suggest subtly a relationship between sex and guilt or shame expressed in terms of cleanliness and dirt or disarray. Huppert's almost offhand, understated comments, for example, her ironic, detached "C'est vrai" (It's true) in answer to her neighbor's excitement about the nativity "getting her every time"; summarizing her detailed retelling of the night of her father's gruesome murder spree with a concise, sardonic "Pas mal, huh" (Not bad, huh); the responses of annoyance written entirely in the look on her face as she reacts to her new brown-skinned grandson, asserting that they are going to need a DNA test as she casts a sidelong glance at the couple's brown-skinned friend Omar prominently present in the hospital room; her impatience at having to find an appropriate resting spot for her mother's remains; and her persistent sense of entitlement and determination invite one to observe her humanness without fully owning the character through an expansive elaboration of motivation. Huppert's characters don't ask that one idealize or unequivocally empathize with them. Instead, these complicated heroines are placed in social worlds where their actions expose the misogyny around them. Despite the accoutrements of women's equality and power, it is still the law of the father that dominates and masculine desire that it services. *Elle* speaks to this contradiction of women's experience, privately and publicly, and Michèle's resistance and struggle in both domains supports *Elle*'s status as a feminist work of art, one vivified and humanized through Isabelle Huppert's persona.

7

CELEBRATING THE OUTLIER

Villa Amalia, L'avenir, In Another Country

Quand l'acteur a une realité très forte dans le paysage du cinéma on peut faire le filme dans la perspective de cet acteur (When an actor has a very strong presence in the landscape of the cinema, it allows a film to be made from the perspective of that actor).

—Benoît Jacquot

Over the course of Huppert's career, several directors seek her out and use her persona specifically as the centerpiece of their films. Although they are narrative fictions, a number of these films can also be considered essays about a woman's demands for freedom and self-definition in a culture still dictated by patriarchal values. Huppert's films increasingly explore existential concerns regarding a woman's search for authenticity and integrity in relation to her life and place in the world. The dramatizations of a character's insistence on self-expression and autonomy, the rejection of roles, conscious or otherwise, build on Huppert's iconic status as an anti-victim, a woman who acts to satisfy her desires as opposed to one dominated by ideology or destiny. This includes a strong ego and "necessary narcissism": a belief in one's own value and worthiness to make choices and act to reinvent oneself accordingly.[1] These feminist mainstays have underpinned Huppert's career and are used, cumulatively, to support and articulate the meaning of a film largely built around her as a central character and persona. As Huppert comments, Benoît Jacquot knows that every good film is a documentary about the actor ("Tout [bon] film est un documentaire autour de l'acteur").[2] Given Huppert's performance style, which makes

154   Chapter 7

space for a character alongside herself, these films are layered explorations of a woman's subjectivity, her response to social contradictions or conflicts shared and experienced by the audience.

Benoît Jacquot's *Villa Amalia* (2009), Mia Hansen-Løve's *L'avenir* (2016), and Hong Sang-soo's *In Another Country* (2012) are examples of films dependent on Huppert's iconic meaning. All three are built entirely on her presence, to explore the idea of negotiating transition or difference. They also use the metaphor of changing direction or a journey, sometimes to a foreign place or to a changed social reality, at times at the expense of a partner, spouse, or father, to articulate a celebration of independence. The films locate the idea of refuge or peace in the valuation and appreciation of one's self, dramatized by the character through the actor.

Villa Amalia

"What is this place?"
"Whatever you want."

Villa Amalia was directed by Benoît Jacquot, with whom Huppert has made seven films. Jacquot, a woman-centered director, uses Huppert's presence and screen persona directly and precisely in creating meaning. As he suggests, "When an actor has a very strong presence in the landscape of the cinema, it allows a film to be made from the perspective of that actor." He describes the script as a kind of letter to the actor: "The actor responds by performing, and it's this response that the director will film," creating what Jacquot describes as "a documentary of the actor at work," which suggests collaborative authorship.[3] *Villa Amalia* has a minimalist, pared down narrative that does not rely on the expectations of realism, plausibility, psychological explanation, and causal action. It unfolds more on the level of allegory or a series of timeless, dream-like states, using abstraction, condensation, improbable coincidence, and the intangibility of music as modes of expression that are dependent on the woman's subjectivity. The film begins from the perspective of a woman in a car in the rain at night, spying; she stands outside the gates of a house and witnesses a man and a woman embracing passionately. The experience is profound and totalizing, and it instigates her trajectory to abandon her identity and re-create her life. When a man she fails to recognize interrupts her, her state of shock is expressed in her air of distraction, blank bewilderment and slow, guarded responses. He identifies her as Eliane Hidelstein, and himself as Georges (Jean-Hugues Anglade), a close childhood friend from her hometown in Brittany; after having initially turned to walk away, she rushes back and hugs him, her eyes welling up with tears. He describes their chance encounter as "miraculous" and "a meeting of two ghosts"; its placement immediately after her discovery of her partner's infidelity and before her extrication from her current identity as Ann Hidden, a successful composer and pianist, is significant to the film's thematic: that life is a process where identities one has outgrown are not easily discarded. Ann's desire to redefine herself by denying elements of her past—evident in her adoption of the professional name "Hidden"—depends on denial and erasure. Georges renames her Ann-Eliane, pointing to this layering, and he will witness her embarking on this new stage in her life that will demand a coming to terms with the past and subconscious impulses that she has suppressed. The betrayal Ann witnesses is like a return of the repressed, a resurfacing of what has formed her as a result of her perception of the betrayal of her father, and, by extension, the "Father" or social norms, and its continuing implications in her life.

Huppert's Ann is an unconventional character not easily accessed; from the start, identification with her is impeded. She is opaque and not forthcoming, as if not fully there in the present. The momentary release of deeply felt sentiment in a hug or tears can be followed by an abrupt resumption of formality. Although one can initially interpret this as Ann being in a state of shock following her eyewitnessing her partner's infidelity, she remains guarded, pointing out her discomfort with George's use of the familiar mode of address "Tu," which surprises him ("You're not serious, Ann-Eliane, I've known you forever!"). She responds with vague platitudes—"C'est vrai" (It's true); "Je suis désolée" (I'm sorry)—empty phrases or social niceties that underline her disengagement from an authentic response. Ann's extreme decision to abandon a successful life and career suddenly ("d'un coup") is perceived as a form of madness or "derangement," as Georges gently suggests, which she acknowledges while refusing to explain. *Villa Amalia* can be related to other postwar

156   Chapter 7

precedents set in motion by a woman's abrupt and complete rejection of her former life and identity that is socially perceived as insanity—for example Irene (Ingrid Bergman) in Rossellini's *Europa '51*, Elizabeth (Liv Ullmann) in Bergman's *Persona* (1966), and even Marion Crane (Janet Leigh) in Hitchcock's *Psycho* (1960).[4] The classic response to their protest is to be confined by others to variations of the attic of Thornfield Hall, be it an asylum, a hospital, or the trunk of a car at the bottom of a swamp. Nevertheless, these films similarly explore existential choices, identifying the woman's decision to withdraw from society as an expression of resistance to their alienation from their lives. Ann's complete extrication from her identity begins with a lengthy section of the narrative demonstrating her disdain for who she is through her dismantling of the accoutrements of bourgeois success. Scenes where Ann quickly arranges the sale of her upscale apartment, car, and piano; abandons her contractual commitments and concert engagements; closes her bank accounts; tries to dispose of personal effects, photographs and CDs related to her life and career that would be considered of sentimental value by burning them; or dumping expensive clothing in trash bags manifest her barely controlled anger and disdain, creating a frisson of discomfort and tension within the viewer, in part because it demonstrates openly her contempt for her life and who she is. Her determination and single-mindedness and the responses of surprise and suspicion she encounters from those uncomfortable with her haste is both admirable and alienating, as is her ability to reduce her life to a knapsack and, the pièce de résistance, to flush her cell phone down a toilet. Ann's refusal of the lifelines of contemporary existence (cell phone, bank accounts, credit cards, email) includes lying to Georges that she is off to Tangiers, despite having entrusted him to help her achieve her ends. The elaborate enacting of these details is necessary to emphasize Ann's complete refusal to compromise and stay put and elicits a response of unease, as if, like Marion Crane, she is suspect simply for her choice of decisively rejecting the expectations of compliance and normalcy. The investigation of her perceived irrationality or madness is the subject of the film.

Huppert's interpretation communicates Ann's state of mind with the precision of a dance performance. Words are minimal and measured; instead, gestures or particular stances or postures, a manner of swimming or walking or vehemently emptying a closet, convey meaning without directly explaining thoughts or motivations. Initially Ann maintains her privacy and secrets. Scenes like the one where she is thinking by the river and gets up to leave when it starts to rain, or leaves Thomas with a slam of the door behind her, walking briskly and with determination, entering a bar and peeling an egg offer the idea of the character/actor thinking, without necessarily pointing out or allowing the viewer access to what she is thinking or contributing to the progression of the narrative. Jacquot's idea of a good film being a documentary about an actor, like Maurizio Ponzi's comment that the Bergman/Rossellini films could also be considered documentaries on a face, describes a different conception of characterization and narrative cinema, where the actor's face or body and presence create a space for raising questions and ideas or an abstracted state of mind as opposed to clarifying motivations that serve the progression of a story.[5] The narrative doesn't give details about Ann and Thomas's (Xavier Beauvois) relationship prior to Ann's discovery of her partner's infidelity or much about Ann's life except when she dismantles it. As Ann tells Georges, "There are no whys." It tells a story about watching a process of making the decision to implement change by withdrawing and vanishing, to begin again at zero. The scenes where Ann enters the concert hall and stops performing suddenly and exits or visits a church and then abruptly rushes out exemplify this. Ann's self-effacement and unwillingness to perform a role is expressed visually through a gradual diminishment of a certain standard of grooming and costume. Her hair is no longer coiffed perfectly, and as she travels her makeup disappears, her clothing needs are minimized to the demands of the location and tossed when she leaves; in Italy she has her hair cut in a style that doesn't require care and reduces her wardrobe to one or two light articles of clothing and sandals, as if paring down to bare essentials. She is no longer complying with the demands of being seen, as a performer or a female participant in the social environment of modern urban life.

Ann's interiority is also expressed through her music, the only constant in her life that accompanies her on her journey. Even without her piano Ann continues composing, and at times her music is used as commentary in the score, its atonality reflective of her own searching. The irregular dissonant sounds that characterize it express the contradictions, turbulence, or deep emotions she feels—for example, when she visits her mother on Twelfth Night. Ann's visit is surreal, dreamlike, and condensed. Her mother appears almost catatonic and silent, as if in a severe state of

158   Chapter 7

withdrawal or depression; Ann serves the traditional cake, the *galette des rois*, celebrating a festivity marked by a reversal of social positions and the rejection of social conventions and order and then crowns her mother as the Twelfth Night's traditional Queen of "Misrule." It is as if the scene stages Ann's trajectory: her departure from the woman's expected place visualized in her mother's state of impotence. When Ann performs her own piano compositions for her girlhood friends from her hometown, they are uncomfortable with her performance and look at each other puzzled, as if unsettled by its elusive, jagged, unexpected, and unmelodic tones. Alfred Deller's rendition of Purcell's "O Solitude," used intermittently in the score, also complements Ann's music with the idea of solitude as "the sweetest choice," the unconventional one Ann pursues. Having completed her farewells by visiting her mother and her brother's grave, she leaves on her journey.

Ann's travels lead to Naples and the island of Ischia off its coast. One day while swimming alone she spots a house perched on a mountain that intrigues her. The scenes in Italy place Ann in an intensely natural world characterized by the sun, the blue sea, and the mountainous terrain. The shot of the house she sees from the sea is from her point of view; however, a few subsequent shots of her climbing up the mountain to get a closer look are taken from behind her, sidestepping point of view and reaction shots, as if avoiding the possibility of overtly objectifying Ann for the spectator. It also allows for images of Ann's determined, strong strides, embodied almost in contradiction to Huppert's petite frame. Similarly, the publicity still for the film is of Ann taken from behind her, purposely blocking the gaze and privileging her looking out at the sea. Aside from the camera's unwillingness to exploit her as an object to be looked at, its tendency is to place Ann in the landscape as a means of establishing an abstracted state of tranquility and peace that she discovers, connected to the physical world as much or more so than to the social.

The villa she finds belongs to the family of an older local woman who lives nearby and who identifies herself as Amalia, like, she explains, her mother and her aunt, who were also named Amalia. At first annoyed by Ann's persistence to converse and what she perceives to be the disingenuousness of polite social discourse, like Ann's conventional "I'm sorry" in response to hearing of the travails of the woman's father and his sister Amalia ("Signora, you're not to blame for the deaths of my relatives"), she

The shot of Ann from behind her emphasizes her subjectivity in the landscape in *Villa Amalia*.

then warms up to Ann and agrees to rent her the house, adding that she is sure her father would have liked her. This leads Ann to reveal that her own father didn't love her, expanding on his departure when she was a child. The comment is unexpected and unusual, coming from someone whose tendency is not to reveal anything personal. Villa Amalia, named after the woman's aunt, for whom it was built, is an ideal rather than an actual place, a woman-centered house removed from the world; the space enables Ann to acknowledge openly her father's abandonment, suggesting the significance of that event to Ann's identity and struggle to reinvent her life outside of attachments, particularly to men. Villa Amalia is the place of solitude that Ann finds and welcomes, without the complications of disappointments and betrayals, without time constraints and obligations to perform for others, a meditative refuge of independence and freedom.

Ann's renaissance can be seen in her willingness to open up and trust others, ironically through a place of relative isolation. The image of Ann swimming alone in the sea visualizes her choice of solitude; on one of these excursions, she has swum far from the shore and develops a cramp. A woman named Giulia (Maya Sansa) in a nearby boat with a friend notices her distress and jumps in to save her. The encounter is akin to the magic of a fairy tale, the young woman-savior's attraction evident in her admiring remark "Where did you get that face? It comes from another world," as if

160   Chapter 7

identifying Ann's foreignness and her beauty with her independence as an outlier. The brush with mortality is life changing for Ann, who is not only physically rescued but also emotionally freed, as if symbolically reborn; the near-death experience triggers an outpouring of words and feelings that have thus far been uncharacteristic to her. Over a drink she discloses her father's identity as a musician and her teacher, his abandonment of the family, her sulking for a year after the death of her younger brother, her mother's encouragement—events long stymied and suppressed. Ann surprises herself with her profuse revelations of her private history, commenting, "Why am I telling you this?," and concluding with her remark that her life presently on the island is not bad with no family, which Giulia concurs is ideal. Unlike Ann's earlier opacity and restraint, Huppert emphasizes the change through her performance, which is markedly more naturalistic and engaged. Ann's friend Carlo disappears from the narrative, and Ann develops a casual physical relationship with Guilia, who is not presented as a substitute partner like Thomas or a long-term solution to Ann's life; in answer to Georges who asks of her later, she simply states, "She left." It is a part of the magic of Villa Amalia, which Ann describes as a place of her own, a utopian idea of possibility, where age or gender or nationality and social rules fall away. When Georges arrives for a visit, he asks Ann, "What is this place?," and she replies, "Whatever you want."

The journey toward liberation extends beyond finding Villa Amalia and necessitates facing the father, an opportunity that arises when she returns to France for her mother's funeral. Although Ann's initial response to hearing of her father's request to see her is to run, as if reverting momentarily to her child-self, she then meets her father with a sense of maturity and empathy, and they are able to have a discussion of their lives over dinner. The Ann of this scene is forthcoming, comfortable in her being, and able to come to terms with her father and his desertion. It is more of a rapprochement than a confrontation, and Ann can see similarities between herself and her father as musicians who reject their former lives and run away, retaining only their music. A number of images in this dinner scene are patterned in a more traditional shot/reverse shot sequencing, with medium close-ups of Ann registering responses to her father that are surprisingly gentle and compassionate, playing against expectation. Although she voices an affinity with her father and his choice to escape, Ann also challenges his inclusion of her in his self-pitying description as being lonely and lectures him in turn that he might have stayed in touch or acted like normal people do. When he responds, "There is no normal existence," she agrees with him. The scene demands a modulated array of emotions from Ann, who is, in part, trying to comprehend his explanation and redeem something of the relationship, feeling sadness at the loss of a parent, the suffering it caused and still causes, hearing her father address her as "ma fille" (my daughter). Huppert's performance is extremely nuanced, communicating meaning in the slightest movement of her eyes, the knitting of her brow, and tearing up, suggesting the finesse of a musician communicating a range of feelings rooted in a deep unconscious place. Huppert manages this with a minimalist subtlety.

The scenes in the restaurant and walking back to her father's hotel are difficult in part because they are almost too compressed in terms of the father's condensed explanation of being a Jew who married a Catholic and felt guilty for betraying the dead by doing so. He describes a void that he couldn't refill with family, and that he could not survive her birth or the death of her brother, to which Ann delicately responds, "Quiet, Papa, I think you're hurting me." Huppert's sensitivity to the demands of the discussion compensates for what is arguably at times underdeveloped or underwritten on the father's part. This is, however, redeemed toward the end of their meeting at his hotel, when Ann's father returns to distancing himself with sardonic comments like that of Ann being like her French

Displaying an intricate range of feelings in *Villa Amalia*.

Catholic mother, who enjoys a good cry; Ann responds with a simple gesture of reaching out to him and gently touching his cheek, an acknowledgment of a shared humanity as well as a sign of compassion and affection that disarms her father just when he is trying to detach himself from her and his past. It also succinctly communicates Ann's freeing of herself through an understanding of herself as an outlier like her father. Although repeating the outlier's disappearance, Ann's journey moves beyond merely running away as a protest; instead, she empathizes with his repudiation of the construct of normality as fitting for all, as is evident in the tenderness she can express. Huppert's Ann is no longer the victim dominated by her father's or her partner's actions and moves toward a more natural or authentic state of being and autonomy.

Although Ann has renovated a studio space for herself on Georges's property, she leaves again for Villa Amalia at the film's close and doesn't commit to returning any time soon. Georges's character in the film is akin to the woman of a traditional melodrama; he is sentimental, less resilient than Ann, and less self-protective, such as when he is beaten up when descending to the town for a night out on Ischia, the intimation being as a result of a failed attempt to pick up younger men. The film ends with a revelation that Georges is dying, a complication that pushes the aspect of melodrama and vulnerability that defines the character, and although it may seem overdetermined (or in line with the fable-like sensibility of the narrative) Ann's unwillingness to sacrifice herself and stay, or promise to return right away, is significant. The final shot of the film provides the reason: Ann is back at Villa Amalia, surrounded by the sea, opening the shutters in a gesture of freedom.

L'avenir

Mia Hansen-Løve's *L'avenir* is a personal, loosely autobiographical film inspired by the director's mother and father, both of them philosophy teachers. Philosophy is central to the film, which addresses fundamental philosophical questions of existence and meaning related to freedom, ethics, and morality. It grounds its inquiry in the concrete details of daily life, in being in relationships and living with integrity and purpose, insisting on learning how to question and reason in order to do so. *L'avenir* stars Isabelle Huppert as its central character and consciousness, and, like Jacquot, Hansen-Løve builds the film around the presence and responses of the actor. This extends authorship to include the concept of collaboration, though it can still be a personal film for both director and actor. Hansen-Løve has stated that she could not imagine anyone but Isabelle Huppert in the film, and in fact the film is completely dependent on Huppert, the persona and her style of performance both inseparable from her person.[6] The philosopher is often an iconoclast who questions ideological truths, holding them up to intellectual scrutiny. Huppert's intellectualism, her ability to communicate a sharp sense of irony, and her iconic identity as a woman who challenges accepted ideas about a woman's place perfectly complements the concerns of the film. Huppert also claims *L'avenir* as a personal film for her, "in the way all films are, reflecting what I think. It's her but it's me—it makes a personal statement."[7] While Hansen-Løve's film follows the tradition of the postwar art film, drawing from the personal in an auteurist sense, she encourages the engagement of an actor with her own distinctive presence and sensibility. *L'avenir* utilizes Huppert's identity as a contemporary woman to explore the idea of a woman's place in the modern world: contemplating the changes of aging and desirability, remaining relevant and true to oneself, being fulfilled intellectually and emotionally. Although Nathalie is a figure of identification in a more traditional sense of a character whose motives are explained, *L'avenir* can't be reduced to a film about an individual whose life changes when her husband of many years leaves her abruptly; it presents Nathalie more emblematically, as a modern woman who questions the choices available to women and the tensions and responsibilities they negotiate in the culture.

L'avenir is an entirely woman-centered film, addressing a subject rarely explored in art: the difficult transitions of a woman's lived experience, particularly when her familial identity as wife/caregiver/mother fall away, leaving a space of sudden obsolescence.[8] Although Nathalie has an identity outside of the family as a teacher, which is related to mothering, as it demands a form of nurturing and transmission of values—Nathalie's son describes her student Fabien (Roman Kolinka) as a preferred son, intellectually and physically—her existential crisis is set off when her husband of twenty-five years announces his departure from the marriage, only after being confronted and pressured by his children to make

164 Chapter 7

a decision and act. The film's subject is Nathalie's having to acclimatize to the kinds of changes for which one is never fully prepared and the disquieting freedom received through loss, while maintaining one's sense of self. In this regard, it is a kind of coming-of-middle-age narrative, of learning to keep sailing in a world no longer perfectly familiar. Hansen-Løve's film is insightful and sensitive to issues pertaining to women and aging and its effects on the woman's cultural relevance, suggesting a maturity that belies the director's age. This may be in part a result of the leeway she gives Huppert and Huppert's interpretation, but it is also attributable to Hansen-Løve's idea that "women of all ages wonder how to find a spiritual fulfillment that doesn't depend on relationships, a peace that doesn't depend on others—not rejecting others or lacking love but finding independence."[9] This brings *L'avenir* close to the Bergman/Rossellini collaborations, which use Bergman to support the thematic of a woman's quest for fulfillment and authenticity in a social world where living with integrity is a struggle. It is a fiction while also a document of an actor's personal truth registered in who they are and how they respond—as Huppert says of her characters, "I play a role, but I am not transformed entirely. . . . It's me more than anyone else."[10] Huppert's presence acts as a guide to the experience of maintaining status and significance as a subject in a culture that curtails and diminishes the value of women as they age and are less needed as nurturers. The film avoids the emotional excesses of melodrama (the husband's sudden abandonment of a lengthy marriage, the mother's death) by relying on Huppert's intelligence, ironic awareness, subtle sense of humor, and restraint, safeguarding the character from being read as a victim of the upheavals in her life and a culture that denigrates older women. Instead, the film encourages a critical perspective and an identification with a woman content with her independence and the freedom she discovers.

The film's opening scene visualizes the idea of a journey, as it begins with a family on a ferry en route to see the resting place of the French writer Chateaubriand. Nathalie is introduced from behind, a choice that allows her privacy and subverts a traditional introduction of the lead protagonist, as she works on a class assignment that poses the question "Can one put oneself in the place of the other?" Nathalie's children are young, barely adolescent. The short scene points to thoughts of mortality in a still distant future and introduces the philosophical thematic of the importance of placing oneself in a broader humanity, a question that assumes a consideration of ethics and principles. The film's title, *L'avenir*, then appears on-screen, and the story jumps several years to a scene where the same couple are in bed, late at night, and the phone rings. The husband, Heinz (André Marcon), advises his wife, "Don't answer. It's your mother." Nathalie ignores him and tries to calm her mother, who is having one of her frequent panic attacks. Disturbed by her mother's distress, Nathalie gets out of bed and gets a snack, perhaps to settle herself, a small detail that indicates the tension that results from these calls. The scene is concise but it introduces the husband's blasé attitude and lack of empathy, the mother's inability to respect boundaries, and Nathalie's unwavering commitment to her regardless.

Putting oneself in the place of another is deeply implicit in the mother/daughter relationship and the complex reciprocity of caring it entails. Mothers are forerunners of their daughters, and on some level, their struggle to cope with increasing vulnerability, loneliness, and aging are a precursor to the reality their daughters will face. The casting of Édith Scob is suggestive, as she was associated most famously with the politicized films of Georges Franju (*Les yeux sans visage* [*Eyes without a Face*], 1960), a director who encouraged a response of critical awareness via irony and an absurdist sensibility, elements that *L'avenir* uses in the treatment of her character. She is attractive, witty, and vibrant and has a kind of ageless beauty; her self-perception as a desiring subject—still shopping for designer clothing and taking acting parts even if it is as a cadaver—makes a point of her unwillingness to accept marginalization or to be caged in like her cat, Pandora. "Old folks make me puke," she confides to Nathalie in the retirement home. (A shot of photographs of Édith Scob on the wall of her apartment at various moments in her life and career as a model and an actor underlines the point.) The tone of irony and at times gentle absurdity tempers the emotionality of her trajectory in the narrative, steering the film away from melodrama. Nathalie is often exasperated with but consistently attentive to and tender toward her mother, refusing to ignore her, leaving her students mid-class after receiving one of her calls, explaining, "It's my mother, she's crazy, I have to go take care of her." Reluctant and in visible pain, she leaves her mother in an upscale retirement home that is permeated, as she says through her tears, "with that fucking smell, the smell of death." When Nathalie is in Brittany to pack up her things from her ex-husband's family's home—a difficult and painful task as it is a place she loves and feels invested in—she attempts to call and check in on her mother in the retirement home. Nathalie leaves the beach house trying to connect to phone service, and Huppert's performance in this scene is modulated precisely to communicate both genuine concern for her mother's emotional and physical well-being and extreme frustration, as she is unable to fully comprehend and ascertain, until she does, that her mother hasn't eaten in three days and risks dying. This is beautifully visualized in Huppert's physicality and the absurdity of her struggling to get to a spot where there is service, walking gingerly over rocks at the shoreline or being pulled down by the sticky wet sand on the beach.

Nathalie's extreme effort and concern contrasts with Heinz, again aloof and detached, who tries to dissuade her from leaving. "It's not a ruse to get you back?" he asks nonchalantly, and she responds, exasperated, "Of course it's a ruse. What should I do? Let her die?," looking at him with a sidelong glance that says everything about the differences between them. The sequence continues with Nathalie's hurried departure to the train station, the sorrow and worry subtly conveyed in her face set against Schubert's "Auf dem Wasser zu singen," a song about the ephemeral passage of time, followed by her arrival at her mother's bedside. She kisses her mother, who, upon seeing her, revives almost magically and immediately regains her appetite, requesting luxury foods like oysters and fresh

Nathalie's predicament is visualized in Isabelle Huppert's physicality in *L'avenir*.

strawberries, as if in celebration. The scene is brief but touching in the way the two, relaxed, enjoy each other's company and watch TV, her mother playfully remarking on President Sarkozy's unattractiveness. The scene attests to the mother's insistence that she is a person, as opposed to an irrelevant social category, her inability or unwillingness to exist apart from her daughter, and the profound love that they share. Nathalie's expression of pleasure as she watches her mother fall asleep quietly says many things: about her understanding and love and the absence of any resentment, their bond defying the modern response of indifference and measuring actions against personal gain.

Heinz's infidelity and announcement to leave the marriage completely surprises Nathalie. After a few initial questions, which elicit minimal guarded responses from Heinz, Nathalie's simple "I thought you'd love me forever" and "I'm an idiot" is followed by her quietly rejecting his claim to always love her. When he later returns home, Nathalie, still in her role as a caring partner, reminds him that lunch is ready, though refuses to accept his invitation to join him. Huppert's performance is pointedly understated and devoid of emotional excess, registering Nathalie's honesty and straightforwardness as the antithesis of Heinz's dissimulation and cool detachment. When Heinz leaves her a bouquet of flowers, an empty gesture meant to signal sincerity and caring, Nathalie disdainfully tosses them into the garbage with an effort that is subtly humorous, because she is angered by the disingenuousness it masks.

L'avenir questions a variety of codes of behavior that seem principled but are often complicated by self-interest. The students who strike for issues pertaining to teachers' retirement disrupt classes and are not particularly attentive to the opinions of a teacher like Nathalie, who crosses the picket line because she doesn't want to shortchange her students and may not agree with them. The new generation of publishers who decide against reissuing Nathalie's texts because they are no longer in line with academic trends and market expectations have little to do with quality or values and are motivated by products and profit, designing books to appeal to consumers as if they were ads for M&Ms, as Nathalie comments. As a figure of identification, Nathalie maintains her integrity and balances the personal with her consideration of the needs of students and family as well as her responsibility as a citizen of a social world that extends beyond her. As she claims at one point, revolution is not her goal—it is to help

168   Chapter 7

young people think for themselves, which implies acquiring the tools to make reasoned decisions for the present as well as the future.

These questions also permeate the ideas of groups directly concerned with radicalism and social change, like the politics of Nathalie's former student Fabien now living in a self-sustaining commune, committed to a life of radical protest to urban capitalist existence. Nathalie has guided him in his career, assisting in getting a paper of his published and lending him books that she feels are of value and significance. Fabien reciprocates and lends her articles he feels are important to him and invites her to visit the commune, but doesn't appreciate her unwillingness to unquestionably support what he does—for example, to consider terrorism as a valid radical response—and ultimately judges her as a bourgeoise who is not genuinely radical in practice. Although the changes in Nathalie's life have given her a sense of total freedom that she describes as extraordinary, she realizes that Fabien's lifestyle, however romanticized, is not a viable choice for her. Nathalie's relationship with Fabien is complicated, as he is, in part, an idealized or alternative son, as her own son notes, as well as a quasi-figure of desire (Heinz seems almost jealous when he turns up at their home, claiming he doesn't like him and calls him a know-it-all who will walk over you if you're in the way—oddly, an apt description of himself) though this is never made explicit. Nathalie soon realizes that she cannot revert to the group's youthful political discussions of collective versus individual authorship and doesn't share Fabien's support of terrorists and anarchists and thinkers like Žižek, or his interest in the Unabomber's manifesto and the disregard for human life they all, at times, condone. Fabien's dismissal of her politics hurts her feelings, as he suspects when Nathalie abruptly decides to return to Paris. The sexual tension in their friendship is never overtly raised, but scenes of Nathalie in a bathing suit at the farm (even if they are taken from behind her and at a respectful distance) seem to be included, perhaps awkwardly, to assert her identity as a still sexually desirable woman. The scene in a movie theater showing Juliette Binoche in Abbas Kiorastami's *Certified Copy* (2010), which Nathalie attends alone one evening and, after which, is followed by a younger man who hounds her, wanting to initiate a sexual pickup, is similarly there to make the same point from a more humorous perspective. Nathalie is fully aware, as she tells Fabien at one point, that, unlike Heinz, who has found a younger woman, women over forty are socially considered "fit for the trash." To the

Celebrating the Outlier   169

film's credit, replacing Heinz with Fabien is not a resolution. More significant is the film's gentle questioning of what radicalism means in a social world where engagement is not always grounded in ethics and a genuine concern for others' needs and differences. As the film's moral center, the film consistently presents Nathalie as grounded in values that shape her thoughtful, reasoned responses.

Huppert's characters generally don't cry readily, so, when they do, the moments are notable. The exteriorization of suffering that crying implies is generally atypical of Huppert's private, non-externally expressive style of characterization and performance. Nathalie cries at various points in the narrative: when she leaves her mother in the retirement home, her final visit to the house in Bretagne, following the funeral, at night in bed at the commune when she decides abruptly that it is time to leave. For Nathalie, crying is a sign of sadness as opposed to an expression of weakness, despair, or victimization and is tempered by the character's ability to see life's ironies and retain control. One example finds Nathalie crying on a bus following her mother's funeral. Her calm words of eulogy extend beyond the funeral itself and are heard as a voice-over against the image of her on the bus, in tears; suddenly she sees her ex-husband on the street with his new lover and, taken aback, laughs aloud at the incongruousness of the moment.

When Nathalie returns home and is surprised to find Heinz having entered unannounced, using a key he has been asked to return, Nathalie objects with a wry "I might have been here with a lover" and does not extend an invitation for him to join her and their children for Christmas dinner, despite his lack of plans. Her seeming reluctance to be generous to him is more precisely an unwillingness to be dishonest and to be taken advantage of, as well as a refusal to sacrifice her principles for polite social niceties. The final scene shows Nathalie tenderly holding her new grandchild, and the lullaby she sings segues into a song about time, loneliness, tenderness, and the need for touch and love. It is an understated, open ending that plays against expectation, gently emphasizing the simple pleasure and sensuous joy of hugging a new member of her family. The moment is suggestive of her being at peace with her life, looking forward to a future that she can yet contribute to meaningfully. It is also in line with the philosopher-teacher who is dedicated to encouraging generations that follow to think critically and responsibly. The casting of Huppert is

Nathalie's contentment holding a grandchild: redefining a woman's role in *L'avenir*.

essential to these scenes: she challenges the cultural assumptions of what women at a certain point in their lives want by combining Nathalie's intellectual fulfillment, which she equates with happiness, along with her strength of character, uncompromising standards, and capacity for love. Cuddling a grandchild does not contradict her independence, nor is it a stereotype of domesticity or marginalization; rather, it offers a portrait of a woman mid-life who is authoritative and comfortable in her mind and body. Interestingly, the publicity still for the North American version of *L'avenir / Things to Come* is very close to the one for *Villa Amalia*: an image of Huppert, shot from behind, a subject looking out at the landscape. These films use Huppert precisely, as a celebration of a woman in transition, autonomous and content with who she is.

In Another Country

In Another Country (2012), shot in South Korea, is the first of three films Hong Sang-soo has made with Isabelle Huppert. *Claire's Camera* (2017) and *A Traveler's Needs* (2024) were shot in Cannes and South Korea, respectively. *In Another Country* is a film entirely reliant on Huppert's star persona and presence, and, given the director's style of filmmaking, one perfectly appropriate to her style of performance. Although Hong Sang-soo claims that the actors are given freedom of interpretation, the films are tightly scripted. Actors receive their lines on the day of shooting and are expected to memorize them in an hour or less. They are not encouraged to prepare and are given little to no explanation about the characters in terms of background or psychology.[11] Rather than three stories about a woman, all named Anne, played by Huppert in the same location, in a country foreign to her, *In Another Country* is more of a humorous essay on manners and sociological perceptions about everyday experience, particularly with regard to gender. Huppert's presence acts as a guide to the film's survey of cultural mores, through the locals' response to her identity as a beautiful foreigner who travels alone. Rather than depending on dialogue, meaning is deduced through the actor's presence in a location. Although the film often utilizes longer takes and little cutting, the use of jarring devices like a rapid zoom or pan, or a specific utilization of color, draws attention to style and presentation, as does the film's employment of repetition—of location, dialogue, and characters—in its structure as a triptych of three different stories. The intention is not to capture reality but rather to suggest that people see things differently, and that reality is subjective. The free mixing of dreams in the middle story, appearing interchangeably with objective reality, as well as the use of repetition in the stories' structure, dialogue, and reappearance of some characters like the director and his pregnant wife, further undermines the idea of an absolute reality. Irony, humor, and the film's playful tone depend on a layering of meaning and perspectives and encourage critical distance. For example, the shared language spoken, English, which is not native to any of the characters, adds an additional layer of estrangement. The Korean spoken is translated and subtitled, so the viewer is privileged to understand what the Huppert characters do not. Rather than encouraging identification with a character's consciousness as a means of following the narrative, the film uses Huppert as an outlier figure to challenge cultural assumptions regarding a woman's place, acknowledging what she has come to represent. Although a very different film, *Claire's Camera* uses Huppert similarly, as an outsider looking more closely at Korean attitudes through the prism of Claire's presence and practice of using a camera to see the world with greater clarity.

In Another Country is structured in three sections. The first concerns a "charming" French director who is visiting a small hotel in a seaside town,

172   Chapter 7

Mahong, as the guest of a Korean director, Jongsoo (Kwon Hae-hyo). In the middle section, the wife of a wealthy businessman from Seoul arrives at the same hotel for a tryst with another Korean director, Munsoo (Moon Sung-Keun), who is late in arriving, and, in the last, a woman whose husband has recently left her arrives at the same hotel with a friend, a Korean professor, Park Sook (Youn Yuh-jung), as a means of recuperating from her husband's infidelity and the end of their marriage. The triptych is framed by a young woman who is the writer of these stories, thus introducing the idea of the film as a product of a female scriptwriter's imagination. The film begins with her and her mother at the hotel, discussing an uncle for whom they have acted as a guarantor; he has disappeared with the money, saddling the family with his debt and disgrace. The young woman wonders hopefully if her uncle might kill himself, while her mother, more resigned, suggests that he said he would turn himself in and comments that her sister married the wrong man. The young woman is next seen writing a script ("to calm my nerves"); rather than pursue an idea about a woman running from debt, she imagines a "charming French visitor—she will be a successful film director like the woman I saw at the Jeonju film festival." The stories present an autonomous woman, a foreigner who challenges conservative patriarchal expectations and traditional values, an inspiring figure created by an angry young woman imagining new possibilities. *In Another Country* references its identity as a film through repetition and a minimalist plot. Huppert acts as different characters within a narrative structure that consists of staying at the same inn, walking to the beach, searching for a lighthouse, discovering an attractive young lifeguard (Yoo Jun-sang). The characters are identified by their situations and are played without the depth of fully realized characters with whom one is expected to identify. Instead, Huppert is both a character and Isabelle Huppert, and thus acts as a catalyst to explore social attitudes while foregrounding a persona and an awareness of acting and being viewed.

Aside from the similarities in all three sections, of the foreigner at ease and slightly bored in a location where she is both admired and suspect because she is a woman traveling alone, each character is differentiated and identified by subtle details of expression, gesture, costume, and performance.[12] The first Anne is most familiar and closest to Huppert in the sense of being a celebrity and director from France, a self-assured, independent artist visualized in casual understated attire and appearance, a colleague and an equal of the director who is her host. The director's very pregnant wife (Moon So-ri) is insecure and threatened by her husband's attentiveness to his guest. Worried about her husband's solicitousness to Anne, she tests him as to whether he finds her more beautiful than the student Wonju or Anne, questioning if she can trust him. When Anne asks for a translation of their interchange, she is told by the director that his wife said that she is beautiful, which Anne questions ("Really? No, I don't think she was saying that"). She is aware of her host's dissimulation of the marital tensions, but moves on when his wife affirms this, with a humorous "OK, so we're all beautiful." In the next scene, shot in a long take, Anne, alone on the veranda smoking a cigarette, is joined by the director, who mentions that his wife is taking a shower before proceeding with his startling comment: "You remember our kiss?" Both face the camera, and, taken aback, Anne responds, "What? What kiss?" Her surprised expression leads him to expand: "You don't remember our kiss . . . in Berlin? In a playground." Anne's response is subtle but funny, as she is composed and attempts to be polite "(Oh, yes, I remember, sure"), though she clearly doesn't, and her face and occasional look away communicates the complete meaninglessness of the kiss, if it did happen, to her. He continues that it was just a kiss, and they are friends, to which Anne agrees, telling him he needn't worry. He adds, as a kind of explanation, that his wife is pregnant, and Anne

Isabelle Huppert's subtle comedic expressiveness: Anne and Jongsoo (Kwon Hae-hyo), *In Another Country*.

174   Chapter 7

answers, "Yes, you don't have to tell me. I can see for myself." He thanks her for understanding, then takes and holds on to her hand while Anne silently conveys the awkwardness of the gesture, and his concern that she might have misconstrued his inability to pursue the relationship, in her manner of smoking, her amused expression and slight look away. Anne's composure and open but direct manner structures the episode. At times, details of cultural difference, like the shot of the director's slightly sickened look when he stands near Anne, who is busy clipping her nails, adds to the humorous tone created by differing standards of what is considered culturally appropriate.

The second character is introduced by her identity as the rich house-wife of a CEO and, as such, is identified by her more carefully coiffed hair, a designer red lace dress, and, most importantly, a pair of kitten-heeled Louboutins, which at times, when she hurries, cause her to walk in short steps, a small detail that is humorous when she is trailing behind trying to catch up with the lifeguard who catches her eye or her lover who does not wish to be spotted publicly with her in Mohang. The visual details underline her status as a fish out of water in the beach town; she is also uninhibited and comes across as slightly eccentric, as indicated during her walk to the beach, when the camera zooms in on her from behind as she stops and turns to let out a bleat of a greeting, two times, to goats nearby.

The third Anne, on a personal quest to find herself after being dumped by her husband is defined by small gestures and details—for example, her manner of imbibing soju to the point of drunkenness, an activity delegated locally to men, like the director whose wife berates him for drinking exces-sively, a sign perhaps of his unhappy married life. Anne ends up indulging herself, when drunk, in some sex with the lifeguard, who serves as an object of sexual desire in all three episodes, in his tent.

Although playing three distinct characters, each is filtered through Huppert's presence and persona, and each are women who privilege their needs first, which is antithetical to conservative ideological expectations of women deferring their desires out of politeness or self-sacrifice. Like men, each evidence an ego or exhibit a narcissism and sense of entitlement that expresses a commitment to oneself, a trait that distinguishes them. In the first episode, when the lifeguard whom Anne has met earlier on the beach sees her later that day and asks if he can perform another song that he has written for her, she is surprisingly abrupt and dismissive and then denies to her hosts that she knows him. Although Anne later seeks him out to offer an apology and a note she has written, excusing herself by explaining that she was tired, she is humanized as a person who puts herself first and will indulge her needs over the expectation of satisfying others. In the second episode, when Munsoo, the long-awaited lover, finally arrives, Anne kisses him passionately, then abruptly stops and slaps him and says, "Oh, so sorry, I love you." She kisses him again and repeats the angry slap, and when he asks, bewildered, why she is doing this, she explains, "Because I love you, you know that," and then repeats the kiss, confounding him, as if her displeasure with his putting his needs first and making her wait is condensed in the meaning of the gestures. In the last episode, Anne meets with a monk, hoping to pose some existential questions that trouble her, and, noting his Mont-Blanc pen, to which he claims to be very attached, asks him if he might gift it to her. When asked why, she says simply, "Because I want it." Her friend, appalled at the selfishness of the request, calls it "not normal." The point of the final episode is that Anne learns to exist as an individual with her own desires and define herself outside of her husband and social expectations. The display of self-centeredness is surprising coming from a woman who is expected to suppress what she wants, and less so from a man who is expected to prioritize himself and his needs. The Huppert characters' appeal is in their uninhibited manner of going after what each wants as subjects who value and prioritize themselves and act accordingly.

In all three episodes, Huppert's characters are often shot from behind, a distinctive recurring stylistic choice emphasizing a woman looking as opposed to a frontal shot of one being viewed. The characters' resistance to subordination—their indulgence in masculine activities, the ego they surprisingly exhibit—are further supported by a style that discourages the objectification of a beautiful woman. For example, in each episode the characters are shot from behind on the road to the beach, moving toward a right-turn arrow at the back of the frame. In the second episode, the camera is twice placed behind Anne as she sits at the water's edge, looking out to the sea, a camera position repeated at the end, when Munsoo finally arrives: it is behind Anne, in the third episode, when she is looking out to the beach before catching sight of the lifeguard, and, most magnificently, behind her in the film's final shot, as she walks away from the camera, alone down the road, visualizing, perhaps, her cryptic message to her friend and the monk: "I'm on my way to the unknown path."

The outlier on her own path: *In Another Country*.

Ironically, the object of desire in all three episodes is the young lifeguard, identified by his youth and physicality, with Anne the subject looking, a reversal of the expectations of the gaze.[13] In a place where, as Anne comments, there is not a lot to do, the lifeguard becomes a distraction. This is emphasized by pans from Anne looking to the lifeguard she is looking at, watching him swim or chasing after him as he emerges from the water. Each Anne asks the lifeguard directions to a lighthouse, in a humorous interchange involving his dramatic hand movements to act out the projected lights, and by the time he understands, he informs her that he doesn't know where it is. Each character flirts with him, asking him if he is cold, and each is then invited to enter his tent, which each, in turn, admires. In the middle episode, Anne declines the offer to enter, but then dreams of her lover's jealousy of her attraction to and flirtation with the lifeguard on the beach, telling her, "You must have a craving for a young body," to which she replies, "Yes, I have, don't you?," placing herself on equal footing, an inversion of the pregnant woman's role of reprimanding her husband for his sexual attraction to Anne or, as she claims, "anything in a skirt." In the last episode, after sending her friend a message of being on her way to the unknown path, and many sojus later, Anne ends up joining the lifeguard in his tent. Her friend and the monk, worried that she has disappeared and may have harmed herself, come to the beach looking for her. The irony is that, while they are seen in long shot looking for her, there is a cut to a slightly high-angle long take of her waking up in the tent next to the lifeguard snoring loudly, with a quizzical look of both surprise and satisfaction. The scene ends with the lifeguard exiting the tent and then being questioned by Anne's friend and the monk as to whether he has seen a foreign woman, and he anxiously denies having seen her.

In the first episode, Anne enters the lifeguard's tent, and he proceeds to sing her a song he has composed inspired by her, a song for Anne. The scene is shot at a distance from the tent, with Anne barely visible, being serenaded by the lifeguard's tribute to a woman searching for a lighthouse in the rain, ending in a crescendo: "Anne, Anne, Anne!" *In Another Country* is Hong Sang-soo's song for Isabelle, and this book is mine, an homage to the woman who has come to personify intelligence, self-possession, and independence. *In Another Country*'s whimsical closing shot is of Anne, taken from behind, the outlier receding alone down the road, on her life journey. It is a perfect metaphor for what Huppert has come to represent as an actress: a woman who is the subject of the film, who owns herself, demonstrating the modernist and feminist dimensions of performance. It is, in every sense, an image of freedom and autonomy.

Notes

Introduction

1 Huppert uses the term "modernist performance" in relation to a distinction she makes regarding the preference for acting that looks inward as opposed to emoting outward. See Francois Boddaert, Pierre-Marc de Biasi, Caroline Eliacheff, Arnaud Laporte, Claude Mouchard, and André Versaille, *Autour d'Emma: Madame Bovary, un film de Claude Chabrol, avec Isabelle Huppert* (Paris: Hatier, 1991), 142.

2 Rachel Donadio, "The Enduring Allure of Isabelle Huppert," *T: The New York Times Style Magazine*, November 30, 2016, www.nytimes.com/2016/11/30/t-magazine/isabelle-huppert-elle-movie-interview.html.

3 András Bálint Kovács, *Screening Modernism: European Art Cinema, 1950–1980* (London: University of Chicago Press, 2007), 11.

4 Susan Sontag claims she sympathizes with Nathalie Sarraute's objection to the way the author of a realist novel leads the reader to feel one "knows" the characters. See Susan Sontag, *Against Interpretation and Other Essays* (New York: Farrar, Strauss & Giroux, 1961), 105–6.

5 Kovács discusses modern cinema's lack of psychological characterisation, citing Roland Barthes's claim that it is the "the most immediate criterion of an art work's modernity." See Kovács, *Screening Modernism*, 65.

6 Kovács claims, regarding Antonioni's films, that landscapes do not necessarily reflect a character's state of mind but can also create a contrast between the characters and the material world in which they move. See Kovács, 152.

7 Darren Waldron uses the example of the closing shot of Pomme facing the camera in Goretta's *La dentellière* (*The Lacemaker*), as an example of the way Huppert's characters can frustrate the viewer's "possession" of the "Other and a sense of unmediated access to the Other's inner world." Darren Waldron, "Intimate Distance: The Face of Isabelle Huppert," in *Isabelle*

180   Notes to Introduction

Huppert: Stardom, Performance, Authorship, ed. Nick Rees-Roberts and Darren Waldron (New York: Bloomsbury Academic, 2021), 24.

8 Julia Kristeva, Christian de Portzamparc, Umberto Echo, Phillipe Sollers, Isabelle Huppert, and Marcel Detienne, *Le plaisir des formes* (Paris: Éditions Du Seuil, 2003), 176; Sontag, *Against Interpretation*, 106.

9 Sontag makes this point in her discussion of Bresson and Brecht (*Against Interpretation*, 184, 188–89).

10 Richard Brody mentions that though Godard "intended her character to suffer," Godard did not permit the actress to express it: Huppert recalled that he wanted his characters to be "neutral" and "sought to remove all psychology." Huppert claimed doing so "revealed the character all the more." The result was a film "on" or "about" her personally as actress. Brody reports Huppert felt "that Godard's methods brought her closer to herself as and, paradoxically, to the character she was embodying, and she found the experience artistically gratifying." Richard Brody, *Everything Is Cinema: The Working Life of Jean-Luc Godard* (New York: Holt, 2008), 425–26.

11 James Quandt in *Robert Bresson (Revised)*, ed. James Quandt (Toronto: Toronto International Film Festival, 2011), 20.

12 Michael Haneke, "Terror and Utopia of Form—Addicted to Truth: A Story about Robert Bresson's Au hazard Balthazar," in *Robert Bresson*, 389.

13 Isabelle Huppert, "Préface," in Xavier Lardoux, *Le Cinéma de Benoît Jacquot* (Paris: Editions PC, 2011), 5.

14 Frank P. Tomasulo, "'The Sounds of Silence': Modernist Acting in Michelangelo Antoinioni's *Blow-Up*," in *More than a Method: Trends and Traditions in Contemporary Film Performance*, ed. Cynthia Baron, Diane Carson and Frank P. Tomasulo (Detroit, MI: Wayne State University Press, 2004), 97.

15 Tomasulo, "Modernist Acting in Antonioni's *Blow-Up*," 95.

16 Patrice Chéreau, "The Abyss as Blank Page," in *Isabelle Huppert: Woman of Many Faces*, ed. Ronald Chammah and Jeanne Fouchet (New York: Harry N. Abrams Inc., 2005), 35.

17 Andrew Higson, "Film Acting and Independent Cinema," in *Star Texts: Image and Performance in Film and Television*, ed. Jeremy G. Butler (Detroit, MI: Wayne State University Press, 1991), 169.

18 Sontag, *Against Interpretation*, 184. Bertolt Brecht makes this point in his "Short Description of a New Technique of Acting Which Produces an Alienation Effect": "The actor does not allow himself to become completely transformed on the stage into the character he is portraying. He is not Lear, Harpagon, Schweik; he shows them. He reproduces their remarks as authentically as he can; he puts forward their way of behaving to the best of his abilities and knowledge of men; but he never tries to persuade himself

Notes to Introduction 181

(and thereby others) that this amounts to a complete transformation." In *Star Texts: Image and Performance in Film and Television*, ed. Jeremy G. Butler (Detroit, MI: Wayne State University Press, 1991), 69–70.

19 Nick Rees-Roberts and Darren Waldron claim that "rather than allowing herself to be 'wholly transformed into character,' she has recurrently stood between the spectator and the character." Rees-Roberts and Waldron, "Introduction—Against Type: Isabelle Huppert's Unorthodox Stardom," in Rees-Roberts and Waldron, *Isabelle Huppert*, 3.

20 Darren Waldron discusses how Huppert's "act of asserting herself through the character blurs the boundary between actor and character, allowing her to channel aspects of her persona to the audience and simultaneously endow that persona with the features she reads into the character." Waldron, "Intimate Distance," 25.

21 Andrea R. Vaucher, "Madame Bovary, C'est Moi!," *American Film* (September–October 1991): 30.

22 Andrew Britton, "A New Servitude: Bette Davis, *Now Voyager*, and the Radicalism of the Woman's Film," in *Britton on Film*, ed. Barry Keith Grant (Detroit, MI: Wayne State University Press, 2009), 27.

23 Kovács, *Screening Modernism*, 96.

24 Chabrol's plans to shoot a film based on Simenon's *The Iron Staircase* (1953) with Isabelle Huppert, mentioned in Stéphane Delorme's interview with Huppert, "Le Plaisir de jouer. Entretien avec Isabelle Huppert," *Cahiers du cinéma* no. 660 (October): 23, never realized because of Chabrol's death, is a Gothic melodrama centered around a woman in a traditionally male position of control who victimizes her emasculated husband. The novel is written from the point of view of the husband, who realizes that he is being slowly poisoned to death in his home by his wife, who has moved on to another lover half her age whom she has known since he was a child. It inverts the structure of the persecuted wife melodrama in its placement of a woman in the role of the husband; the woman also usurps the man's place, running a business she inherited from her father, where her husband (and the father of her lover) are her employees. Like the Gothic mode and its mining of the subconscious, Simenon's *The Iron Staircase* explores the idea that the spouse who indulges desires that threaten the life of the marital partner is monstrous; the narrative, however, is complicated by the fact that despite what the husband confirms regarding his suspicions, he enjoys his dependent position in the marriage and does not want to lose his wife. It would have been interesting to see Chabrol/Huppert's iteration of this Gothic melodrama realized, and the film's attitude toward the wife. Casting Huppert as the transgressive woman who

Notes to Introduction

will fulfill her desires at any cost would complicate Simenon's limiting the novel to the husband's voice and consciousness.

25 Kovács, *Screening Modernism*, 260.

26 Kovács, 38–39.

27 Kovács, 222.

28 Huppert discusses the importance of mise-en-scène as a true partner to performance in her interview with Stéphane Delorme, "L'instant présent: Entretien avec Isabelle Huppert," *Cahiers du cinéma*, June 2016, 8.

29 Isabelle Huppert, "Paroles avec Antoinette Fouque," *Cahiers du cinéma*, March 1994, 45.

30 Huppert claims that she doesn't do any external work with regard to facial expressions, that these originate from the interior. Stéphane Delorme, "L'Instant présent: Entretien avec Isabelle Huppert," *Cahiers du cinéma* (June 2016), 11.

31 Peter Debruge, "Oscar Nominee Isabelle Huppert Looks Back at Her Early Career," *Variety*, February 3, 2017, variety.com/2017/film/features/oscar -nominee-isabelle-huppert-1201974850/.

32 The name "Jean Dabin" suggests the actor Jean Gabin, connecting the lover to an idealized fantasy, like the movie stars that decorate Violette's mirror. He is also feminized like Marie Latour's lover Lucien in *Une affaire de femmes*, suggesting a displacement of the characters' affections for women.

33 Although the narrative distinguishes Baptiste Nozière from her biological father, he has raised her and is presented as a father figure and parent. The murder remains an attempt to kill the father both literally and symbolically, a figure whom Violette views as an impediment to her independence.

34 "*Violette*: An Enigma Preserved," *Washington Post*, December 29, 1978, www.washingtonpost.com/archive/lifestyle/1978/12/29/violette-an -enigma-preserved/5805841c-0322-4f0f-bd4c-6482c00d33c1/.

35 Thierry Klifa, "Isabelle Huppert, ma vie d'actrice," *Studio Magazine*, September 2002, 64.

36 Britton, *Britton on Film*, 41.

37 Robin Wood, *Hollywood from Vietnam to Reagan* (New York: Columbia University Press, 1986), 317.

38 Steven Bach, *Final Cut: Dreams and Disaster in the Making of Heaven's Gate* (New York: William Morrow, 1985), 191.

39 Bach, *Final Cut*, 413.

40 "Interview with Michael Cimino, 1980," *Heaven's Gate* (1980), Criterion Collection, DVD edition, 1980, booklet, 24.

41 This is playfully acknowledged in Huppert's role as head of the house of Dior in *Mrs. Harris Goes to Paris* (2022).

Notes to Chapter 1   183

42 Both of the following reports for *British Vogue* emphasize Huppert's uniqueness and originality. See Alice Carey, "Obviously Isabelle Huppert Is Now a Balenciaga Campaign Star," *Vogue UK*, July 23, 2021, www.vogue.co.uk/news/article/balenciaga-campaign-isabelle-huppert-justin-bieber; Liam Hess, "Isabelle Huppert Steals the Show in a Deceptively Simple Gown," *Vogue*, July 9, 2021, www.vogue.com/article/isabelle-huppert-cannes-balenciaga-dress.

43 Serge Toubiana, "Foreword," in Chammah and Fouchet, *Isabelle Huppert*, 14.

44 Alice Newbold, "At 68, Isabelle Huppert Is the Coolest Person at the Balenciaga Show," *Vogue UK*, March 6, 2022, www.vogue.co.uk/news/article/isabelle-huppert-balenciaga-show. Huppert's appearance on the red carpet in Balenciaga at Cannes in 2023 was a reiteration of the rocker chick look.

45 "Verhoeven described Huppert a 'pure Brechtian actor' in that she puts distance between herself and the audience without trying to seduce it or seek its sympathy." See Donadio, "Enduring Allure of Isabelle Huppert." The Balenciaga campaign similarly alludes to this distance and unwillingness to seduce the viewer which contributes to her image as a woman in control.

46 Antoinette Fouque states that this gap that Huppert maintains, being both the character and herself, "perceptible in all your creations . . . is the creative part you take on; this is your writing. It's very modern. You are definitely the most resolutely, absolutely modern actress, because you maintain the gap within a divided subject in your films." Antoinette Fouque, "Dialogue with Isabelle Huppert" (December 15, 1993), in *There Are Two Sexes: Essays in Feminology*, ed. Sylvana Boissonnas (New York: Columbia University Press, 2015), 97. One can argue that she maintains the same gap in her still photographs to the same effect.

47 Toubiana, "Foreword," 14.

48 Chéreau, "Abyss as Blank Page," 37.

49 Chéreau, 37.

Chapter 1

1 "In all the films I've made, I've always played women whose journeys were a metaphor for a certain condition of women. I don't know if it can change the world, but, in any case, it can't hurt." Kristeva et al., *Le plaisir des formes*, 195.

2 Fouque, "Dialogue with Isabelle Huppert," 103.

3 Toubiana, "Foreword," 9; Chéreau, "Abyss as Blank Page," 35.

4 This comment is made in the context of still photography but is applicable to her performance style in the cinema as well. Toubiana, "Foreword," 13.

5 Kristeva et al., *Le plaisir des formes*, 194.

184 Notes to Chapter 1

6 Toubiana, "Foreword," 13.

7 "Je suis active dans la production de mon absence." Isabelle Huppert, "Isabelle Huppert auto-portrait(s), Mots avec Jean Baudrillard," *Cahiers du cinéma*, March 1994, 120.

8 Huppert, "Mots avec Jean Baudrillard," 120.

9 "J'aime l'idée qu'une actrice peut être à la fois sujet et objet, qu'elle peut désirer en même temps qu'elle séduit." Huppert explains that she likes the idea that an actress can be both subject and object, that she can desire at the same time that she seduces. Huppert, 119.

10 Huppert explains that by being both subject and object in her films, she is able to create a space in which she can stand back, having, what she terms, a double gaze. Huppert, "Paroles avec Antoinette Fouque," *Cahiers du cinéma*, March 1994, 37.

11 Toubiana, "Foreword," 10.

12 Isabelle Huppert, "Editorial," *Cahiers du cinéma*, March 1994, 5.

13 Instead of inhabiting another's life and becoming someone else, Huppert describes the role of the actor as an exploration of herself, a process of self-discovery, "un engagement totale de ma personne." Huppert, "Paroles avec Antoinette Foque," 38. She also discusses the undefinable line between the person and the character: "To be oneself and not oneself." Delorme, "L'instant présent," 10.

14 Joan Dupont, "Still Waters," *Film Comment* 46, no. 6 (November–December 2010): 40.

15 Boris Kachka, "Brooklyn Hearts Huppert," *New York Magazine*, October 22, 2009, nymag.com/arts/theater/features/60239/.

16 Joan Dupont, "Still Waters," 41.

17 Isabelle Huppert, "Conversation avec Claude Chabrol et Emmanuèle Bernheim," *Cahiers du cinéma*, March 1994, 57

18 Huppert, "Paroles avec Antoinette Fouque," 46.

19 Huppert suggests that rather than understanding Erika in *La Pianiste* as incoherent, she creates a character that leaves it up to the viewer to fill in the spaces or gaps that the performance intentionally withholds. Kristeva et al., *Le plaisir des formes*, 188.

20 Huppert, "Paroles avec Antoinette Fouque," 40.

21 Chéreau, "Abyss as Blank Page," 37.

22 Godard uses the same terms referring to a type of image suggesting neutrality, commenting, "I didn't express (*exprimé*) much, but I impressed (*imprimé*—'printed' or 'registered') quite a lot of things." Brody, *Everything Is Cinema*, 429.

23 Boddaert et al., *Autour d'Emma*, 142.

Notes to Chapter 1   185

24 Boddaert et al., 142.
25 Robin Wood, *The Wings of the Dove* (London: BFI Modern Classics, 1999), 17.
26 Wood, *Wings of the Dove*, 19.
27 Kristeva et al., *Le plaisir des formes*, 192.
28 The Sternberg/Dietrich collaborations, Max Ophüls's, Otto Preminger's, Fritz Lang's, and Douglas Sirk's melodramas, as well as Hitchcock's *Marnie* and *Vertigo* (as two of many examples), might be considered modernist, or realist art at the edge of modernism, in the way that style presents a layered perspective, producing a commentary. The point is to interrogate the woman's position from an analytical position of empathy and distance, opening a discussion.
29 Huppert, "Mots avec Jean Baudrillard," 120.
30 Wood describes Preminger's melodramas as "anti-melodramatic melodramas," citing the final moments of *Angel Face* (1952), though melodramatic in content, in terms of "Preminger's rigorous (and non-judgmental) refusal of melodramatic effect." Many of Huppert's films can also be considered similarly, as anti-melodramatic melodramas. Wood, *Wings of the Dove*, 9–10.
31 Kristeva et al., *Le plaisir des formes*, 189.
32 Donald Chase, "A Day in the Country," *Film Comment* 27, no. 6 (November–December 1991):14.
33 Jean-Paul Sartre, "Introduction," in *The Maids and Deathwatch: Two Plays*, by Jean Genet (New York: Grove, 1954), 19.
34 Huppert, "Paroles avec Antoinette Fouque," 38
35 Mick Lasalle, *The Beauty of the Real: What Hollywood Can Learn from Contemporary French Actresses* (Stanford, CA: Stanford University Press, 2012), 80.
36 Huppert, "Paroles avec Antoinette Fouque," 45.
37 Jean-Michel Frodon, "Isabelle Huppert: 'Un pacte de croyance,'" *Cahiers du cinéma* no. 603 (Juillet–Août 2005): 30.
38 Boddaert et al., *Autour d'Emma*, 93.
39 Chase, "Day in the Country," 11.
40 Kristeva et al., *Le plaisir des formes*, 179.
41 Huppert mentions how Godard "always films actors and their personalities, their story" and for that reason, calls her character Isabelle: "He got who I was." Dupont, "Still Waters," 38.
42 Chase, "Day in the Country," 13.
43 Huppert's rejection of creating a character outside of herself intensifies the aspect of autoreferentiality in her work, as her characters raise questions

186   Notes to Chapter 1

about the boundaries between actor and role. This is not the same as the idea of a "star vehicle," a narrative built upon the foundation and expectations of a star persona, which does not foreground style and construction. Some of Huppert's recent work is less meditative on process than others; Jean-Paul Salomé's *La Daronne* (*Mama Weed*, 2020), for example, is more of a standard star vehicle, self-reflexive in its use of familiar elements of the persona within the conventions of a caper/comedy. Huppert's character, Patience, plays a translator who works for the police, in need of money to help pay for mounting debts related to her mother's care and her own bills as a widow raising two daughters. She decides to augment her income through a sting where she scams the drug dealers her department is trying to catch in the act and attempts to profit selling their hash. Although *La Daronne* utilizes the concept of masquerade and role-playing in Patience's plan to impersonate a wealthy woman dressed in religious Muslim attire, it is a more traditional character that Huppert creates. Nevertheless, the film can be considered a star vehicle in the way Huppert is cast as an outlier who appears alienated from her life, shares an affinity with a minority Arabic culture, decides to resist the "law" in order to pursue what she needs, becomes aligned with other women outside of the law like her Chinese landlady, and heads a female-centered family that consists of herself, her daughters, and her mother. Her potential love relationship with her supervisor in the ministry is undermined directly by her subversion of his attempt to arrest the drug dealers. *La Daronne* is, overall, a lesser film in Huppert's oeuvre, but it is interesting to what extent it relies on her persona as an independent woman who resists patriarchal authority and has the courage to reinvent herself.

44 A poster of Huppert announcing *Women in Motion* at the 2017 Cannes Film Festival specifically references a likeness to Garbo, as does Chéreau, "Abyss as Blank Page," 37; Robert Wilson's Video Portrait, 2005, recreates Steichen's photograph of Greta Garbo, titled *Greta Garbo, Hollywood, 1938.*

45 Huppert, "Paroles avec Antoinette Fouque," 40.

46 Toubiana, "Foreword," 14.

47 Britton, "New Servitude," 41.

48 One might compare this to Jean Seberg at the end of Godard's *Breathless* (1960), rubbing her finger across her lip, quoting Jean-Paul Belmondo quoting Humphrey Bogart, a sign that announces that she is insisting on defining her destiny.

49 Catherine Dousteyssier-Khoze describes Audran, like Huppert, as often playing the part of "an outwardly cold, self-contained, 'silent,' unreadable female character" in Catherine Dousteyssier-Khoze, "Huppert and

Chabrol: Opacity, Dissonance, and the Crystal Character," in Rees-Roberts and Waldron, *Isabelle Huppert*, 142.

50 Ginette Vincendeau, *Stars and Stardom in French Cinema* (New York: Continuum, 2000), 117.

51 Vincendeau, *Stars and Stardom*, 120, 130.

52 Vincendeau, 126.

53 Isabelle Huppert, "Préface," in *Le Cinéma de Benoît Jacquot*, by Xavier Lardoux (Paris: Éditions PC, 2011), 5. Peter Brunette quotes Maurizio Ponzi's description of the Bergman-Rossellini collaborations similarly as "documentaries on a face." Peter Brunette, *Roberto Rossellini* (Berkeley: University of California Press, 1987), 139.

54 Huppert makes this point specifically with regards to *La Pianiste*, where, she explains, her performance intentionally leaves blank spaces for the viewer to fill in. Kristeva et al., *Le plaisir des formes*, 188.

55 "Ms. Huppert also tends to mime her lines with fervent comic exaggeration, suggesting a visitor from Planet French Music Hall." Ben Brantley, "Classy Dames in Desperate Straits," *New York Times*, August 10, 2014, www .nytimes.com/2014/08/10/theater/cate-blanchett-and-isabelle-huppert-in -the-maids.html.

56 Huppert specifically states that her conception of Erika in *La Pianiste*, unlike Jelinek's in the novel, was not meant to be parodic. Kristeva et al., *Le plaisir des formes*, 188.

Chapter 2

1 "*Things to Come* Press Conference, Isabelle Huppert & Mia Hansen-Løve NYFF 54," YouTube video, 24:05, December 65, 2016, www.youtube.com/ watch?v=wRO-DR-9V-cYouTube.

2 Anita Gates, "Anna Karina, Star of French New Wave Cinema, Is Dead at 79," *New York Times*, December 15, 2019, www.nytimes.com/2019/12/15/ movies/anna-karina-dead.html.

3 He makes this assertion in a Dick Cavett interview included in the Criterion Collection's edition of *Every Man for Himself* (2015).

4 Richard Brody, *Everything Is Cinema: The Working Life of Jean-Luc Godard* (New York: Holt, 2008), 417–23. Richard Brody states that the film was about Godard and Miéville's relationship. (417) He reports that "Anne-Marie Miéville was often present on the set, taking still photographs and discussing with Godard the work at hand." Their tensions were in the open—according to William Lubtchansky, "they argued all the time"— and affected Godard's relations with his colleagues (423).

188   Notes to Chapter 2

5 See, for example, special issue on Jean-Luc Godard, *Camera Obscura* 34, no. 231 (Fall 1983).

6 Laura Mulvey and Colin MacCabe conclude their chapter "Images of Woman, Images of Sexuality," with the comment that Godard's investigation "is, finally, a masculine investigation," in Colin MacCabe, *Godard: Images, Sounds, Politics* (Bloomington: Indiana University Press, 1980), 87.

7 *Scénario de Sauve qui peut (la vie)* (1979) included on the Criterion Collection's *Every Man for Himself*, Blu-Ray edition, 2015.

8 Two back-to-back 1980 appearances by Godard on *The Dick Cavett Show* are included on the Criterion Collection's *Every Man for Himself* DVD (2015).

9 Brody, *Everything Is Cinema*, 426.

10 Brody, 425.

11 John Berger distinguishes between naked ("to be oneself") and nude ("to be seen naked by others and yet not recognized for oneself"). John Berger, *Ways of Seeing* (New York: Viking, 1972), 54.

12 One can argue that Duras's refusal to be seen, like Dietrich in Maximilian Schell's *Marlene* (1984), has a similar effect, undermining or counterpointing the visual image, allowing the woman to maintain control.

13 Godard compares his "starting point for the framing and body movements" to Bonnard's works, using an image of a woman looking out a window as illustration in *Scénario de Sauve qui peut (la vie)* (1979).

14 Yosefa Loshitzky claims "the film's most memorable (and disturbingly funny) metapornographic image is that of the sex-chain machine, the *combinatoire* scene used 'as a mild pastiche of de Sade's more elaborate combinations,'" citing Janet Bergstrom, "Violence and Enunciation," *Camera Obscura* 34, no. 231 (Fall 1983): 28. Yosefa Loshitzky, *The Radical Faces of Godard and Bertolucci* (Detroit, MI: Wayne State University Press 1995), 153.

15 Brody, *Everything Is Cinema*, 437.

16 Interview with Isabelle Huppert, included on the Criterion Collection's *Every Man for Himself*, 2015.

17 Brody, *Everything Is Cinema*, 417. Brody states: "Godard was intent on making the film on the basis of an ongoing dialogue with its participants. The production would create a set of personal relationships that the film would reflect. *Sauve qui peut (la vie)* was even more permeable than Godard's previous films to the people who worked on it and to his life while making it; the film would embody a new era of intimate politics" (417).

Nevertheless, Brody reports there were tensions, and despite Godard's invitation to the actors to contribute to the production of *Passion*, as Huppert noted, "he depends on others, but he doesn't take into account that

Notes to Chapter 3   189

the people with whom he works and on whom he depends are under the influence of a power relationship" with him (441).

18 Brody, *Everything Is Cinema*, 426. Huppert claimed that "he wanted his actors to be 'neutral'"; "He had us speak like oracles. . . . He doesn't want an interpretation he wants the affirmation of a thought."

Chapter 3

1 Huppert uses the term "archetype of dissatisfaction" to describe Emma in Boddaert, De Biasi, and Eliacheff, *Autour d'Emma*, 126.

2 Chéreau attributes to Huppert "a conscious assumed narcissism that fascinates" and "a necessary narcissism." Chéreau, "Abyss as Blank Page," 36–37.

3 Huppert, "Conversation avec Claude Chabrol et Emmanuele Bernheim," 57.

4 Iconic maternal melodramas like *Blonde Venus* (1932), *Stella Dallas* (1937), and *Mildred Pierce* (1945) suggest that the woman's real crime might be the irrelevance of the husband to her happiness. Huppert (like Helen Farraday / Marlene Dietrich in *Blonde Venus*) is particularly adept at naturalizing the woman's/mother's indulgence of her own needs and, more importantly, her agency and willingness to act on satisfying these without apology or regret. The threat of emasculation that this erasure implies is particularly dire; if she thrives outside of the family, she demonstrates the husband's inutility and obsolescence, both of which are intolerable to the husband and to society.

5 Chabrol makes a similar point earlier when Jasmine's sister-in-law leaves the courtyard with the two orphaned children and is then followed by one of Lulu's clients and, finally, by Marie, who, dashing past her children, stops to tell her son to take care of his sister and then rushes off to see her lover.

6 Scene comments by Claude Chabrol, *Une affaire de femmes*, Home Vision Entertainment, DVD, 2004.

7 Marie's understanding of the misogyny that condemns her remains partial, failing to include the implications of this scene in the park and its broader indictment of the occupation, which suggests that she shares the general population's values; her loss of Rachelle remains personal and not political in this sense, further demonstrating that Chabrol's film is representative of the average citizen's point of view, as opposed to that of a notorious individual.

8 This comment echoes her earlier declaration to Lucien that "he will make her burn in hell," illustrating Marie's inability to negotiate her autonomy and sexual needs in a social world which prohibits and punishes the expression of female sexuality.

9 Interview with Producer Marin Karmitz, *Une affaire de femmes*, Home Vision Entertainment, DVD, 2004.

190   Notes to Chapter 4

10 At times, Marie's actions and delivery, viewed from a perspective of distance from the character, produces the layering of irony and, at times, subtle humor. Scenes like the one where Marie tries to convince a reluctant Fernande that her husband might be old hat to her but would be new to Fernande, or the one where she is chased playfully by Lucien around the living room, or when she describes her method of birth control to Jasmine as hardly ever sleeping with her husband, or preparing for a rendezvous with her lover and spritzing her underarms and between her legs with perfume and then returning to add some more, attest to Huppert's ability with understated comedy.

Chapter 4

1 "C'est en tout cas pour moi un des aspects les plus émouvants du personnage: le désespoir engendré par le vide." Boddaert et al., *Autour d'Emma*, 138.

2 Chabrol claims he wanted to avoid the risk of having the viewer identify with Charles. Boddaert et al., 39–40.

3 Boddaert et al., 132.

4 Huppert explains the awareness of the unconscious is what constitutes the modernity of the novel. "Cet inconscient qui cherche à se faire entendre, et que Flaubert s'est attaché à dépeindre minutieusement, c'est la modernité du roman, cette conscience d'un inconscient" (This unconscious trying to make itself heard, and that Flaubert sets out trying to depict meticulously, is the novel's modernity, this awareness of the unconscious). Boddaert et al., 126.

5 Huppert claims the film presents a vision of feminine hysteria before psychoanalysis in the way the unconscious speaks through the body ("Une façon de faire parler l'inconscient, pars le corps"). Boddaert et al., 134.

6 Vaucher, "Madame Bovary, C'est Moi!," 30.

7 Huppert, "Conversation avec Claude Chabrol et Emanuele Bernheim," 57.

8 Boddaert et al., *Autour d'Emma*, 126.

9 Boddaert et al., 138.

10 Gustave Flaubert, *Madame Bovary*, trans. Lydia Davis (New York: Viking Penguin, 2010), 168.

11 Boddaert et al., *Autour d'Emma*, 127. Isabelle Huppert points out that another way for Emma to fill her void is by way of the fantasy of conducting herself as a man, evident in the way she can at times be brutal, appear in masculine-like attire, or demonstrate her "taste for conquest" (138).

12 Huppert claims this arrogance makes Emma more modern. Huppert, "Paroles avec Antoinette Fouque," 42.

Notes to Chapter 5   191

13 Emma demonstrates a spiritual earnestness that she doesn't perceive as being contradictory to the choices she makes—for example, seeking guidance from the priest for the afflictions of her soul, praying in the cathedral moments before joining Léon for a tryst in a private cab, passing the nuns in the convent who trigger a lost promise of achieving fulfillment or happiness.

14 Antoinette Fouque, "Dialogue with Isabelle Huppert," 103.

Chapter 5

1 Huppert claims that Haneke identified with her in the same way that one can describe François Truffaut identifying with the actor Jean-Pierre Léaud: "Il s'est reconnu en moi." Kristeva et al., *Le plaisir des formes*, 179.

2 Huppert mentions that Haneke described Jelinek's novel as a sarcastic parody; she preferred the film's interpretation not be parodic. Kristeva et al., 188.

3 Dennis Lim, "Austrian Filmmakers with a Heart for Darkness," *New York Times*, November 27, 2006, www.nytimes.com/2006/11/27/arts/27iht-ausfilm.3682336.html.

4 Haneke uses mise-en-scène to visually illustrate these boundaries, separations, and spaces that confine and entrap Erika. For example, the emphasis on closed doors and windows, cage-like elevators, closed office space, and the separated rooms of the Kohut apartment underline the motif of confinement common to the melodrama. Space is also gendered as in the male-dominated porn rooms or the hockey arena or defined by class distinctions as in the salons of the wealthy and the conservatory versus the drive-ins, thus underlining the social hierarchies that structure the social world of the narrative.

5 Haneke claims to have made the film with Huppert in mind for the lead, "sans elle le film n'existerait pas": in *Michael Haneke à propos de La Pianiste de Serge Toubiana*, MK2 Curiosity, 2003, www.mk2curiosity.com/film/a-propos-de-la-pianiste (link not available).

6 Haneke's penchant for filming Erika from behind in a number of scenes—for example, in the coatroom where she sits and thinks, rubbing her ear and flexing her shoulder, before standing and enacting her plan to insert a broken piece of glass in her student's coat pocket—suggests an intentional subversion of the viewer's expectation to see Erika frontally and read her motivation.

7 Kristeva et al., *Le plaisir des formes*, 195.

8 Alison Taylor argues that Huppert's ability to reveal the surfacing of interior emotions through minute gestures and bodily movements dramatizes

192 Notes to Chapter 6

Erika's struggle to suppress her feelings. Alison Taylor, "Isabelle Huppert in *The Piano Teacher*," in *Close-Up: Great Cinematic Performances*, vol. 2, *International*, ed. Kyle Stevens and Murray Pomerance (Edinburgh: Edinburgh University Press, 2018), 217.

9 Julia Kristeva comments on how Huppert maintains a distance—for example, even when she is performing a character who is mad, it is as if she is "citing" this madness. Kristeva claims it is achieved through techniques using gesture, voice, and so on, and the effect is to promote an analytical response that raises questions. Kristeva et al., *Le plaisir des formes*, 190.

10 One might say Haneke's *The White Ribbon* (2009) is similar in the way the film's title refers to the symbol of humiliation and violence that is the parent's response to the child's sexuality.

11 This is like, in Hitchcock's *Marnie*, Marnie's habit of slipping from adult to child; Marnie's mother also suspects and rejects Marnie's identity as a sexual woman, igniting similar skirmishes like the scene in the mother's kitchen, where the pecans spill onto floor.

12 This is revisited in *The White Ribbon*; the children absorb and reiterate the punishment and violence prevalent in the culture.

13 Susan Sontag, "Fascinating Fascism," in *Under the Sign of Saturn* (New York: Farrar, Strauss & Giroux, 1972), 93.

14 Elfreide Jelinek, *The Piano Teacher* (New York: Weidenfeld & Nicholson, 1988), 86.

15 Sontag, "Fascinating Fascism," 105.

16 Jelinek, *Piano Teacher*, 233.

17 Huppert claims that Haneke does not allow Erika to commit suicide, as one often finds in the tradition of the melodrama. Instead, he permits her to survive ("Haneke l'autorise à vivre"). Kristeva et al., *Le plaisir des formes*, 189.

Chapter 6

1 Adam Nayman, "The Rules of the Game: Paul Verhoeven's *Elle*," Cinemascope Online, 2016, cinema-scope.com/features/elle-paul-verhoeven-france-special-presentations/ (accessed November 9, 2023). *Elle* is also comparable to Buñuel's oeuvre in its subtle comedic tone, used as irony or humor, which serves to distance the viewer without veering into parody.

2 The animus expressed in this review, particularly directed at Isabelle Huppert, is breathtaking. Haskell takes issue with how Huppert "prefers discomfiting an audience over pleasing it," adding that "there has been a hardening of the bitch persona, the ice queen who never melts." Referring to Huppert and Verhoeven, she suggests that the film can be seen as "two

Notes to Chapter 7   193

people [Huppert and Verhoeven] mercilessly exploiting their own dark talents to a point of self-parody." Haskell is angered by Huppert's unwillingness to provide some "nugget of truth," or "solution to the riddle," instead "withholding, refusing" through her "enigmatic portraits of—among others—a prostitute, abortionist, murderer (patricide) and psycho piano teacher." The entire piece is fueled by a hardly suppressed rage and a complete unwillingness to engage with or understand Huppert's style of performance and the films she stars in, and the different kind of relationship with the viewer they set up, which is distinct from that of more traditional narratives. See Molly Haskell, "Agents Provocateurs: Isabelle Huppert and Paul Verhoeven Dive Back into the Deep End of Coy Perversity in *Elle*," *Film Comment*, 38, no. 6 (November–December 2016): 40.

3 Kate Taylor, "For Actress Isabelle Huppert, a Question of Revenge," *Globe and Mail*, November 17, 2016, www.theglobeandmail.com/news/actress-isabelle-huppert-on-the-complexity-of-revenge-inelle/article32894682/.

4 Verhoeven claims that *Elle* is about "a woman who refuses to be a victim. I think that's the essence of the whole story" and Huppert confirms that Michèle "doesn't want to be a victim and the way she reacts to the rape, she doesn't consider herself as a victim." "A Tale of Empowerment: Making *Elle*" included in the Sony Pictures Home Entertainment Blu-Ray DVD of *Elle*, 2017.

5 Michèle's gesture is like Erika's placement of the broken glass in a young pianist's pocket as a punishment for having gained the attentions of the young student she desires in *La Pianiste*.

6 One can see this complex conjoining of desire and prohibition through a long history of the cinema and the woman's novel. In Murnau's *Nosferatu* (1922), for example, Ellen's dubious sacrifice, inviting Nosferatu into her bedroom, clearly expresses her sexual desire.

7 Georg Simmel, "The Metropolis and Mental Life," in *The Blackwell City Reader*, 2nd ed., ed. Gary Bridge and Sophie Watson (Maldon, MA: Wiley-Blackwell, 2010), 106.

8 Britton, "New Servitude," 41.

9 In some ways, the ritualized treatment of the assaults are like the ceremonies/rituals in Genet's *The Maids*, where frustration and fantasies of power are expressed in sadistic scenarios that repeat in a loop without completion.

Chapter 7

1 Chéreau, "Abyss as Blank Page," 37.

2 Huppert, "Préface," 5.

194   Notes to Chapter 7

3 Lardoux, *Le Cinéma de Benoît Jacquot*, 8.

4 In *Persona*, Elizabeth, like Ann, is an artist who makes the decision to with-draw from her life and her refusal to perform or even speak, becomes an expression of her resistance, strength, and search for authenticity. Elizabeth similarly retreats to an island, cut off from her social world, as part of her "cure"; although the film suggests the possibility of a lesbian relationship between Alma and Elizabeth, it is a direction that Bergman does not or cannot explore. The Bergman-Rossellini films *Stromboli* (1950), *Europa '51* (1952), and *Viaggio in Italia* (1954) similarly follow a narrative trajectory where the protagonist rediscovers herself through her immersion in a for-eign environment (like *Villa Amalia*, also in Italy) which is intensely phys-ical and closer to the natural world.

5 Brunette, *Roberto Rossellini*, 139.

6 Kate Taylor, "Director Mia Hansen-Løve's Search for Independence in *Things to Come*," *Globe and Mail*, December 1, 2016. www.theglobeandmail .com/arts/film/mia-hansen-loves-search-for-independence-in-things-to -come/article33122817/.

7 "*Things to Come* Q&A, Mia Hansen-Løve and Isabelle Huppert, NYFF 54," YouTube video, 15:01, March 14, 2017, www.youtube.com/watch?v= QJu9Cz7gYjI.

8 Huppert's character in Florian Zeller's play, *The Mother* (directed by Trip Cullman and staged at the Atlantic Theatre in New York, February 20–April 13, 2019) faces a similar dilemma, discovering her obsolescence when her family no longer need her.

9 Taylor, "Director Mia Hansen-Løve's Search for Independence."

10 Huppert makes this comment in an interview with Ruth La Ferla: "Isabelle Huppert: The Best Way to Please Is Not to Please," *New York Times*, February 23, 2017, www.nytimes.com/2017/02/23/fashion/isabelle-huppert -oscar-nominee-elle.html.

11 These comments are made in "Director's Dialogue with Hong Sangsoo at NYFF55," included in the DVD *Claire's Camera*, Blu-Ray edition, Cinema Guild, 2017.

12 The concept of traveling, like wandering, is typically a masculine privilege and activity. The woman who leaves home veers into the male domain. Additionally, as a woman traveling alone, Anne is warned of the need to be wary of men.

13 Huppert is often paired, transgressively, with younger men in her films. In *Souvenir* (2016), Liliane's theme song, "Joli garçon, je dis oui," sums this up.

Bibliography

Bach, Steven. *Final Cut: Dreams and Disaster in the Making of Heaven's Gate.* New York: William Morrow, 1985.

Bálint Kovács, András. *Screening Modernism: European Art Cinema, 1950–1980.* Chicago: University of Chicago Press, 2007.

Bellaïche, Carole, *Isabelle Huppert par Carole Bellaïche.* Paris: Éditions de la Martinière, 2019.

Berger, John. *Ways of Seeing.* New York: Viking, 1972.

Boddaert, Francois, Pierre-Marc de Biasi, Caroline Eliacheff, Arnaud Laporte Arnaud, Claude Mouchard, Claude, and André Versaille. *Autour d'Emma: Madame Bovary, un film de Claude Chabrol, avec Isabelle Huppert.* Paris: Hatier, 1991.

Brantley, Ben, "Classy Dames in Desperate Straits." *New York Times,* August 10, 2014. www.nytimes.com/2014/08/10/theater/cate-blanchett -and-isabelle-huppert-in-the-maids.html.

Brecht, Bertolt. "Short Description of a New Technique of Acting Which Produces an Alienation Effect." In *Star Texts: Image and Performance in Film and Television,* edited by Jeremy G. Butler, 66–79. Detroit, MI: Wayne State University Press, 1991.

Britton, Andrew. *Katharine Hepburn: The Thirties and After.* Newcastle upon Tyne: Tyneside Cinema, 1984.

Brody, Richard. *Everything Is Cinema: The Working Life of Jean-Luc Godard.* New York: Holt, 2008.

Brunette, Peter. *Roberto Rossellini.* Berkeley: University of California Press, 1987.

Butler, Jeremy G., ed. *Star Texts: Image and Performance in Film and Television,* Detroit, MI: Wayne State University Press, 1991.

Chammah, Ronald, and Jeanne Fouchet, eds. *Isabelle Huppert: Woman of Many Faces.* New York: Harry N. Abrams, 2005.

196 Bibliography

Chase, Donald. "A Day in the Country." *Film Comment* 27, no. 6 (November–December 1991): 7–14.

Chéreau, Patrice. "The Abyss as Blank Page." In *Isabelle Huppert: Woman of Many Faces*, edited by Ronald Chammah and Jeanne Fouchet, 35–43. New York: Harry N. Abrams, 2005.

Debruge, Peter. "Oscar Nominee Isabelle Huppert Looks Back at Her Early Career." *Variety*, February 3, 2017. variety.com/2017/film/features/oscar-nominee-isabelle-huppert-1201974850/

Delorme, Stéphane. "L'Instant présent: Entretien avec Isabelle Huppert." *Cahiers du cinéma*, 723 (June 2016): 6–16.

———. "Le plaisir de jouer: Entretien avec Isabelle Huppert." *Cahiers du cinéma*, 660 (October 2010): 22–24.

Donadio, Rachel. "The Enduring Allure of Isabelle Huppert," *T: The New York Times Style Magazine*, November 30, 2016. www.nytimes.com/2016/11/30/t-magazine/isabelle-huppert-elle-movie-interview.html.

Dousteyssier-Khoze, Catherine. "Huppert and Chabrol: Opacity, Dissonance, and the Crystal Character." In *Isabelle Huppert: Stardom, Performance, Authorship*, edited by Nick Rees-Roberts and Darren Waldron, 137–55. New York: Bloomsbury Academic, 2021.

Dupont, Joan. "Still Waters: Isabelle Huppert Discusses Her Career with Joan Dupont." *Film Comment* 46, no. 6 (November–December 2010): 34–41.

Flaubert, Gustave. *Madame Bovary*. Translated and with an introduction and notes by Lydia Davis. New York: Penguin, 2010.

Fouque, Antoinette. "Dialogue with Isabelle Huppert" (December 15, 1993). In *There Are Two Sexes: Essays in Feminology*, edited by Sylvana Boissonnas, 94–112. New York: Columbia University Press, 2015.

Frodon, Jean-Michel. "Isabelle Huppert: 'Un pacte de croyance.'" *Cahiers du cinéma* no. 603 (July–August 2005): 28–30.

Genet, Jean. *The Maids and Deathwatch: Two Plays*. New York: Grove, 1954.

Grant, Barry Keith, ed. *Britton on Film*. Detroit, MI: Wayne State University Press, 2009.

Higson, Andrew. "Film Acting and Independent Cinema." In *Star Texts: Image and Performance in Film and Television*, edited by Jeremy Butler, 155–82. Detroit, MI: Wayne State University Press, 1991.

Haneke, Michael. "Terror and Utopia of Form—Addicted to Truth: A Story about Robert Bresson's *Au hazard Balthazar*." In *Robert Bresson (Revised)*, edited by James Quandt, 385–93. Toronto: Toronto International Film Festival, 2012.

Haskell, Molly. "Agents Provocateurs: Isabelle Huppert and Paul Verhoeven Dive Back into the Deep End of Coy Perversity in *Elle*." *Film Comment* 52, no. 6 (November–December 2016): 38–41.

Higson, Andrew. "Film Acting and Independent Cinema." In *Star Texts: Image and Performance in Film and Television*, edited by Jeremy G. Butler (Detroit, MI: Wayne State University Press, 1991),

Huppert, Isabelle. "Conversation avec Claude Chabrol et Emmanuèle Bernheim." *Cahiers du cinéma*, 477 (March 94): 52–57.

———. "Éditorial." *Cahiers du cinéma*, 477 (March 94): 5.

———. "Isabelle Huppert auto-portrait(s), Mots avec Jean Baudrillard." *Cahiers du cinéma*, 477 (March 94): 113–20.

———. "Paroles avec Antoinette Fouque." *Cahiers du cinéma*, 477 (March 1994): 36–46.

———. "Préface." In *Le Cinéma de Benoît Jacquot*, by Xavier Lardoux, 5. Paris: Éditions PC, 2011.

Jacobowitz, Florence, "*Un barrage contre le Pacifique* / *The Sea Wall*." *Cine-Action*, 76 (2008): 31–34.

———. "*La Cérémonie*: 'The Last Marxist Film' by Claude Chabrol." *CineAction*, 39 (1995): 36–43.

———. "*Nue Propriété* with Isabelle Huppert." *CineAction*, 71 (2007): 40–42.

———. "Rethinking History through Narrative Art." *CineAction*, 34 (1994): 4–20.

———. "*Special Treatment* / *Sans queue ni tête*." *CineAction*, 82–83 (2010): 34–36.

———. "*Le temps du loup* / *Time of the Wolf*." *CineAction*, 70 (2006): 46–50.

———. "*White Material*: A Film by Claire Denis." *CineAction*, 80 (2010): 44–46.

Jelinek, Elfreide. *The Piano Teacher*. New York: Grove Atlantic, 2009.

Joudet, Murielle, *Isabelle Huppert: Vivre ne nous regarde pas*. Paris: Capricci, 2018.

Kachka, Boris, "Brooklyn Hearts Huppert." *New York Magazine*, October 22, 2009. nymag.com/arts/theater/features/60239/.

Klifa, Thierry. "Isabelle Huppert, Ma vie d'actrice." *Studio Magazine* 181 (September 2002): 62–73.

198   Bibliography

Kristeva, Julia, Christian de Portzamparc, Umberto Eco, Philippe Sollers, Isabelle Huppert, and Marcel Detienne. *Le plaisir des formes*. Paris: Éditions du Seuil, 2003.

La Ferla, Ruth. "Isabelle Huppert: The Best Way to Please Is Not to Please." *New York Times*, February 23, 2017. www.nytimes.com/2017/02/23/fashion/isabelle-huppert-oscar-nominee-elle.html.

Lardoux, Xavier. *Le Cinéma de Benoît Jacquot*. Paris: Éditions PC, 2011.

Lasalle, Mick. *The Beauty of the Real: What Hollywood Can Learn from Contemporary French Actresses*. Stanford, CA: Stanford University Press, 2012.

Loshitzky, Yosefa. *The Radical Faces of Godard and Bertolucci*. Detroit, MI: Wayne State University Press 1995.

Mulvey, Laura, and Colin MacCabe. "Images of Woman, Images of Sexuality." In *Godard: Images, Sounds, Politics*, edited by Colin MacCabe, 79–103. Bloomington: Indiana University Press, 1980.

Nayman, Adam. "The Rules of the Game: Paul Verhoeven's *Elle*." Cinemascope Online. Accessed December 22, 2023. cinema-scope.com/features/elle-paul-verhoeven-france-special-presentations/.

Quandt, James, "Introduction." In *Robert Bresson (Revised)*, edited by James Quandt, 1–23. Toronto: Toronto International Film Festival, 2012.

Rees-Roberts, Nick, and Darren Waldron. "Introduction—Against Type: Isabelle Huppert's Unorthodox Stardom." In *Isabelle Huppert: Stardom, Performance, Authorship*, edited by Nick Rees-Roberts and Darren Waldron, 1–20. New York: Bloomsbury Academic, 2021.

Sartre, Jean-Paul. "Introduction." In *The Maids and Deathwatch: Two Plays*, by Jean Genet, 7–32. New York: Grove, 1954.

Sontag, Susan. *Against Interpretation and Other Essays*. New York: Farrar, Strauss & Giroux, 1961.

——. *Under the Sign of Saturn*. New York: Farrar, Strauss & Giroux, 1972.

Taylor, Alison. "Isabelle Huppert in *The Piano Teacher*." In *Close-Up: Great Cinematic Performances*, Vol. 2, *International*, edited by Kyle Stevens and Murray Pomerance, 217–27. Edinburgh: Edinburgh University Press, 2018.

Tomasulo, Frank P. "'The Sounds of Silence': Modernist Acting in Michelangelo Antoinioni's *Blow-Up*." In *More than a Method: Trends and Traditions in Contemporary Film Performance*, edited by Cynthia Baron, Diane Carson and Frank P. Tomasulo, 94–125. Detroit, MI: Wayne State University Press, 2004.

Toubiana, Serge. "Foreword." *Isabelle Huppert: Woman of Many Faces*, edited by Ronald Chammah and Jeanne Fouchet, 9–14. New York: Harry N. Abrams, 2005.

Vaucher, Andrea R., "Madame Bovary, C'est Moi!" *American Film* (September–October 1991): 28–31.

Vincendeau, Ginette. *Stars and Stardom in French Cinema*. London: Bloomsbury, 2000.

Waldron, Darren. "Intimate Distance: The Face of Isabelle Huppert." In *Isabelle Huppert: Stardom, Performance, Authorship*, edited by Nick Rees-Roberts and Darren Waldron, 21–39. New York: Bloomsbury Academic, 2021.

Wood, Robin. *Hollywood from Vietnam to Reagan*. New York: Columbia University Press, 1986.

———. *The Wings of the Dove: Henry James in the 1990s*. London: British Film Institute, 1999.

Index

Note: Page numbers appearing in *italics* refer to figures.

abstraction, 3, 5, 34, 37–39, 41, 154
Abus de faiblesse (*Abuse of Weakness*), 38
Une affaire de femmes (*Story of Women*),
  81–97, *86*, *89*, *95*; on abortion,
  81–87, 89–91, 95–97; archetype
  of dissatisfaction in, 82; on capital
  punishment, 81, 93, 95–97; comedic
  elements, 190n10; criminal deviance in,
  13, 81, 82; critical reception of, 96–97;
  female relationships in, 17, 50, 88–90;
  feminization of male characters in, 91,
  182n32; identification with characters
  in, 83; minimalist performance style
  in, 94, 97; on motherhood, 82, 85–87,
  93–96, 102; patriarchy and, 25, 81,
  83, 97, 108; politics of agency in, 46;
  sexuality in, 85, 91–92, 108; specifically
  developed for Huppert, 28, 81;
  unconscious in, 40–41, 83, 89; Vichy
  France, 25, 81, 84, 85, 97
agency: characterization and, 2, 6, 181n19;
  masculinity and, 23; in maternal
  melodrama, 189n4; oppression and,
  34, 45; politics of, 44–46, 61, 74; in
  resistance to objectification, 37; self-
  determination and, 3
Les ailes de la colombe (*The Wings of the
  Dove*), 10–11
Aimée, Anouk, 53

Akerman, Chantal, 52
alienation: Friedan on, 99; interiority and, 4;
  madwoman figure and, 42; oppression
  and, 7, 41, 110; politics of agency and,
  44, 45; resistance to, 156; sexuality and,
  65, 117, 123, 126, 145; social context
  and, 6, 107; unconscious, 100–102
Andrews, Benedict, 27
Angel Face, 185n30
anti-victimhood, 11, 27, 37, 139, 149,
  153, 193n4
Antonioni, Michelangelo, 5–7, 179n6
Astruc, Alexandre, 8
Audran, Stéphane, 52, 53, 186n49
authoritarianism, 81, 97
authorship, 3, 8–9, 154, 163, 168
autonomy: in adolescence, 118; authentic
  state of, 162; expressions of, 20, 26,
  67, 136; of Huppert, 1, 2, 17, 30,
  34, 35; prostitution and, 65, 67, 79;
  representations of, 27, 129; women's
  bodies and, 82, 85, 87
L'avenir (*Things to Come*), 162–70, *166*,
  170; comedic elements, 167, 168;
  mother-daughter relationship in,
  165–67, 169; negotiation of transition
  in, 163–64, 170; philosophical themes,
  162–65; specifically developed for
  Huppert, 28, 154, 163

202   Index

Bach, Steven, 20
Bachmann, Ingeborg, 43–44, 116
Balenciaga campaign, 28–30, *29*,
    183nn42–43
Un barrage contre le Pacifique (*The Sea
    Wall*), 8, 17, 42
Barthes, Roland, 179n5
Baudelaire, Charles, 65, 107
Baudrillard, Jean, 42, 65
Baye, Nathalie, 61, 70
Bella addormentata (*Dormant
    Beauty*), 48
Bellaïche, Carole, 27, 30–31, 51
Bellocchio, Marco, 48
Belmondo, Jean-Paul, 75, 186n48
Benjamin, Walter, 65
Berger, John, 68, 188n11
Bergman, Ingmar, 156, 194n4
Bergman, Ingrid: Hitchcock and, 54;
    Renoir and, 54; Rossellini and, 45,
    53–54, 74, 156, 157, 164, 187n53,
    194n4
Bergman, Ingrid, films of: *Europa '51*, 54,
    74, 156, 194n4; *Stromboli*, 54, 194n4;
    Viaggio in Italia, 54, *55*, 194n4
Bier, Bertrand, 10
Binoche, Juliette, 54–55, 168
Blanchett, Cate, 45, 55–56, *56*
Blonde Venus, 189n4
Blue Angel, The, 124
Bolognini, Mauro, 48
Bondy, Luc, 17
Bonnaire, Sandrine, *40*
Bovarysme, 8, 34, 82, 99, 107, 108
Brantley, Ben, 55, 187n55
Breathless, 75, 186n48
Brecht, Bertolt, 6–7, 36–37, 55, 69, 128,
    180n9, 180–81n18
Breillat, Catherine, 38
Bresson, Robert, 4–6, 180n9
Britton, Andrew, 7, 16, 50, 148–49
Brody, Richard, 180n10, 187n4,
    188–89n17

Brunette, Peter, 187n53
Buñuel, Luis, 26, 52, 139, 144, 192n1

caméra-stylo, 8, 60
capital punishment, 81, 93, 95–97
Carmet, Jean, 15, *17*
Carrie, 13
Cavett, Dick, 66, 187n3, 188n8
La Cérémonie, 17, 39, *40*, 42, 45, 50
Chabrol, Claude: Audran and, 52; *La
    Cérémonie*, 17, 39, *40*, 42, 45, 50;
    director-actor partnerships, 8–9, 47;
    Hitchcock's influence on, 13, 146;
    interiority in works of, 4, 16, 25,
    83; *L'ivresse de pouvoir*, 16–17, 50;
    New Wave movement and, 25; *L'Oeil
    de Vichy*, 81; unrealized film based
    on *The Iron Staircase*, 181–82n24;
    X-ray analogy of performance, 38, 83,
    101. See also *Une affaire de femmes*;
    Madame Bovary; *Violette Nozière*
Le chagrin et la pitié (*The Sorrow and the
    Pity*), 97
Chammah, Lolita (Huppert's daughter),
    31
Chammah, Ronald, 27, 30
Champlin, Charles, 20
characterization: agency and, 2, 6,
    181n19; demonstrative approach to,
    6, 54, 180–81n18; in *Elle*, 9, 140–42;
    feminist approach to, 9; Godard on,
    5, 59, 78–79, 189n18; Haneke on, 5,
    117, 191n6; Huppert's persona and,
    13, 66, 181n20; in *In Another Country*,
    172, 174–75; insertion of self in roles,
    2, 6, 27, 46–48, 59, 181n20; Jacquot
    on, 5, 157; landscapes and, 4, 179n6;
    in *Madame Bovary*, 25, 47, 100–105,
    190nn11–13; in melodrama, 7–8, 41,
    45, 118, 162; minimalism and, 79, 172;
    mise-en-scène and, 8, 9, 182n28; in
    Passion, 47, 79; in *La Pianiste*, 117–18,
    137, 184n19, 191n6, 191–92n8;

psychological, 3–6, 179n5, 180n10; in *Sauve qui peut (la vie)*, 5, 47, 79, 180n10; in *Villa Amalia*, 155–58, 162. *See also* identification with characters; interiority

Chéreau, Patrice, 6, 30–31, 35, 39, 48, 186n44, 189n2

Cimino, Michael, 1, 10, 18, 21, 23–24

Claire's Camera, 170, 171

class: boundaries of, 20, 22; disparities related to, 42; gender and, 45, 93, 94, 100, 112, 136; middle class, 69, 116; mobility and, 121; patriarchy and, 3, 17, 100; politics of, 45, 73, 93–94; privilege and, 19, 93–94, 103, 122–23, 131; working class, 11, 12, 15, 73–75, 79, 117

conservatism, 19, 97, 172, 174

Coup de foudre / Entre Nous, 16, 17, 50

critical reading, 6, 9, 54

Cukor, George, 115–16

Cullman, Trip, 27, 194n8

cutting (self-harm), 40, 119, 127–28, 132, 136

La Daronne (Mama Weed), 186n43

Davis, Bette, 50

death penalty. *See* capital punishment

Defurne, Bavo, 17

democracy, 19, 22, 23, 116

Deneuve, Catherine, 52

Denis, Claire, 4, 5, 8

La dentellière (The Lacemaker), 1, *10*, 10–12, *12*, 23, 179n7

De Palma, Brian, 13

Destry Rides Again, 18–19

Deux (Two), 28

Deux ou trois choses que je sais d'elle (Two or Three Things I Know about Her), 64–65

Devil Is a Woman, The, 51

Dietrich, Marlene: Huppert compared to, 30, 50–52; photographic career, 28; Sternberg and, 18, 50–51, 185n28

Dietrich, Marlene, films of: *Blonde Venus*, 189n4; *Destry Rides Again*, 18–19; *The Devil Is a Woman*, 51; *Dishonored*, 51, *52*; *Marlene*, 188n12; *Morocco*, 51–52

Discreet Charm of the Bourgeoisie, The, 139

Dishonored, 51, *52*

distanciation strategy, 6

Doinel, Antoine, 12

domesticity, 20, 101, 103, 170

double gaze, 184n10

Dousteyssier-Khoze, Catherine, 186n49

Dreyer, Carl, 72

Duras, Marguerite, 4, 52, 61–64, 71, 188n12

Dutronc, Jacques, 61–62, 71

Eclipse, 7

L'école de la chair (The School of Flesh), 17

8 femmes (8 Women), 56

Elle, 139–51, *141*, *147*, *149*; abstraction in, 38; anti-victimhood in, 149, 193n4; award for Huppert's performance in, 57; characterization in, 9, 140–42; comedic elements, 142, 151, 192n1; critical reception of, 57, 140, 192–93n2; feminism and, 151; Gothic melodrama and, 7, 139, 141; identification with characters in, 140–42; *Marnie* compared to, 146–48; phallic erasure in, 16, 149, 150; *La Pianiste* compared to, 193n5; sexuality in, 139–49, 151; spectator estrangement and, 26; unconscious in, 141

emasculation, 50, 91, 92, 181n24, 189n4

Entre Nous. See Coup de foudre / Entre Nous

equality: in democracies, 19, 22; in relationships, 116, 126; for women, 3, 33, 64, 141, 151

Europa '51, 54, 74, 156, 194n4

204   Index

European art films: authorship and, 3, 8, 163; director's vision in, 21, 27; search for authenticity in, 44–45; social experience and, 33; unconscious in, 8. *See also specific films*
Exorcist, The, 13

facial expressions, 9, 39, 182n30
fascism, 13, 44, 81, 84, 116, 127
Les fausses confidences (*False Confessions*), 17
femininity, 53, 101, 103, 121, 133, 190n5
feminism: *Une affaire de femmes* and, 81, 82, 97; anti-victimhood and, 37, 139, 153; characterization and, 9; *Elle* and, 151; on fetishism, 51; *Madame Bovary* and, 99–100, 113; melodrama and, 115; politics and, 1, 25, 94; radical, 33; *Sauve qui peut (la vie)* and, 63; second wave, 33, 44; self-determination and, 27. *See also* women
fetishism, 51, 119, 144
Flaubert, Gustave, 7, 25, 47, 99–101, 106–7, 113, 190n4
Fonda, Jane, 18, 61
Ford, John, 21
Fouchet, Jean, 27, 30
Fouque, Antoinette, 183n45
Les 400 coups (*The 400 Blows*), 12
Franju, Georges, 165
Frankie, 28
Friedan, Betty, 44, 99
Friedkin, William, 13

Gabin, Jean, 182n32
Garbo, Greta, 30, 48–50, *49*, *51*, 186n44
Gaslight, 115–16
gender: class and, 45, 93, 94, 100, 112, 136; clothing styles and, 28; constructions of, 24; crossing gender lines, 21, 23, 69; hierarchy of, 112–13; oppression based on, 87, 94, 97, 137; politics of, 33, 42, 133; roles

related to, 48, 64, 101, 108. *See also* men; women
Genet, Jean, 45, 46, 55–56, 193n9
genres. *See specific film genres*
Girardot, Annie, 118, *132*
Giraud, Marie, 81
Godard, Jean-Luc: *Breathless*, 75, 186n48; on characterization, 5, 59, 78–79, 189n18; cinematic influences on, 188n13; *Deux ou trois choses que je sais d'elle*, 64–65; director-actor partnerships, 9, 47, 78, 185n41, 188–89n17; on *imprimer* vs. *exprimer*, 39, 49, 184n22; interiority in works of, 24, 59; *Letter to Jane*, 61; Miéville and, 62, 187n4; minimalism and, 11, 12; prostitution analyzed by, 64–70, 188n6; *Tout va bien*, 59–61, 69; *Vivre sa vie*, 64–66. See also *Passion*; *Sauve qui peut (la vie)*
Goldin, Nan, 27
Goretta, Claude, 1, 179n7
Gothic melodrama, 7, 115, 139, 141, 181–82n24
Grannam, Katy, 29
Greenberg, Clement, 3
Greta, 56–57
Gvasalia, Demna, 28

Haneke, Michael: on characterization, 5, 117, 191n6; director-actor partnerships, 8–9, 47, 191n1; *Happy End*, 17; Hitchcock's influence on, 13, 146; interiority in works of, 4, 117; modernist filmmaking and, 115; *The White Ribbon*, 192n10, 192n12. See also *La Pianiste*
Hansen-Løve, Mia, 154, 162–64
Happy End, 17
Haskell, Molly, 57, 140, 192–93n2
Heaven's Gate, 18–24, *21*, *24*; critical reception of, 18; identification with characters in, 23; self-definition

of characters in, 10; sexuality in, 20–21, 23; western conventions and, 9, 19–22, 24; on women's place in society, 1, 20, 22

Hepburn, Katharine, 50

Higson, Andrew, 6

Hitchcock, Alfred: Bergman and, 54; *Blackmail*, 13; on criminal deviance, 13; influence on cinematic practices, 7–8, 13, 117, 146; *Psycho*, 13, 146–48, 156; *Rebecca*, 116; *Shadow of a Doubt*, 13, 146; *Vertigo*, 185n28. See also *Marnie*

Hong Sang-soo, 9, 48, 154, 170–71, 177

Honoré, Christoph, 17

horror films, 13, 139. *See also specific films*

8 femmes (8 Women), 56

Huppert, Isabelle: autonomy of, 1, 2, 17, 30, 34, 35; critical reception of, 55, 57, 140, 192–93n2; Dietrich compared to, 30, 50–52; Garbo compared to, 30, 48–50, 186n44; on *imprimer* vs. *exprimer*, 39, 49; insertion of self in roles, 2, 6, 27, 46–48, 59, 181n20; photographic career, 27–31, 36; privacy of, 1, 30–31, 34–35, 79; on self-discovery through acting, 46, 184n13; social media presence, 27; as subject and object, 35–37, 117, 184nn9–10; theatrical career and collaborations, 27. *See also* Huppert, Isabelle, persona of; modernist performance style; *specific films and plays*

Huppert, Isabelle, persona of: anti-victimhood and, 11, 27, 37, 139, 153; characterization and, 13, 66, 181n20; films making use of, 17–18, 48, 117, 151, 153–54, 163, 170; narcissism and, 56, 82, 153, 189n2; paradoxes attributed to, 2; self-definition and, 10, 153; stereotypes associated with, 56, 140, 192n2

hysteria, 7, 41–44, 100–101, 120, 190n5

identification with characters: abstraction and, 38; in *Une affaire de femmes*, 83; challenges to expectations of, 2–7, 35, 179n7; in *Elle*, 140–42; in *Heaven's Gate*, 23; in *Madame Bovary*, 100, 190n2; in *The Mother*, 27; objections to, 179n4; in *La Pianiste*, 117; in *Sauve qui peut (la vie)*, 62; social context and, 16, 25, 34; in *Villa Amalia*, 155; in *Violette Nozière*, 16

I Heart Huckabees, 56

In Another Country, 170–77, *173*, *176*; characterization in, 172, 174–75; sexuality in, 174, 176–77; specifically developed for Huppert, 48, 154, 170; triptychal organization of, 171–74

infidelity, 73, 155, 157, 167, 172

interiority: elements associated with, 4, 34; elusiveness and, 4, 25, 26; facial expressions and, 39, 182n30; melodrama and, 41; minimalism and, 39, 48, 117, 141; modernist performance style and, 39–41, 59; music as expression of, 157–58; opacity resulting from, 5, 16; personas of actors utilized for, 24; unconscious and, 4, 5, 34, 39–41; X-ray analogy, 38, 83, 101

Isabelle Huppert: La femme aux portraits (Woman of Many Faces) (Chammah and Fouchet), 27, 30

Isabelle Huppert par Carole Bellaïche, 30–31

L'ivresse de pouvoir (Comedy of Power), 16–17, 50

Jacquot, Benoît: *Les ailes de la colombe*, 10; on characterization, 5, 157; director-actor partnerships, 8–9, 154; *L'école de la chair*, 17; on films as documentaries about actors, 54, 153, 154, 157. See also *Villa Amalia*

James, Henry, 40

206   Index

Jelinek, Elfriede, 45, 116, 128, 131, 136, 187n56, 191n2
Jones, Jennifer, 100
Jordan, Neil, 56–57

Karina, Anna, 59, 65, 66
Karmitz, Marin, 97
Keaton, Diane, 18
Kovács, András Bálint, 7, 179nn5–6
Kristeva, Julia, 118, 192n9
Kurys, Diane, 16

Lafitte, Laurent, 141, *141*
Lafosse, Joachim, 17
Lang, Fritz, 115, 185n28
Lassalle, Jacques, 27
Léaud, Jean-Pierre, 47, 191n1
Letter from an Unknown Woman, 103
Letter to Jane, 61
Losey, Joseph, 10
Loshitzky, Yosefa, 188n14
Lubtchansky, William, 187n4

MacCabe, Colin, 188n6
Madame Bovary, 53, 99–113, *106*, *111*, *113*; archetype of dissatisfaction in, 101, 189n1; Bovarysme, 8, 34, 82, 99, 107, 108; characterization in, 25, 47, 100–105, 190nn11–13; feminist reading of, 99–100, 113; hysteria in, 100–101, 190n5; identification with characters in, 100, 190n2; minimalist performance style in, 105; patriarchy and, 100, 108, 109, 112–13; sexuality in, 51, 53, *53*, 105–8; unconscious in, 100–101, 109, 190nn4–5
Maids, The, 27, 45–46, 55–56, *56*, 187n55, 193n9
male privilege, 26, 93–94, 97, 112, 194n12. *See also* men
Malina, 42–44, *44*, 116
Ma mère (*My Mother*), 17

Marlene, 188n12
Marnie: criminal deviance in, 13, 16; *Elle* compared to, 146–48; male dominance in, 116; melodrama and, 185n28; *La Pianiste* compared to, 118, 131, 192n11; sexuality in, 119, 146, 192n11
masculinity: agency and, 23; ethos of, 122–23; fascism and, 13; fetishism and, 51; football and, 69; hierarchy of, 6; power and, 30, 103, 122, 151; privileges of, 194n12; prostitution and, 65, 188n6; in Vichy France, 81, 84, 85, 97; violence and, 140, 141; in westerns, 20
Medea, 27, 41
melodrama: abstraction and, 41; anti-melodramatic, 185n30; anti-naturalist, 7, 41; characterization in, 7–8, 41, 45, 118, 162; confinement motif in, 191n4; emotional excesses of, 164; Freudian-feminist, 115; Gothic, 7, 115, 139, 141, 181–82n24; hysteria and, 7, 41–44; interiority and, 41; maternal, 189n4; modernist performance style and, 7, 41–44, 115, 142, 185n28; tropes associated with, 25–26, 42, 115, 192n17. *See also* woman's film; *specific films*
men: emasculation, 50, 91, 92, 181n24, 189n4; misogyny, 26, 99, 110, 145, 151, 189n7; obsolescence in woman's film, 42, 50, 90, 189n4. *See also* gender; male privilege; masculinity; patriarchy
Miéville, Anne-Marie, 62, 187n4
Mildred Pierce, 189n4
minimalism: in characterization, 79, 172; clothing styles and, 28; in expressions, 1, 94, 97, 105, 161; interiority and, 39, 48, 117, 141; naturalism and, 11, 12, 23; in postwar performances, 52

Minnelli, Vincente, 100
mise-en-scène: actor collaboration with, 48; characterization and, 8, 9, 182n28; complexity of, 77, 118; confinement motif and, 191n4; hysteria expressed through, 43, 100; New Wave movement and, 53; openness to interpretation, 115
misogyny, 26, 99, 110, 145, 151, 189n7
modernist performance style, 33–57; absence as resistance in, 35–37; abstraction in, 3, 5, 34, 37–39, 41, 154; acknowledgment of camera and, 11–12, *12*, 75, *76*; collaboration and, 46–48; elements of, 3–4, 179n1, 179n5; interiority and, 39–41, 59; melodrama and, 7, 41–44, 115, 142, 185n28; politics of agency and, 44–46; precedents for, 48–57; woman's film and, 7, 8. *See also* characterization; minimalism
Montand, Yves, 60, 61
Moreau, Jeanne, 52, 53
Morocco, 51–52
Mother, The, 27, 194n8
mother-child relationships, 93–96, 189n4; *Une affaire de femmes*, 82, 85–87, 102; *L'avenir*, 165–67, 169; *Elle*, 142–44; *Madame Bovary*, 53, 102, 108; *La Pianiste*, 118–26, 129–32; *Villa Amalia*, 157–58, 160; *Violette Nozière*, 16
Mrs. Harris Goes to Paris, 182n41
Mulvey, Laura, 188n6
Murnau, F. W., 193n6
mystery of Huppert. *See* privacy

New Wave movement, 7–8, 25, 52–53
Nicloux, Guillaume, 48, 56
Nosferatu, 193n6
nouveau roman, 4, 6
nudity vs. nakedness, 68–69, 188n11
Nue Propriété (Private Property), 17

objectification: dehumanization and, 145; in fashion industry, 28, 30; resistance to, 36–37, 65, *68*, 175; sexuality and, 23, 65, 109, 122; voyeurism and, 117
L'Oeil de Vichy (The Eye of Vichy), 81
O'Hagan, Colo Tavernier, 81
Ophüls, Marcel, 97
Ophüls, Max, 103, 185n28
oppression: agency and, 34, 45; alienation and, 7, 41, 110; freedom from, 3, 26; gender-based, 87, 94, 97, 137; patriarchy and, 15, 17, 25, 43, 100; race-based, 81, 97; resistance to, 13, 17, 44, 65; sociocultural context, 115, 116, 121, 122
Orlando, 27
Ozon, François, 56

Panh, Rithy, 8
parole de femmes, 63, 64, 71
Passion, 71–79, *75–76*; on centrality of director, 60, 71, 77; characterization in, 47, 79; director-actor partnership in, 78, 188–89n17; minimalist naturalism in, 12; rejection of dominant story in, 72–73; sexuality in, 74
Passion of Joan of Arc, The, 72
patriarchy: *Une affaire de femmes* and, 25, 81, 83, 97, 108; authoritarianism and, 81; class and, 3, 17, 100; constraints of, 50, 153; cultural effects of, 1, 33, 42, 100; in film industry, 66; hysteria and, 42; *Madame Bovary* and, 100, 108, 109, 112–13; oppression and, 15, 17, 25, 43, 100; resistance to, 3, 17–18, 33, 172, 186n43; *Sauve qui peut (la vie)* and, 61, 63; sexual control and, 13, 134; violence and, 148; *Violette Nozière* and, 13, 15
Persona, 156, 194n4
phallic erasure, 16–17, 149, 150

208   Index

La Pianiste (*The Piano Teacher*), 115–37, 120, 125, 132; characterization in, 117–18, 137, 184n19, 191n6, 191–92n8; *Elle* compared to, 193n5; Huppert as subject and object in, 35, 117; identification with characters in, 117; interpretation by spectators, 137, 187n54; madwoman figure in, 42; *Marnie* compared to, 118, 131, 192n11; melodrama and, 7, 25–26, 115; mother-daughter relationship in, 118–26, 129–32; parody in, 45, 187n56, 191n2; phallic erasure in, 16; phallic woman in, 123–27, 130; pleasure and punishment in, 125–36; politics of agency in, 45; sexuality in, 40, 117–35; sociocultural context, 116–17, 191n4; specifically developed for Huppert, 28, 117, 191n5; unconscious in, 40–41

Pinckney, Darryl, 27

politics: of abortion, 81; of agency, 44–46, 61, 74; of class, 45, 73, 93–94; feminist, 1, 25, 94; of gender, 33, 42, 133; of male dominance, 26; sexual, 61

Ponzi, Maurizio, 157, 187n53

pornography, 63, 118–19, 123, 126, 133, 191n4

Preminger, Otto, 115, 185n28, 185n30

privacy, 1, 30–31, 34–35, 79

prostitution: in *Une affaire de femmes*, 85, 89, 91; autonomy and, 65, 67, 79; *Heaven's Gate* and, 20, 21; as metaphor for alienated labor, 65; *Sauve qui peut (la vie)* and, 36, 62, 64–70; *Violette Nozière* and, 16

Quandt, James, 5

Quartett, 27

Les 400 coups (*The 400 Blows*), 12

Queen Christina, 50, 51

racial oppression, 81, 97

rape: in *Elle*, 139–42, 144–48, 151; in *Heaven's Gate*, 21; in *La Pianiste*, 122, 131, 134, 135; in *Violette Nozière*, 15

Rebecca, 116

Rees-Roberts, Nick, 181n19

La règle du jeu (*The Rules of the Game*), 77–78, 139

La Religieuse (*The Nun*), 56

Rendell, Ruth: *A Judgment in Stone*, 45, 50

Renoir, Jean, 54, 77–78, 139

Resnais, Alain, 52

Riva, Emmanuelle, 53

Rossellini, Roberto: Bergman collaborations, 45, 53–54, 74, 156, 157, 164, 187n53, 194n4; *Europa '51*, 54, 74, 156, 194n4; influence on cinematic practices, 7–8; *Stromboli*, 54, 194n4; *Viaggio in Italia*, 54, 194n4

Russell, David O., 56

Sachs, Ira, 28

Salomé, Jean-Paul, 186n43

Sarraute, Nathalie, 4, 179n4

Sauve qui peut (la vie) (*Every Man for Himself*), 1, 60–71, 67–68; characterization in, 5, 47, 79, 180n10; director-actor partnership in, 78, 188n17; as essay film, 59–60; feminist debates regarding, 63; Huppert as subject and object in, 36; identification with characters in, 62; minimalist naturalism in, 12; *parole de femmes* and, 63, 64, 71; patriarchy and, 61, 63; resistance through absence in, 36; sexuality in, 36, 61–70, 188n14; *Tout va bien* compared to, 60–61; on women's place in society, 1, 63

Schell, Maximilian, 188n12

Schroeter, Werner, 9, 28, 43, 44

Schygulla, Hanna, 72, 76

Scob, Édith, 165
Seberg, Jean, 186n48
self-definition, 10, 26, 34, 42, 153
self-determination, 3, 10, 27, 33, 82
self-harm. *See* cutting
self-reflexivity, 3, 41–42, 48, 70, 186n43
sexuality: in *Une affaire de femmes*, 85, 91–92, 108; alienation and, 65, 117, 123, 126, 145; in coming-of-age narratives, 11; desire and, 62, 76, 106, 119, 174, 193n6; in *Elle*, 139–49, 151; freedom and, 10, 33; in *Heaven's Gate*, 20–21, 23; Huppert's confidence with, 3; identity and, 13–14, 115, 118, 127, 131; in *In Another Country*, 174, 176–77; in *Madame Bovary*, 51, 53, *53*, 105–8; in *Marnie*, 119, 146, 192n11; in *Nosferatu*, 193n6; objectification and, 23, 65, 109, 122; in *Passion*, 74; patriarchal control and, 13, 134; in *La Pianiste*, 40, 117–35; politics of, 61; pornography, 63, 118–19, 123, 126, 133, 191n4; repression of, 10, 13, 106, 116, 118, 122, 127, 132; in *Sauve qui peut (la vie)*, 36, 61–70, 188n14; in *Violette Nozière*, 13–16, *17*; in *The White Ribbon*, 192n10. *See also* prostitution; rape
Seyrig, Delphine, 52, 53
Simenon, Georges: *The Iron Staircase*, 181–82n24
Simmel, Georg, 145–46
Sirk, Douglas, 115, 185n28
Sontag, Susan, 127, 129, 179n4, 180n9
Souvenir, 17, 194n13
spectators and spectatorship: actor relationships with, 7, 30; assessment of thoughts and feelings, 5; centrality of voyeurism to, 115; challenges to expectations of, 2, 140; critical reading and, 6, 9, 54; engagement of, 6, 25, 26, 39, 54; estrangement of, 6, 26, 36, 117; interpretations by, 54, 137, 187n54;

modernist reconceptions of, 34; objectifying gaze of, 36; pleasures of, 2, 35. *See also* voyeurism
Stanwyck, Barbara, 50
star vehicles, 186n43
Steichen, Edward, 48, *49*, 186n44
Stella Dallas, 189n4
Sternberg, Josef von, 18, 50–51, 124, 185n28
La storia vera della signora dalle camelie (Lady of the Camelias), 48
Stromboli, 54, 194n4

Tavernier, Bertrand, 9
Tavernier, Nils, 84, 91
Taylor, Alison, 191–92n8
Toubiana, Serge, 29, 30, 35–37, 49–50
Tout va bien, 59–61, 69
Traveler's Needs, A, 170
Truffaut, François, 12, 47, 191n1
La Truite (The Trout), 10–11

unconscious: abstraction and, 38; in *Une affaire de femmes*, 40–41, 83, 89; alienation and, 100–102; in *Elle*, 141; in European art films, 8; interiority and, 4, 5, 34, 39–41; in *Madame Bovary*, 100–101, 109, 190nn4–5; in *La Pianiste*, 40–41; in *Violette Nozière*, 13, 15, 23, 40–41
unknowability of Huppert. *See* privacy

Valley of Love, 48
Les Valseuses (Going Places), 10–11
van Hove, Ivo, 27
Verhoeven, Paul: on anti-victimhood, 193n4; Haskell's criticisms of, 192–93n2; on Huppert, 2, 183n44. *See also Elle*
Viaggio in Italia, 54, *55*, 194n4
Vichy France, 25, 81, 84, 85, 97
victimhood, 26, 33, 45, 118. *See also* anti-victimhood

210 Index

viewers. *See* spectators and spectatorship

Villa Amalia, 154–62, *159*, *161*; abstraction in, 154; characterization in, 155–58, 162; cinematic influences on, 54, 156, 194n4; existentialist journey and, 45; female relationships in, 50, 159–60; identification with characters in, 155; minimalist performance style in, 161; phallic erasure in, 17; specifically developed for Huppert, 28, 154

Vincendeau, Ginette, 52–53

Violette Nozière, *14*, *17*; award for Huppert's performance in, 16; as coming-of-age narrative, 10–11; criminal deviance in, 13–16, 182n33; female relationships in, 50; feminization of male characters in, 14; identification with characters in, 1, 16; madwoman figure in, 42; nouveau roman and, 4; patriarchy and, 13, 15; phallic erasure in, 16; sexuality in, 13–16, *17*; unconscious in, 13, 15, 23, 40–41

Viridiana, 144

Vivre sa vie (*My Life to Live*), 64–66

Vlady, Marina, 65

voyeurism: camera positions from behind characters, 88, 110, 158, *159*, 164, 170, 175–77, *176*, 191n6; centrality to spectatorship, 115; Huppert's mitigation of, 30, 35, 50; objectification and, 117; pleasure of, 35, 123, 139, 147; pornography and, 119, 123, 126

Waldron, Darren, 179n7, 181nn19–20

westerns, 9, 19–22, 24, 62. *See also specific films*

White Material, 4, 5, 7–8, 17, 28, 42, 45–46

White Ribbon, The, 192n10, 192n12

Wilson, Robert, 27, 48, 186n44

woman's film: characterization in, 8, 118; male obsolescence in, 42, 50, 90, 189n4; modernist performance style and, 7, 8; negotiation of transition in, 154, 163–64, 170, 194n8; phallic erasure in, 16–17, 149, 150; tropes associated with, 42. *See also specific films*

women: abortion, 81–87, 89–91, 95–97; autonomy over bodies, 82, 85, 87; Bovarysme and, 8, 34, 82, 99, 107, 108; domesticity, 20, 101, 103, 170; equality for, 3, 33, 64, 141, 151; femininity, 53, 101, 103, 121, 133, 190n5; hysteria and, 7, 41–44, 100–101, 120, 190n5; misogyny, 26, 99, 110, 145, 151, 189n7; motherhood, 53, 82, 85–87, 93–96, 102, 189n4; *parole de femmes*, 63, 64, 71; phallic, 123–27, 130; stereotypes of, 12, 20, 170. *See also* feminism; gender; sexuality

Wood, Robin, 18, 40, 185n30

Les yeux sans visage (*Eyes without a Face*), 165

Zeller, Florian, 194n8

Zweig, Stefan, 103